Role of Women in Turkish Politics

Isabell J. Ackermann

Abstract

This study offers a case study of women's political participation and representation in pro-Kurdish politics in Turkey since 1990s. Kurdish women have been double oppressed in Turkey due to both their ethnic identity and gender identity. They have been mobilized by the Kurdish national movement for the Kurdish national cause and joined both Kurdish armed and political struggles from the early 1990s. From the foundation of the first pro-Kurdish political party, the People's Labour Party *[Halkın Emek Partisi- HEP]* in 1990, Kurdish women have actively been involved in pro-Kurdish party politics. However, the pro-Kurdish party failed in promoting egalitarian gender values, policies and supporting women's inclusion in decision-making until the end of 1990s except the election of the first Kurdish woman deputy, Leyla Zana in 1991. Women's participation and representation in pro-Kurdish party politics have significantly advanced numerically since 1990s. In contrast to the general picture of women's underrepresentation in Turkey's politics, the proportion of Kurdish women representatives has been increasing in representation bodies. Therefore, this research aims to examine the Kurdish case through conducting an intensive field research in order to explain the reasons and factors behind these developments.

This research is an empirical case study, primarily based on qualitative analysis of face-to-face in-depth semi-structured interviews of female political activists and participant observations held during field research. On the basis of empirical data gathered from field research and an analysis of pro-Kurdish party characteristics, its gender policies and female political activists' roles in representation bodies, this study argues that the pro-Kurdish politics has gradually been feminizing which refers to an increase in women's both descriptive and substantive representation since the beginning of 2000s. The changes and developments in terms of women's representation in pro-Kurdish politics are framed as a process of feminization; which can simply be defined as a process for women to be included in political decision-making both in numbers and ideas for representing women's interests. In this regard, this thesis searches for answers for two essential questions: how has the pro-Kurdish party politics been feminized and what difference has been made in pro-Kurdish politics since women are increasingly taking part in decision-making processes. Thus, this study assesses whether descriptive representation links to women's substantive representation in pro-Kurdish politics.

The examination of Kurdish women's representation based on the *feminizing politics* approach does not only theoretically contribute to broaden the scope of *feminizing politics* but it also broadens the scope of the concepts of descriptive and substantive representation included in this approach. In this respect, this thesis will demonstrate that the analysis of the Kurdish women case in the context of feminizing politics presents several insights about the women's political representation and put forth how political parties and actors strategically interact in changing women's political representation.

TABLE OF CONTENTS

Dedication..2
Abstract...3
Acknowledgements...5
Notes on Translation...9
Chapter One – Introduction: Changes in Kurdish Women's Political Participation and Representation: Bridging the Gender Gap in Pro-Kurdish Politics..10
Aims of Thesis...15
Research Questions..16
Arguments...17
Rationale...17
Theoretical Framework..18
    Feminizing Politics...18
    Types of Political Representation: Descriptive and Substantive..........23
    Women's Interests..26
Methodology..30
The Structure of the Thesis...38
Chapter Two – Literature Review of the Study...................................41
Women's Participation in Guerrilla Movements.......................................41
Kurdish Guerrilla Movement and Women's Participation........................55
Women and (Kurdish) Politics in Turkey..56
Chapter Three – The Actors Promoting *Feminization* in Pro-Kurdish Politics..67
Introduction: *Feminization* of pro-Kurdish Politics as a Multifaceted Process..........67
The Role of Kurdish National Movement...70
    A Brief History of the PKK..72
    PKK, Öcalan and Women: Shift in Ideology and Discourses.............74
    Öcalan's Political Project: *Democratic Confederalism*......................80
    Women in the PKK..82
The Pro-Kurdish Political Parties since 1990s and their Gender Approach............87
    Women's Participation in pro-Kurdish Political Parties.......................93
    Changes in Gender Approach of pro-Kurdish Parties.........................95

Party Program and Statutes: Shift in Approach towards Women and Women's Issues...97
A New Period for Pro-Kurdish Politics: *Feminization* Progressing..............106
Women's Arguments and Aims for *Feminizing* Politics..116
Conclusion: Women as the main dynamics of democratization.........................123

Chapter Four – Obstacles to *Feminizing* (pro-Kurdish Party) Politics..............128
Introduction...128
Political Factors...132
Socio-economic Factors...146
Cultural Factors...154
State Politics: pro-Kurdish Politics 'High Risk Area'...161
Women's Experiences of Gendered Violence..169
Conclusion..172

Chapter Five – Strategies and Opportunities for *Feminizing* pro-Kurdish Party Politics..174
Introduction...174
The Change of Form of Intra-party Women's Organizations: Commissions- Branches- Assemblies...177
The Expansion of 'Autonomous' Women's Organization: DÖKH (Democratic Free Women Movement / Demokratik Özgür Kadın Hareketi).......................................188
The Implementation of the Quotas..198
Why did quotas appear in pro-Kurdish politics?..200
Equal Participation in Leadership Positions: Co-chairship..............................210
Training: the School of Politics for Women...214
Networking Activities..223
Conclusion..240

Chapter Six – The Feminization of Politics in Practice...............................242
Introduction: Make a difference in (pro-Kurdish) Politics?................................242
Practice of Politics: Women Activists in Offices..248

    Feminizing the Parliamentary Politics..251

    Feminizing Local Governments...265

Conclusion..284

Chapter Seven – Conclusion: Findings and Theoretical Implications...........287

Findings..288

The Role of Gender Equality Strategies in *Feminizing* pro-Kurdish Politics..........295

Theoretical Implications: Re-Defining *Feminizing Politics* in Kurdish Context.........305

CHAPTER ONE

Introduction

Changes in Kurdish Women's Political Participation and Representation: Bridging the Gender Gap in Pro-Kurdish Politics

The election of Leyla Zana in 1991 marked the first appointment of a Kurdish woman to the Turkish parliament. Kurdish women have made significant changes in the political sphere in terms of their participation and representation in pro-Kurdish politics in particular and in Turkey's politics in general since her election. Leyla Zana has become a symbol of the struggle for Kurdish national rights since she was sentenced to 14 years in prison for 'illegally' adding Kurdish words to her official oath and wearing the red, yellow, and green colours of the Kurdish national movement[1] in her headband at the swearing in ceremony in the Turkish Grand National Assembly [TBBM- Türkiye Büyük Millet Meclisi] in1991. Zana was released in June 2004 and re-elected to the parliament in 2011. Zana's case as the first elected Kurdish female political activist highlighted two important issues concerning Kurdish women. On the one hand, it exposed discriminatory policies against Kurdish women and on the other it demonstrated the increase of Kurdish women's political activism in Turkey. Women who had been involved in politics in Turkey up to the 1990s were drawn from the Turkish secular elite who predominantly belonged to the leftist and secular political parties and had abstained from exposing their ethnic or other identities, such as their

---

[1] It is an ethno-political movement that seeks to obtain Kurdish national rights. It consists of organizations and actors who regard themselves as working on behalf of and for the reconstruction of a Kurdish nation. The leading organization is the PKK which will be examined in details in Chapter 3.

religious identity, in public. Zana's case was the starting point for the changes that were proceeding in Kurdish women's political activism and representation.

Kurdish women have been further oppressed in Turkey due to both their ethnic identity and their gender identity. They faced state oppression because of their ethnic identity and they belonged to a society [Kurdish society] which was traditionally patriarchal in which women had a subordinate status compared to men. Therefore, they were faced with family and social oppression due to their gender identity. At the beginning of the 1990s a new group of Kurdish women who claimed their distinct cultural and ethnic identity emerged. This new group of Kurdish nationalist women mobilized for the Kurdish national cause and participated in protest movements and joined the Kurdish armed struggle carried out by the PKK [Partiya Karkerên Kurdistan/ Kurdistan Workers Party].

From the establishment of the first pro-Kurdish political party, the People's Labour Party [Halkın Emek Partisi- HEP][2] in 1990, Kurdish women began to actively

---

[2] In this research pro-Kurdish parties are regarded as one of Kurdish national movement organizations that defend Kurdish cultural and political rights within the legal framework of Turkish state. Watts refers to pro-Kurdish political parties as challenger parties. She defines a challenger party "as a party that mobilizes political identities or programs viewed by authorities as posing a fundamental challenge to the ideological or organizational basis of the ruling establishment."(Watts, 2010: 16). Although the term is not used during analysis but I consider the roles of pro-Kurdish political parties in parallel to this definition. An analysis on the pro-Kurdish party politics includes a number of party names due to the fact the Kurdish parties have been repeatedly closed by the Constitutional Court with the allegation that they make separatist ethnic politics and have been re-founded immediately with a different name over the line of same ideology. Besides that in the last two general elections, these parties decided to run as independent candidates in the elections so that they can overcome the major obstacle they face, namely the 10 % electoral threshold. Because of that I would prefer to use the term the pro-Kurdish parties instead of the party name. The names of the pro-Kurdish parties since 1990 are; HEP (People's Labour Party), DEP (Democracy Party), ÖZDEP (Freedom and Democracy Party), HADEP (People's Democracy Party), DEHAP (Democratic People's Party), DTP (Democratic Society Party), BDP (Peace and Democracy Party). For a detailed analysis of pro-Kurdish political parties since 1990s see: Nicole F. Watts (2010) *Activists in Office: Kurdish Politics and Protest in Turkey*. United States of America, Seattle, WA: University of Washington Press. Nicole F. Watts, "Activists in Office: Pro-Kurdish Contentious Politics in Turkey" *Ethnopolitics*, Vol. 5, No.2, 125-144, June 2006. Another work is Şeref Kavak's published MA thesis, which makes a comprehensive examination of pro-Kurdish Democratic Society party. Şeref Kavak (2012) *Kurdish ethno-political transformation in Turkey: Democratic Society Party (DTP) experience (2005-2009): a pro-Kurdish party between ethnic & nonethnic political agenda*. Saarbrücken: LAP: Lambert Academic Publishing.

join successive pro- Kurdish political parties. However, until the end of 1990s pro-Kurdish political parties failed not only in promoting egalitarian gender values and policies, but also in supporting women's inclusion in politics. Kurdish women's participation and representation in political parties have substantially changed numerically with the passing of time. In comparison with the general picture of women's representation in politics in Turkey, women's representation in pro-Kurdish politics has significantly advanced especially since the year 2000.

The statistics concerning women's representation in national politics in Turkey show that female representation on the national level had considerably increased at the last two general elections [2007 and 2011]. However, it is relevant to find out the distribution of number elected female representatives to the political parties. In the 2007 national elections 50 female MPs[3] were elected and the pro-Kurdish party, which entered the elections with independent candidates and despite the 10% election threshold 8 of its 21 seats (38%) were held by women. In the June 2011 national elections 550 parliamentarians were elected and only 78 of them were female[4]. The pro-Kurdish party which campaigned for its independent candidates obtained 31 seats in the Parliament and 11 of these were held by women which makes it the party with the highest percentage of female representation in the parliament (35%).

---

[3] AKP: 30 out of 341 (9%); CHP: 10 out of 112 (9%); MHP: 2 out of 71 (3%),
"50 Kadın Meclis'te" http://www.ucansupurge.org/arsiv (Accessed on 19 May 2011) and statistics for national elections can be found online at www.belgenet.net.

[4] AKP 327 (45 female -13,8%) CHP 135 (19 female- 14,07 %) MHP 53 (3 female- 5,6%) Independent 35 (31 of them joined the Pro-Kurdish party and 11 of them are female, which corresponds 35%). Statistics for June 2011 general election can be found at
http://www.ysk.gov.tr/ysk/docs/2011MilletvekiliSecimi/turkiye/milletvekilisayisi.pdf.
"78 Kadın 472 Erkek Vekil Meclis'te" http://bianet.org/bianet/siyaset/130697-78-kadin-472-erkek-vekil-mecliste (Accessed on 17 May 2011).

These developments in pro-Kurdish politics in favour of the election of women raise the issue of the gender gap in politics in Turkey. Although women gained the right to vote and run for office for the first time in the 1930 local elections and in the 1935 general elections, in Turkey the history of women's political representation reveals a situation in which female representation began promisingly but did not continue to improve.[5] The percentage of women in the Turkish parliament varied from election to election but did not exceed the 1935 levels until the 2007 general elections. A proportion that nearly equal to that of 1935 was observed only in 1999 at 4, 2 %. While no remarkable change could be noted in the 2002 elections, the percentage of women in the parliament doubled in the 2007 elections, when 9,1 % of the legislative seats were occupied by female representatives. The highest percentage was achieved in the 2011 general elections but 14% can never be interpreted as constituting gender equality.

Although the issue of women's under representation in politics revolves mostly around the distribution of seats in the parliament, there is also a serious political gender gap in other areas such as local governments and central government. In the 2004 local elections 18 female mayors[6] were elected of which 9 were members of the pro-Kurdish party. In the latest local elections in March 2009 there were no women mayors in the 16 metropolitan municipalities and there were only 18 women (0, 9 %) among the 2,093 mayors throughout Turkey. The pro-

---

[5] The most frequently repeated fact is that Turkish women obtained political rights even before most of their Western European counterparts. At that period of time (1930s), French women, for instance, lacked these rights and the women in England were not as successful as the Turkish women in obtaining seats in the parliament. After the first general elections they could run for office, the Turkish women hold 4,5 % of the parliament while the percentage of female parliamentarians in England changed between 0,1 % and 2,4 % in the same period (Tekeli 1981: 299).

[6] 18 female mayors out of 3.225, Ayşe Durukan "Kadın Siyaset ve Karar Mekanizmalarında Yok" ttp://bianet.org/bianet/kadin. (Accessed on 19 May 2011).
CHP: 5, AKP: 2, SHP (Social Democrat People's Party): 1, DYP (True Path Party): 1.

Kurdish party had 14 of those 18 female mayors[7]. In the local elections, even if the number of female mayors throughout the country remained low, the pro-Kurdish political party nonetheless provided the overwhelming majority of those mayors.

These statistics of women's representation point out that the problem in Turkey is that women are absent in the decision-making processes in general. Although there are still serious issues regarding women's political participation and representation in pro-Kurdish party politics, the results of the latest elections are significant in identifying the impact of pro-Kurdish parties and the role of female political activists in advancing women's representation in pro-Kurdish politics. Based on field research conducted with female political activists and the examination of pro-Kurdish party characteristics and its gender policies and analysis of female political activists' activities in representation bodies, this study has revealed significant developments in women's descriptive representation and the advancement of women's substantive representation in pro-Kurdish party politics. On this basis, this study argues that pro-Kurdish party politics has gradually been feminizing since the beginning of 2000 in particular.

This thesis seeks to investigate how pro-Kurdish party politics has been feminized. I contend that women's representation in pro-Kurdish politics, in the sense of the number of elected women in the parliament and in local governments, and number of women in the party's internal decision-making positions, has increased. The inclusion and integration of women, as both a reality and as an idea, in political decision-making processes has made a significant difference to the political climate in favour of women.

---

[7] 18 female mayors out of 2.948, AKP: 2, CHP: 1, DP (Democrat Party): 1, "Belediye başkanı kadınlar: 81'de 2" http://www.ucansupurge.org/arsiv (Accessed on 16 April 2011) and statistics for local elections can be found online at www.yerelnet.org.tr.

The Kurdish case in relation to developments in narrowing the gender gap in pro-Kurdish politics provides a substantial case study for exploring the factors and mechanisms determining women's representation. While women's representation is a very important issue in creating a gender-egalitarian society for Kurds in particular, it is also a significant issue in Turkey's democratic process in general because, as statistics demonstrate, women's representation has been strikingly low in Turkey's politics. Therefore, any change that any political party makes in advancing women's representation, regardless of its size, is worth exploration. In this sense, the Kurdish case is an impressive case for scholars, practitioners and women rights advocates. Furthermore, analysing the Kurdish case in the context of feminization of politics contributes to the literature on women and political representation broadly and political parties' roles in promoting gender equality in politics more particularly.

Aims of Thesis

This study aims to expand current knowledge regarding the factors that contribute to gender equity in politics and to the academic debate on gender and party politics. In particular, it seeks to explore which are the factors that determine the number of women elected to representation bodies as well as their advance in gender equity in pro-Kurdish politics in general. Since it is evident that the proportion of women elected to representation bodies through pro-Kurdish parties has gradually increased since the 1990's, an analysis at party level and women's agency will contribute to a deeper understanding of the factors that explain women's changing presence in these representation bodies. Through this analysis, this study will contribute to current scholarship that seeks to understand how women's agency interacts with institutions (political party) to shape and influence general political outcomes in the specific case of the Kurdish political position in Turkey.

The empirical findings of this research will provide concrete, practical recommendations for political parties, activists and organizations seeking to promote women's representation and gender equality in politics at large. In addition, understanding how party rules and procedures influence the number of women elected and the role of women's agency in shaping political parties' attitudes can elucidate on the mechanisms that exclude women from political institutions. This study will also present suggestions on the ways in which a political party can reduce gender inequalities in politics and how women rights advocates concerned with the promotion of gender equality in politics.

Research Questions

This research mainly aims to answer the questions of how pro-Kurdish party politics has been feminized and how feminization is occurring. Accordingly, I will attempt to respond to a number of questions during this analysis, which can be listed as:

- Who is pushing for feminization and why? What is the role of the party? What is the role of women activists?
- How are women political activists and the political party trying to bring about feminization? Which strategies have been pursued both by the party and women activists to feminize politics?
- What are the obstacles they encountered?
- What are the results of the actors' efforts in pushing for feminization?

Arguments

Based on my empirical research conducted with Kurdish female activists and on an analysis of pro-Kurdish parties, I argue that there is a strong tendency of *feminization* within pro-Kurdish politics. Feminization in the Kurdish context will be explained in depth in the following sections and concisely refers to an increasing gender equity in pro-Kurdish politics; women have become significantly involved in the decision-making processes both in numbers and in ideas, while a substantial number of women have been elected to representative bodies that raise women's concerns and demands, claim for gender equality in all areas, and act in the interest of women. In terms of party-level factors such as organizational structure, ideology, party women activists and gender-related policies, it is possible to assert that the pro-Kurdish party has played a central role in facilitating a remarkable increase in female representation and an enhancement of women's political position. In addition, this is also one of the fundamental aspects, which differentiates pro-Kurdish party politics from that of the mainstream political parties in Turkey. The alternative position of the pro-Kurdish party, whose discourses, regulations and policies raise public attention on gender inequality in the political arena, offers ways in which such inequality may be overcome.

Rationale

There is no empirical work on the role of pro-Kurdish political parties in enhancing women's political representation in Turkey and there is little work on the pro-Kurdish parties in general. Although there exists a great deal of empirical research focused on national level patterns of women's political representation in Turkey, these analyses do not explore the fact that individual parties might vary greatly in the proportion of women representatives (Arat, 1989 & 2005; Talaslı, 1996; Güneş-Ayata, 2001; Saktanber, 2002; White, 2002; Turam, 2008). Parties differ in the number of women they nominate, where they rank women on party lists, and the proportion of women that they send to representation bodies. However, until quite recently, there have not been many differences among major political parties in Turkey in terms of female representation. But today it can be observed that political parties play a role in the composition of representative bodies. Thus, we must understand how political parties differ in encouraging or discouraging women's access to representative bodies. In this regard, as the pro-Kurdish party has become the most successful party in terms of the proportion of women elected to representative bodies in recent elections, it is worthy of study for its contributions to the scholarship concerning party politics and women's political representation.

Theoretical Framework

In order to examine the argument that pro-Kurdish party politics has gradually been feminizing since 1990s in Turkey, a number of theoretical notions are employed. In this regard, one of the substantial works that belongs to Joni Lovenduski (2005) contributes to determine the theoretical approach of this study as seen below.

Feminizing politics

Lovenduski's work *Feminizing Politics* (2005) shapes the argument, structure and conceptual framework of my research to a considerable extent. Therefore, I consider it to be an approach, which includes a variety of explanations, concepts and views, which enable me to contextualize the Kurdish case. Since my research attempts to explain how pro-Kurdish party politics has been feminized Lovenduski's work which focuses on British politics is very relevant in many respects. First of all, it helps me to explain what feminizing politics means and thus it enables me to explain the feminization of politics in the Kurdish context and to present what the Kurdish case contributes to this both as a concept and approach. Secondly, theoretical explanations and empirical references which are utilized by Lovenduski to explain how politics could be feminized in the British case provided me with an explanation as to how pro-Kurdish party politics has been transformed in favour of women. It also provided an explanation to some other questions related to the main issues, such as what is the role of political parties in the feminization process. For example, Lovenduski mentions a number of strategies for overcoming obstacles to feminization. Some of these strategies such as equality guarantees or positive discrimination treats, which include quotas, even though they refer to a British context, are applicable to an examination of the feminization process in the Kurdish case.

Lovenduski's work of *Feminizing* Politics is based on the development in women's representation in the UK after the 1997 elections when substantial numbers of women elected by the Labour Party through the implementation of a quota system. From this period forward, as Lovenduski's study indicates, the feminization of politics has been greatly assisted in the UK (2005, 1). In my research, I am analysing a similar process in Kurdish politics in Turkey and therefore it is useful to first of all find out how Lovenduski explains the concept of feminizing politics and then to consider how she analyses the feminization of politics in the British context.

Lovenduski defines the concept of feminizing politics as *"the insertion and integration of women, both in terms of numbers and ideas, into a process"* (2005: 12-13). As seen from this definition, which is introduced at the beginning of the book, and in the rest of her analysis, she regards feminization as a process. She emphasizes that feminizing politics is about more than increasing the numbers of women in political institutions; it is about how institutions, processes and procedures are affected by changing the numbers of women, about what else happens when the numbers of women change. That is to say, her understanding of feminizing politics goes beyond the numerical increase of women in politics; the equalization in the numbers of women in political institutions or in representative bodies is only one dimension of the feminization of politics. In her work, the feminization of politics refers to the transformation of politics, as women's concerns and perspectives move towards the centre of the political agenda (Lovenduski 2005, 12). These definitions of feminization by Lovenduski provide significant criteria, which will be used to examine the Kurdish case.

What makes her work, of exploring how the male world of politics is becoming feminized, particularly interesting is that it exposes the factors, strategies, opportunities, and actors, which make possible the transformation of politics in favour of women. Furthermore, this exploration identifies obstacles inherent to a male dominated system, which impede the—feminization of politics. Since the feminization of politics in the Kurdish context also refers to removing male domination in the political arena by empowering women through involvement in the decision-making processes, Lovenduski's work presents some basic guidelines for the examination of the Kurdish case despite the huge differences between the cases.

Furthermore, even if Lovenduski provides a series of general concepts to help explain the feminization of politics, such as increased representation, the number of women in key roles, and the changes caused by their presence in the general political arena, her analysis, being limited to the British context, cannot be applied without reservation to the Kurdish case. Although the feminization of politics is addressed in both cases, there are, however, many differences, which influence the content and meaning of feminization, which need to be differentiated. Lovenduski focuses on the feminization of parliamentary politics whereas this research examines feminization in the politics of one political party and thus including an analysis of the party's local and parliamentary politics. In addition, since Lovenduski examines the major political parties, British national politics is addressed with regard to the role of those parties in the representation of women. In my research, however, I only focus on the pro-Kurdish political parties, which are small in terms of their size and were politically marginalized especially in 1990s due to carrying a contentious politics in Turkish politics. These parties have been significantly different from the major political parties in Turkey with regard to their support to enhance gender equality in politics. In Lovenduski's work, feminization refers mainly to two points: increasing the number of women in representative bodies and the promotion of women's interests, concerns and perspectives within the political process. In her analysis, these changes refer to the transformation of politics, and this is process of feminization. However, Lovenduski's analysis of the British case does not involve large-scale changes but in the Kurdish case one would expect to have to make larger changes to address their particular issues. The obstacles, needs, issues and interests of women in the Kurdish case are not the same as those of British women and it is this, which differentiates the two cases. Therefore, the meaning and content of the feminization are differentiated as a matter of course.

In the case of pro-Kurdish party politics, I frame the changes and developments that have occurred within Kurdish politics as a process of feminization similarly to Lovenduski. However, in my analysis, although the feminization is addressed on the political level, its impacts and intentions go beyond politics. Feminization is not defined just in terms of changing, transforming and reforming political institutions or the advancement of women's position in these institutions. It is a process of transformation that leads to the enhancement of gender equity not only in politics but also in society more generally. In my view, as the statements of the professional female political activists who were interviewed related to this research make it clear, '*feminizing* politics' in the Kurdish case is a project started in the political domain but intended to extend to the whole of society and for the purpose of changing gender relations throughout the society. The efforts of female activists in the political arena and their projects, works and campaigns address women's issues and aim to empower women in society as a whole. In other words, in this research, I define feminization as a process, which starts in pro-Kurdish party politics and goes beyond the representative bodies, in the sense of equitable institutional politics, in a process which seeks to transform society as a whole. The broader aims behind the efforts to feminize politics are to make structural changes in society in order to create a gender-egalitarian society. Basically, feminization is regarded a step to transform society at large.

Since feminization is regarded as a process of transforming politics and political institutions to include women in equal numbers to men and with ideas and perspectives it is necessary to assess how this process is evolving. Thus, a variety of theoretical notions are employed to explain the process of feminization in the Kurdish case. There are two key concepts in Lovenduski's definition, which are of value in explaining this process of feminization: these are descriptive representation and substantive representation. These two concepts enable to understand feminization both in terms of numbers and ideas.

Types of political representation: descriptive and substantive

Political representation cannot be fully understood within the context of democratic elections alone. Hannah Pitkin (1967) specifies four different types of political representation: authorized, descriptive, symbolic, and substantive. Lovenduski defines Pitkin's four categories of representation. She defines them as *authorized,* where a representative is legally empowered to act for another; *descriptive,* where the representative stands for a group by virtue of sharing similar characteristics such as race, gender, ethnicity or residence; *symbolic,* where a leader stands for national ideas; and *substantive,* where the representative seeks to advance a group's policy preferences and interests (2005: 3).

In an effort to carry out a comprehensive analysis of the roles that female representatives play in politics and representative bodies, I particularly concentrate on the descriptive and substantive type of representation. The distinction and relation between descriptive and substantive representation will make clear whether increasing the number of female activists make any difference for women's representation; the term distinguishes whether women in politics symbolically represent women or whether they are active in their advocacy of women's rights. Furthermore, this distinction contributes to explain the feminization process as well. A number of theorists have distinguished between descriptive and substantive representation. Hanna F. Pitkin (1967) differentiates between representation as 'acting on behalf of' and representation as 'standing in for.' According to Pitkin, the crucial dividing line in forms of representation is the distinction between 'standing for' and 'acting for' representation. One of the widely accepted definitions of substantive representation is explicitly Pitkin's (1972: 209): substantive representation is 'acting in the interest of the represented, in a manner responsive to them'. This definition raises three criteria for substantive representation. First of all, it is about representative acts as opposed to, for instance, intentions or attitudes. Secondly, the results of these representative acts should be in the interest of the represented. Thirdly, the representatives should be responsive towards the ones they represent. Applying this to the substantive representation of women, Pitkin's definition suggests that women's interests and female citizens are central to the representative process (Celis, 2009: 3). Besides, according to Lovenduski, the notion of substantive representation refers to the content of the decisions of representatives. The substantive representation of a group means the representation of the interests of that group (2005: 18). In addition, Anne Marie Goetz and Shireen Hassim respectively define descriptive and substantive representation as 'feminine presence' and 'feminist activism' respectively (2003: 5). In Lovenduski's view, descriptive representation (proportionate, pictorial or microcosmic representation) highlights that women should participate in decision making in proportion to their membership of the population. That is to say, women should represent women in accordance with their presence in the population (2005: 17). Furthermore, Mansbridge (1999) notes that 'in descriptive representation, representatives are in their own persons and lives in some sense typical of the larger class of persons whom they represent' (quoted in Lovenduski, 2005: 17).

There are many substantial points that these definitions put forward. First of all, all of these definitions of descriptive and substantive representations specify the clear distinction between descriptive and substantive representations with regard to the transforming impact of substantive representation. An increase in the descriptive representation contributes to the transformation of dominant gender hierarchies if those representatives act on women's interests and advocate for policies and programs that improve women's quality of life; if such activity is present then substantive representation is in play. Thus, the relationship between women's political representation and the furtherance of women's interests constitutes the distinction between women's descriptive and substantive representation. Basically, the question of whether women's interests are represented or not, dictates what form of representation is exercised by representatives. Put in different words, there is substantive representation if women's interests are represented; if not, then descriptive representation is in play. Furthermore, all of the definitions mentioned above are built up around the issue of 'women's interests', or 'on behalf of women'. That is to say, the concept of 'women's interest' is crucial, though not easy to define.

These notions of representations are significant in many respects in order to analyse women's representation in pro-Kurdish politics in Turkey. The debates about types of political representations, which are mainly descriptive or substantive, illuminate the role of women in politics and political institutions. Since feminization is concisely defined as the inclusion and integration of women both in numbers and ideas in the political processes, it is relevant to explore what roles women undertake in political institutions. That is to say, the presence of women in politics and representative offices serves to demonstrate that women have equal numbers with men (descriptive) and/or ensures that women's interests are represented by women themselves (substantive). Furthermore, although these concepts primarily describe women's presence in representative offices I also take them into account in evaluating the role of women activists in the party. These concepts assist to explain the extent to which female activists within the party are able to influence the feminization of party politics. In other words, by evaluating their roles in terms of the different types of representation it is possible to find out how much female activists concern to enhance women's position in politics by their activism within the party. Furthermore, discussions concerning the relations between descriptive representation and substantive representation enable to explore the extent to which an increase in the number of female activists creates an impact in raising awareness of transforming gender relations in politics among female activists.

Women's interests

As mentioned above the notion of women's interests is necessary to explain the extent to which the substantive representation of women is achieved. There are, however, a number of discussions about what women issues are. In the 1980s, the discussions were held by Sapiro, Diamond and Hartsock, and Jónasdóttir. According to Sapiro (1981), the 'private distribution of labour', that is the tasks of giving birth to and providing care for children, means that women occupy a different socio-economic position to men, which in turn produces specific interests that are politically 'representable'. Diamond and Hartsock (1981) have a broader view of women's interests. According to them, women's common interests are not the result of the division of tasks inside the household, but of the gendered division of productive labour (Diamond and Hartsock 1981: 194-196). Jónasdóttir (1988), who reconciled these two points of view, stated that women's interests derive their origins from the gendered reality that predominantly coincides with the gendered division of labour.

This definition, however, is not adequate to include all gender differences within the concept of interests. In Jónasdóttir's view, what is in the interest of women is *"interesse"* (literally to "be amongst") or being present in the decision-making process and this denotes control over the conditions of choice rather than the consequences of choice.

Several scholars have also been involved in debates about what constitutes women's interests in the 1990s onwards. One of those who contributed to the debates at that time was Anne Phillips (1995, 1998), who disapproved of the idea of universal women's interests and needs. Nonetheless, she maintains that women do have peculiar life experiences generating gendered interests that require representation. Other scholars emphasize that the question is not merely the inclusion of women's interests, but also the gendering of the general interest (Lovenduski, 2005: 19). In contrast to Phillips, Iris Marion Young (1997, 2000) puts forward the idea that representing women is not about interests and needs but about social perspectives. Her argument suggests that issue of representation needs to accommodate the way in which people interpret things and events from within their structural social situation. This view asserts that social groups, which are constituted around differences such as gender, race, nationality and religion, cannot be identified and thus represented through the promotion of common interests or through similar ideas. Thus, women cannot be represented as a group on the basis of the interests and ideas of society as a whole; the representation of a social group connotes the representation of the social perspective of that group from its particular structural position in society.

Melissa Williams (1998) put forward a similar argument. She states that, cultural and structural barriers lead to the marginalization of women. The representation of women requires that the point of view of women, or the women's 'voice', is made present in political decision-making. The presence of the voice of women not only ensures that a policy for the marginalized group is established, but also enables an evolution to take place in the minds of the dominant groups. Thus, overcoming discrimination is a key issue in her approach to substantive representation. Furthermore, Lena Wängnerud (2000) also remarks that the substantive representation of women has a feminist 'direction'. This argument asserts that the purpose of the substantive representation of women is to increase women's autonomy. In view of Wängnerud's comments, the process of representing women is formed by three elements: 1) the recognition of women as a social category; 2) the recognition of a power imbalance between men and women; 3) the wish to implement a policy that increases the autonomy of female citizens.

Another classification regarding women's interests, which can be applied to the Kurdish case belongs to Maxine Molyneux (1985), who coined the concepts of practical and strategic gender interests. Practical gender interests are those needs which are formulated from the concrete conditions women experience in their engendered position within the sexual division of labour which derives from their practical gender interests for human survival (Moser 1989:1803). According to Molyneux, the 'practical gender interests are given inductively and arise from the concrete conditions of women's positioning by virtue of the gender division of labour and are usually a response to an immediate perceived need' (Molyneux (1985:233). They do not generally involve a strategic goal such as women emancipation or gender equality. She also added that they cannot themselves challenge the prevailing forms of gender subordination, even though they arise directly out of them. Conversely, according to Molyneux, the 'strategic gender interests' derive from 'an analysis of women's subordination and from the formulation of an alternative, more satisfactory set of arrangements' (1985:232). They are formulated from the analysis of women's subordination to men. They focus on the fundamental issues related to women's/men's subordination and gender inequities. 'The demands that are formulated on this basis are usually termed 'feminist' as is the level of consciousness required to struggle effectively for them' (1985: 233). In addition, Moser (1989:1803) added that women's subordination varies depending on the cultural and socio-political context within which they are formulated. Therefore, gender strategic interests are contextual.

However, the strategic gender interests are long-term, usually not material, and are often related to structural changes in society in terms of women's status and equity. According to Molyneux (1985:233), in general the gender strategic interests may include all or some of the aspects of practical gender interests, such as the abolition of the sexual division of labour; the alleviation of the burden of domestic labour and childcare; the removal of institutionalized forms of discrimination such as rights to own land or property; access to credit; the establishment of political equality; freedom of choice over childbearing; adoption of adequate measures against male violence and control over women; the sexual exploitation of women and coercive forms of marriage. For feminists, these are women's real interests. These theoretical approaches regarding women's interests enable one to contextualize the interests of female political activists in pro-Kurdish politics in order to analyse the process and level of feminization.

Kurdish women's interests and many other points about the growth of Kurdish women's representation in politics, such as the actors and mechanisms behind this growth, have been obtained through field research conducted with female political activists, as will be explained in detail below.

Methodology

This thesis overwhelmingly relies upon primary data that has been collected through field research. Since this thesis mainly focuses on how pro-Kurdish party politics has been feminized, conducting research with female political activists was essential in order to reveal what role women and the party play in the process of feminization. That is to say, female political activists who have been involved in pro-Kurdish politics were regarded as main subjects of the research. Therefore, I had to carry out an extensive fieldwork in order to explore female political activists' experiences and collect primary resources concerning female political activists.

Two basic qualitative research methods were employed during field research. The first method is participant observation, which allows the research worker to secure her data within the mediums, symbols, and experiential worlds, which have meaning to her respondents. Its purpose is to prevent imposing alien meanings upon the actions of the subjects.[8] "*Since participant observation has the greatest potential to uncover contextualized, honest data, otherwise inaccessible, it ontologically and epistemologically underpins human quests for understanding multiple realities of life in context*" (Rossman & Rallis, 2003).[9] Thus, it was employed in order to make observations with regard to women's political activities, processes of political

---

[8] Arthur J. Vidich, "Participant Observation and the Collection and Interpretation of Data", p. 354. http://www.jstor.org (Accessed on 14 January 2011).

[9] Jun Li. (2008) "Ethical Challenges in Participant Observation: A Reflection on Ethnographic Fieldwork." *The Qualitative Report*, 13(1): 100-115. p. 101. Retrieved from http://www.nova.edu/ssss/QR/QR13-1/li.pdf. (Accessed on 14 January 2011).

involvement, position of women within the party and relations among activists both male and female. This meant fieldwork included participant observations in women's council meetings, committee meetings, demonstrations, congresses, conferences and gatherings where women took charge or simply participated in and training programs. This gave me the opportunity to engage with political activists and observe their different types of involvement. In addition, I have tried to capture the voices of women who have devoted their energies to politics.

The second method is in-depth interviews, which are the type of interviewing usually used in qualitative research. The purpose of in-depth interviewing is neither simply to get answers to questions, nor to test hypotheses. At the root of in-depth interviewing is an interest in understanding the experiences of other people and the meaning they attribute to their experience. Interviewing provides access to the context of people's behaviour and thereby provides a way for researchers to understand the meaning of that behaviour as Irving E. Seidman has explained (1991). The main source of obtaining primary data was through a series of interviews I carried out which were semi-structured, open-ended and informal. These were done with female activists and politicians, including members of Parliament who were in office between 2007 and 2011, mayors, members of municipality councils, president and members of provincial women's branches, party activists, and the representatives of women's NGOs affiliated with parties. In-depth interviews conducted with these female activists and politicians aimed to explore their experiences and to understand political involvement and activism in their own terms in order to interpret the motives behind their engagement and the changes that may evolve over time within the party politics.

During the field research, I had access to female activists through personal relationships, Kurdish networks, and visiting pro-Kurdish party branches. Through my previous researches regarding Kurdish women and Kurdish movement I have already met many activists who have joined pro-Kurdish political and social-cultural organizations. Based on these experiences I have an idea where and how to start my research. I used my former contacts to reach out women activists during my field research. Furthermore, during my visits to the branches of the party, the members of women assemblies of the party in particular and Kurdish political activists, whether male or female, provided great assistance in reaching these women. Many of interviewees after the meeting directed me to those they knew could be willing to have interview or to share information about women's organization at both political level and social.

In order to uncover obscured aspects of the case, to identify actors and to understand the internal dynamics of the Kurdish case, I conducted field research four times in different periods in various Kurdish populated cities such as Diyarbakır, Mardin, Batman, Van, Muş and Şırnak and as well as Ankara and Istanbul, the largest Turkish cities. I first started my field study in March 2009 during the local elections[10] campaign in Turkey. This first round of research, which was conducted when the elections campaigns were quite intensive, was different from the other fieldwork because I had the unique opportunity to intensively observe the role and engagement of female activists in political activities, and elections work and to observe female candidates' relations with the constituents. Due to the time limitations and geographical restrictions of the election campaigns, only 8 out of 41 women candidates in Diyarbakir and Mardin in the Kurdish region of Turkey were

---

[10] Local elections were held on 29th March 2009. The election competition was mainly between pro-Kurdish party DTP and the ruling party AKP in the Kurdish region of Turkey.

monitored and 6 of them were interviewed. Out of 6 female mayor candidates, 4 were elected as mayor and they were interviewed again after they became mayor. All interviews with female mayor candidates were conducted in their polling districts during March 2009.

After my research during local elections campaigns in March 2009 I went to for field research again in summer (July and August) 2009, April 2010 and summer (August and September) 2010 respectively focusing on the whole of the political engagement and political activities of Kurdish women. In my last visit to Turkey, which was not in fact for research but to visit to the political parties' branches, I carried out 2 more interviews for a total of 45 female activists in January 2012. Although it was my aim to access all female politicians in office (8 MPs and 14 mayors) who held positions in representative bodies during field research, I was only able to interview 14 of them; 2 MPs (Diyarbakır the MP Gülten Kışanak was interviewed in August 2009 in Diyarbakir and the Istanbul MP Sebahat Tuncel was interviewed in September 2009 in Istanbul) and 12 mayors. These 12 mayors were interviewed in their official places, namely municipality, with the exception of the mayor of Viranşehir district of Şanlıurfa, Leyla Güven, who was interviewed in Tunceli during Munzur Festival (30 July – 2 August 2009). The rest who were members of the women's assemblies of the party and female activists who hold different positions within the party and the members of various women's NGOs affiliated with parties such as Gökkuşağı Women Association (Gökkuşağı Kadın Derneği) and Selis Women Association (Selis Kadın Derneği) were interviewed mainly in Kurdish region such as Diyarbakır, Mardin, Batman and Şırnak and the two largest cities of Turkey, Istanbul and Ankara.

The interviews with the female activists of the party provided a major source of data for this research. The total of 45 in-depth interviews, which lasted 1 hour on average covered diverse information about female political activists. During in-depth interviews open-ended questions were directed to female political activists focusing on their biographies, social backgrounds, political career and attitudes toward their party and their position in the party, personal resources, relations to the constituency, parliamentary activities, and their representation of roles. These interviews provided information on current political engagement, activism, ideologies and actions that have formed the perspectives of the involved participants. The interviews were recorded after asking permission and later they were all transcribed in order to be used efficiently during analysis. Furthermore, when possible, informal and 'off-the-record' conversations were conducted with political activists as well.

During all periods of research I also participated in various events and activities such as the Munzur festival (Dersim/ Tunceli, 30 July- 2 August 2009), Kurdish women conference (Diyarbakır, 24-25 April 2010), Diyarbakır provincial organization congress, politicians' public statements and demonstrations against state violence and training programs. I met MPs, mayors and female activists during these events that gave me opportunity to arrange interview with them. For instance, I accessed to MP Gültan Kışanak during Munzur Festival, who later accepted my interview request. My participation in many different events and activities enabled me to make observations on women's involvement in different arenas. Their visibility was obvious and their commitment to eliminate male domination in all those areas was felt very strong.

Overall, the outcomes of the research were quite satisfactory in terms of collecting large amount of data; however, there were some methodological limitations to this research. Although I have some advantages in sharing the same gender and ethnic identity and in speaking the same languages as the respondents (Turkish and Kurdish), I still faced difficulties during my research. It was quite hard to arrange meetings and to persuade activists to be interviewed. This difficulty was due to their heavy schedule, changeable programme and their political agenda as Kurdish party activists, it was thus hard to arrange meetings and to convince them to interview; and this was especially true in 2009. In comparison to mayors, MPs were not keen to be interviewed because of their position, which makes them not easily accessible and unwilling to allocating time for non-political demands. Mayors, who are one of the targeted groups, were the easiest to access and to persuade to interview. They made more time for meeting and most of them were willing to share more detailed information than MPs. Additionally, it was easy to arrange meeting because they have a certain place, the municipality, where they need to be most of time.

There are complicated issues that have created difficulties in convincing political activists to interview, especially female activists who do not have an elected position. The primary reason seems to be that of security. In other words, pro-Kurdish politics is still a high-risk area due to state politics and oppression. Some of them have court cases; some of them have been arrested and imprisoned before. Most of them have family members who have faced such cases. Moreover, some of them implied that they might not able to give an informative interview due to continuous surveillance by state authorities over their political activities. Basically, because of these reasons, many female activists within the party were not disposed to give interviews. Due to these concerns of female political activists regarding security issues, some of them requested that their real names would not be mentioned and that any information, which might reveal their identity would not be shared in my thesis. Thus, during my analysis, I do not mention the names of female activists apart from some MPs and mayors when it was required and it can't cause harm for female activists.

Furthermore, there were issues concerning using participant observation for obtaining data. While this method enabled me to form an opinion about how women organize their activities, work within the party, and improve their political situation, it presented problems in terms of the lack of boundaries between researcher and participants. Sometimes my role changed from that of outside observer to that of participant. Sharing the same gender and ethnic identity as the subjects of my study most of the time put me in the position of an involved insider. On the other hand, being there for the purpose of research caused some female activists to treat me as an outsider and consequently only sharing limited information and not allowing my participation in some activities and meetings.

Nonetheless, and despite the barriers I faced during my field research, the methods used have provided me with a very valuable data-set that cannot be obtained from any other sources. However, while the primary data, which is based upon women's expressions, experiences, and my observations is central to the analysis of this thesis, I do nonetheless make use of other sources to explore the processes of feminization in pro-Kurdish party politics. That is to say, besides the personal experiences of women, it is necessary to consider external factors and other sources include information about female political activists. These factors are: party policies, strategies, and ideology, Kurdish national movement's ideology and its discourses addressing women, social-economic and political conditions. For this, the written sources, leaflets, periodical publications, journals, newspaper's archives,

TBMM's (Turkish Grand National Assembly) website and the political party's documents have been used in the analysis.

A few issues need to be clarified regarding data collected from field research and its usage during analysis. I want to clarify that the study acknowledges variations among Kurdish women. However, it regards them as a single group for the sake of analytical rigour. Another point, which needs to be mentioned, is that the aim of the study is to reveal the political experiences of women regarding their role in transforming pro-Kurdish party politics in favour of women. Therefore, this study does not include the political experiences of men or aims at a comparison of the political experiences of women with those of men involved in pro-Kurdish legal politics since the 1990s. The influence and role of male political activists on the struggle to access political power for women is derived from the experiences of female activists. However, while male political activists were not targeted during my research, in my visits to party offices and during my participation in the party's activities and election campaigns in the March 2009 local elections I met many male political activists and I had discussions and conversations with them, providing me with general idea about views and attitudes of the party's male activists toward gender equality in politics and in society.

As an additional point, based on my observations and data obtained through field research, I refer to those women who have been involved in pro-Kurdish legal politics since the 1990s as 'political activists'. During analysis I also use the terms 'female MPs' and 'female mayors' in order to explain their political roles in representative bodies. Women's causes, goals and activities are determinative factors for naming them as political activists. The field research explored the idea that women involved in pro-Kurdish politics are typically challengers to policies and practices, trying to achieve a goal, not to obtain power for themselves. Their activism is for their cause, which is obtaining Kurdish rights and women's rights and goes beyond conventional politics. They are characteristically dynamic, eager, innovative, and committed to struggle for their causes. Based on these findings, using the term 'female political activists' for these women actively involved in pro-Kurdish politics will help to explain their role in the feminization of pro-Kurdish politics and provides useful material for further analysis.

Structure of the Thesis

This thesis proceeds in the following way. Chapter 2 focuses on the literature review of the study. This chapter examines the scholarship in various areas; women's participation in guerrilla movements in general, Kurdish guerrilla movement and women's participation, and women and (Kurdish) politics in Turkey in order to explain increasing Kurdish women's activism in political arenas. It aims to reveal the lack of studies concerning the Kurdish women in general and their growing political activism in particular, which lead transformations in women's political representation. Chapter 3, which is entitled "The Actors Promoting Feminization in Pro-Kurdish Politics", focuses on factors behind the increase in women's descriptive representation in pro-Kurdish party politics and the transformation of pro-Kurdish party politics in favour of women. The chapter concentrates on the impacts of three actors that contribute to the feminization of pro-Kurdish party politics in different ways: the stance of the Kurdish national movement, and the relationship between the political party and female political activists. Firstly, the role of the Kurdish national movement is examined with regard to its ideology and discourses, which influence both women and the political party. Secondly, the chapter explores how the party characteristics and ideology influence the party's behaviour, opportunities and decisions by supporting women's equality in politics. The chapter argues that the party's gender ideology, which is shaped by the Kurdish national movement, is an important determinant in increasing Kurdish women's presence in politics. Thirdly, this chapter addresses the role of female political activists by referring to the role of agency in pressuring the political party to make changes in favour of women and mobilizing and encouraging women to take the initiative in the political sphere.

Chapter 4 title is "Obstacles to *Feminizing* (pro-Kurdish Party) Politics" and it explores the obstacles and factors, which determine the level of women's political participation and representation and that of Kurdish women in particular. This chapter focuses on the political, socio-economic and cultural factors and state politics: pro-Kurdish politics "high risk area as an obstacle specific to Kurdish case", that prevent women from participation in political life and increase in women's political representation. It asserts that political institutions and culture in Turkey are characterized by a cultural traditional masculinity that has been a major obstacle for women who intend to have a political career.

Chapter 5 which is entitled "Strategies and Opportunities for *Feminizing* pro-Kurdish Party Politics" seeks to find out what strategies have been used by the party and activists and what gender related policies are employed in order to transform pro-Kurdish party politics in order to obtain gender equity in politics. By analysing strategies that have determined gender composition, it argues that the agency of women has been a critical factor behind the feminization of pro-Kurdish party politics and provides an opportunity for women to negotiate their positions within the party and also to challenge the male dominated nature of politics and political organizations in Turkey.

Chapter 6 which is entitled "The Feminization of Politics in Practice" addresses the outcomes of increasing women's representation in political decision-making through an analysis of the activities of female representatives in representation offices. It aims to find out to what extent the substantive representation of women has been obtained and specifically to what extend women's interests are represented by women political activists in the representative institutions. It argues that women political activists make distinguishable differences in the political arena through their representative roles by acting in favour of women, and that this proves that feminization in pro-Kurdish politics is happening.

Chapter 7 concludes by commenting upon the evidence drawn from this study of the particular case of Kurdish women's political participation and representation in pro-Kurdish politics since 1990s. It brings together the various findings and connects them to the larger theoretical implications.

CHAPTER TWO

Literature Review of the Study

This research focuses on women's political participation and representation in pro-Kurdish politics, which requires a comprehensive literature review on various subjects in order to contextualize the Kurdish women's political activism, as well as to point out the lack of studies on that subject. In this respect, this chapter concentrates on a number of selected guerrilla movements around the world and women's participation and roles within these movements. Then, the Kurdish guerrilla movement is examined on the basis of its role in mobilizing Kurdish women that would assist to explain the emergence of women's political activism in the further analysis. This study contends that the increasing women's political activism is the one of major factors behind feminization of pro-Kurdish party politics. Thereafter, the scholarship on women and politics in Turkey in general and pro-Kurdish politics and Kurdish women in particular, is addressed in order to present to what extent the Kurdish case is different, in terms of promoting women's political participation and representation in Turkey's politics in the following chapters.

Women's Participation in Guerrilla[11] Movements

There are a number of examples of guerrilla movements around the world such as: Zapatista Army of National Liberation (EZLN) or Zapatistas - Chiapas, Mexico, Sandinista National Liberation Front – Nicaragua, Shining Path – Peru, Eritrean

---

[11] Guerrilla means "little war". A guerrilla group is a political organization operating in both rural and urban areas that employs armed battle for the aim of changing societal structure (Reif, 1986: 147).

Liberation Front or ELF – Eritrea, Basque Fatherland and Liberty (ETA) - Spain, Irish National Liberation Army (IRA) Ireland, Liberation Tigers of Tamil Eelam (Tamil Tigers) - Sri Lanka, that women have participated in. Examining the patterns of women's participation in the selected guerrilla struggles, will offer a global perspective to understand the women's participation in the guerrilla struggle of Kurds, led by the PKK, which has mobilized women to join the national struggle since the end of 1980s intensively. With this in mind, this section will examine women's involvement in selected Latin America guerrilla movements as discussed with highlighting the areas where women have made distinct contributions.

The role of women in guerrilla movements, which mainly come from Latin America countries such as: Uruguay, El Salvador, Nicaragua, Peru, Colombia, Mexico and Cuba, will be focused on in the following paragraphs. Although women account for a much smaller proportion of guerrillas than men, a number of scholars have put their attention on the growing numbers and importance of women in these roles. These studies mainly address the reasons behind women's participation in guerrilla movements, roles of women in guerrilla organizations, their levels of participation and roles of guerrilla organizations in mobilizing women (Griset & Mahan, 2003; Chinchilla, 1997; Waylen, 1996; Alison, 2004; Gonzalez-Perez, 2006; Reif, 1986). Certainly, the level of recognition and respect women received from the groups they work for has varied from one group to another, as the literature presents.

Chinchilla (1997: 207) asserts that Latin America has experienced few politically active women before the late 1960s and that female guerrillas appeared as a consequence of restive urbanites and because of frustration with leftist political parties that ignored women's issues and as a reaction against the failure of women's activism in Cuba and anti-colonial nationalism. In an extensive analysis of gender and Third World politics, Waylen (1996: 74) put forward that women became more active in guerrilla warfare during the 1970s because they were more unobtrusive than males, they represented broader community participation, and incorporated a feminist agenda into the cause. Griset & Mahan (2003: 158) contend that women carry out a variety of roles within guerrilla organizations, from simply supportive to active leadership functions.

Several scholars have proposed that women are more active in national liberation movements than in traditional military forces. Sharoni (2001: 86) states that, 'National liberation movements have been portrayed as the least hospitable places for women, despite the fact that women in national liberation movements . . . seem to have had more space to raise questions about gender inequalities'. Alison's (2004: 452) in- depth study of female combatants concurs, that finding such 'anti-state nationalisms are more likely to be receptive to women's non- traditional involvement . . . than institutionalized state nationalisms'. Similarly, Gonzalez-Perez (2006) asserts that non-traditional combat forces are more open to women's participation and, in addition, argues that levels of female participation in both guerrilla activities and terrorism are determined by the goals of the organization as a whole and the group's opponent. According to Gonzalez-Perez (2006) domestic oppression generates higher levels of participation among women, while guerrilla groups focused on combatting international factors such as: imperialism, capitalism, and globalization fail to bring forth this raised intensity of activity among women. In her analysis, Gonzalez-Perez (2006) seeks to address why some nations exhibited high levels while others did not. In this regard guerrilla organizations are divided into two groups on the basis of their agendas, because these different agendas have a direct impact on the role of women within them. These are domestically orientated guerrilla organizations and those with international agendas. Guerrilla activity in the developing nations of Uruguay, El Salvador, Nicaragua, Peru, Colombia, Mexico and Cuba are examined on the basis of these classifications in order to explore the roles of women within these movements as follows.

In Uruguay, Tupamaros, was formed in 1962 which used guerrilla warfare as well as terrorist attacks on civilians in an effort to overthrow the national government in the 1960s and 1970s (Porzecanski, 1973). The Tupamaro guerrilla movement targeted to overthrow the oligarchic rule of Uruguay and eliminate government repression through the establishment of a socialist society. These goals concentrated on domestic objectives rather than international goals. Georges-Abeyie (1983: 75) cites that although Uruguay did not display a strong feminist tradition, it experienced 'considerable feminist input in terrorist organizations'. In addition, there are studies that indicate that the Tupamaros strongly encouraged, the active participation of women within the organization. Within the Tupamaros, women participated at all levels, from supportive roles to more active service as warriors and leadership roles. Reif (1986: 157) states that all troops had at least one or two women as members, and that their duties included both support and combat functions. According to Reif (1986: 157), 'women participated in substantial numbers in the Tupamaros'; she notes Tupamaro arrest records from 1966 that show fully 10% of the membership was female; by 1972, that percentage had increased to over 25%. The fact that the Tupamaros developed specific policy positions on women's issues provides support to the assertion of active female involvement at all levels. The Tupamaros' political platform promoted the direct participation of women in guerrilla activities as well as the elimination of gender discrimination in society as a whole. Reif (1986: 157) contends that the Tupamaros' objectives of free access to education and fair distribution of income as well as the nationalization of health care, elderly care and food production were 'effectively adopted strategies to recruit women'.

In El Salvador, the main opposition to the military and industrial oligarchy emerged in the civil war of 1979–92 and was consisted of two guerrilla movements, the Farabundo Marti Front for National Liberation (FMLN) and the Democratic Revolutionary Front (FDR). The FMLN itself was indeed a merger of five existing political and guerrillas movements that pursued direct democratic political participation by the people, land reform, economic reform, government intervention in the economy and restructuring of the military and police (Reif, 1986: 157; Montgomery, 1995: 103–105). The FMLN–FDR reportedly had 40% female membership in the total group and records demonstrate that between 30% and 40% of the armed fighters were women as well. During the demobilization process at the end of the civil war, United Nations observers presented around 5,000 female members out of 15,000 troops. Among the women, 55% served as guerrillas in armed warfare, while fewer than 30% carried out organizational and domestic duties, and only 15% participated in health and medical care (Heyzer, 2004: 2). Other sources reveal significant numbers of women in high-ranking leadership positions and that women consisted 40% of the revolutionary council (Reif, 1986: 157). They shared in decision- making processes and the performance of tasks that were traditionally gender-assigned, thereby filling not only the basic roles but also warriors and leadership positions.

Another guerrilla movement, the revolutionary Sandinista National Liberation Front (FSLN) formed in 1961 to overthrow the oppressive dictatorship of the Somoza family and its brutal National Guard and form a liberal reform government in Nicaragua. It successfully overthrew the Somoza regime through a guerrilla warfare lasting 18 years (Reif, 1986: 158). That indicated the goals of the FSLN were domestic in nature, limited to internal change rather than external transformations beyond the national borders as the above-mentioned movements. Furthermore, with regard to the women's participation to the movement, the Association of Women Confronting the National Problem (AMPRONAC) established by a leader of the FSLN helped recruit many women into the Sandinista army. Scholars evaluate that women comprised one-third of all heads-of-households during this period (Reif, 1986: 158). Disenfranchised politically and economically by their national government and forced into assuming full responsibility for their families, they were promising candidates for the cause. Women rapidly moved from support positions within the FSLN to battle and leadership roles, sometimes filling as many as half of the leadership posts in battle. By the end of the 1970s, women consisted 30% of the Sandinista guerrilla army and functioned in battle and leadership roles in addition to support positions (Reif, 1986: 158). In addition, Reif (1986: 158) links the success of the Sandinistas' appeal to women to its willingness to create internal policies of respect and support for women, made all the more important by their deviation from the traditional Latin machismo of Somoza society.

The Sendero Luminoso (SL) or Shining Path of Peru provides an example of a guerrilla organization known worldwide as one of the most brutal. Its objectives were mainly domestic in that organization which sought to collapse the institutions of the Peruvian government and replace them with a revolutionary peasant regime (Griset & Mahan, 2003: 162). Many scholars argue that the SL was initially led by a guerrilla, the late Torre Guzman, known as Comrade Norah. Although other sources acknowledge her husband, Abimael Guzman, with its founding, the data evidently demonstrate that, during the 1980s, 'a large number of women [were] involved at all levels of the organization right up to the top positions in both the regional commands and the National Central Committee' (Palmer, 1995: 277). Inside sources pointed out that Abimael Guzman 'relied heavily on a select group of female cadres' (Speck, 1992). Although critics argued that the women were valued for their loyalty rather than their intellect and that their roles were those of administrators, not strategists, information revealed after Guzman's arrest in 1993 that SL leadership had long been controlled by women such as Edith Lagos, Laura Zambrano, and Elena Iparraguirre, who could 'maintain order and keep a secret' (Speck, 1992). In her research of the SL, Tarazona-Sevillano (1990: 76–78) brings out that the group strongly urged female membership and that women 'historically played a leading role' in the SL, especially lower class women for whom the SL represented 'a battle for gender equality', enabling women 'to strike back violently at the traditional system that oppresses them'. She links the SL's strength and longevity to its widespread female participation, commenting that women were 'frequently charged with the responsibility for delivering the fatal shot in the assassination squad operations'.

Colombia's Fuerzas Armadas Revolucionario de Colombia (FARC) or Colombian Revolutionary Armed Forces which began in 1964 is acknowledged as one of the largest and best-equipped guerrilla forces in history (International Policy Institute for Counterterrorism, 2004). FARC's objectives, which mainly include political reform, elimination of government corruption, more investment in rural social programs, and reduction of Colombia's military and defense spending, which are domestic in orientation.

From 2004 on, the four-decade civil war in Colombia, continued as the longest in the Americas with over 150,000 casualties, including over 5,000 police, and 2.5 million displaced persons (Gruner, 2003: 30). However, many of the FARC members responsible for its guerrilla warfare are women. In 1974, FARC had fewer than 900 members, and a mere handful was female. By the year 2000, approximately 30% of the 15,000 FARC members were women; within two years, women consisted between 40% and 45% of the 18,000 FARC members. Female guerrillas mention the poverty and lack of economic, political, and social rights for women in Colombian society as reasons to join FARC (Hodgson, 2000b: 6; Cala, 2001). Colombia's nation wide unemployment rate is over 20%, and rural traditions reject education for girls, both of which are classic preconditions for guerrilla activity, according to Georges-Abeyie (Hodgson, 2000b; Georges-Abeyie, 1983: 84). Furthermore, according to FARC guerrillas, the movement offers them freedom and equality from the oppressive macho culture of traditional Colombian society. In this respect, Maria Eugenia Vasquez asserts: 'In a country where women are usually ignored, [guerrillas] are surrounded by symbols that give them an identity' (Hodgson, 2000b). Joaquin Gomez, leader of a FARC battle division, states that women are fundamental and valued in the 'people's war'; as such, FARC has actively recruited women since the early 1990s (Cunningham, 2003: 179). The guerrillas contend that their roles are equal to those of the men in FARC, performing guard duty, patrolling, gathering intelligence, fighting in combat, and serving as field commanders (Cunningham, 2003: 179; McDermott, 2002). Within FARC they undertake significant roles; they collect intelligence information, lead guerrilla troops in combat, and make policy decisions.

Finally, as an example of guerrilla movement the Ejército Zapatista de Liberación Nacional (EZLN) or Zapatista Army of National Liberation is a revolutionary leftist group based in Chiapas, the southern state of Mexico. The EZLN provides a model of one of the best-organized and politically effective guerrilla movements today. It declared war on the executive branch of the Mexican government and the Mexican Army in 1994, for political and economic discrimination against the indigenous peoples of Mexico and announced the establishment of political, economic and social equality throughout Mexico as its major objective. In this regard, the researches pointed out that the extreme poverty of the Chiapas region has contributed to the high levels of female participation in the EZLN because the women of Chiapas suffer disproportionately from the burdens of poverty and discrimination (Camp, 1996: 91; Goetze, 1996: 4; Millan, 2002: 3). As Mansbridge (2001) notes, 'the indigenous women of Mexico are the most marginalized group in that country'. Thus, women have been active in the EZLN since its inception and have brought with them a strong desire to protect the opportunities not afforded to them in the external community. In fact, they often function as warriors, rising to high-ranking levels of the guerrilla army, where they command both male and female soldiers (Millan, 2002: 3). They also become dominant forces, creating policy on women's social and economic rights and contributing to negotiations with the Mexican government (Cevallos, 2001; Franco, 2001; Goetze, 1996: 6–7; Rashkin, 1996: 12–13).

These above-mentioned groups, which are representative of the most effective guerrilla movements in the post-WWII world, do not oppose the external forces of imperialism or the inequities of global capitalism. On the contrary, they target the governments of their own nations and seek to overthrow, reform, or secede from the state. In rejecting the traditional power structure and its control, these groups also challenge its restrictions on women's activities and limited gender roles. Women have actively been involved in armed struggle of these groups that open opportunities to eliminate gender inequalities. Similarly, Kurdish guerrilla struggle began in 1984 after the establishment of the PKK ((Kurdistan Workers' Party; a Marxist-Leninist guerrilla organization) in 1978 to fight against oppressive and assimilation policies of the Turkish state and its denial of Kurdish rights. Thus, Kurdish guerrilla movement is a domestically oriented in terms of its objectives. The movement that combats for self-determination, political and cultural rights of Kurds open opportunities for women's emancipation through mobilizing women around the Kurdish cause and encouraging them to join the guerrilla movement that will be explained in details in the below analysis.

While the guerrilla movements discussed above thus far exhibit a domestic orientation, seeking to change or reject their national governments and reform domestic policies, the Cuban revolutionaries of 1959 represent an organization with a more international agenda. Despite the Cuba's guerrilla movement aimed to remove the Batista regime, it was internationally oriented, directed against Western capitalism and the forces of US imperialism that had dominated Cuba since the Spanish–American War of 1898. In this regard, although supporters associate the spread of international socialism and Castro's Communist Revolution with mobilizing Cuban working-class women, even Cuba's revolutionaries accept that Cuban women did not actively participate in the guerrilla activities of the revolt Gonzalez-Perez (2006). The President of the Federation of Cuban Women and Fidel Castro's sister-in-law, Vilma Espin, stated that very few women actually participated in the Cuban struggle and that 'campesino [rural peasant] women were generally not organizationally active until mobilized by the Federation after the insurgency period' (Reif, 1986: 155–156). Jaquette's (1973: 346–347) study of women in revolutionary movements in Latin America discusses only three Cuban women who were active in battle: Fidel Castro's secretary, Celia Sanchez; Vilma Espin, wife of Castro's brother, Raul Castro; and Haydee Santamaria, the wife of a Communist Party leader. Jaquette describes the revolution as a 'conscious attempt by Fidel and other members of the elite to transform the status of women in Cuban society', but does not address the converse, the attempt of revolutionary women to transform society. In addition, though Rowbotham (1972: 223–225) discusses the formation of a Red Army battalion of women in Cuba, she states that battle conditions were viewed unsuitable for women and quotes Che Guevara as stating that the men were not used to following a female commander. Reif's (1986: 155) analysis of interviews and letters from Cuban revolutionaries concludes that 'women performed basically support and relief roles, providing 'support rather than combat performance', as 'women in the guerrilla army did housekeeping and supply assignments'. In her study of women in the Cuban Revolution, Cole (1994: 299–307) discusses the bad situation of women prior to the revolution and the subsequent effect on women, but offers no evidence of any female participation in revolutionary activities. Similarly, Molyneux's (2000: 293–294) examination of the Federation of Cuban Women elucidates the impact of the revolution on women rather than their role in the revolution. As part of the international socialist revolution against capitalism and US dominance, Castro's Cuba perceived changes in women's status as a result of the revolution rather than an active force within the political transformation.

The literature concerning a number of selected guerrilla movements mentioned above demonstrates that domestically oriented guerrilla movements such as the Tupamaros of Uruguay, FMLN and FDR of El Salvador, Sandinistas of Nicaragua, Shining Path of Peru, the ELN, EPL, and FARC of Colombia, and the

Zapatistas of Mexico actively recruit and foster the participation of women at all levels of the organization, providing upward mobility from service as sympathizers to the higher ranks of warrior and dominant forces. The domestically oriented guerrilla movements examined in this study, incorporate women's issues and concerns into their group's internally focused agenda, further encouraging female participation. The increasing numbers and levels of women's involvement have a cyclical effect, inducing the group to become more responsive to women's objectives, thus attracting still more women. On the other hand, those guerrilla organizations that refuse women or assign them to subservient support roles demonstrate a focus on international agendas and external enemies. The Communist revolutionaries of Cuba allowed female participation, but in a form strictly regulated by the males of the organizations. Much as the dominant society assigns women a traditional gender role, these internationally oriented guerrilla groups also restrict women's activities.

In comparison to guerilla movements in Latin America countries examined above which are differentiated in terms of the levels of women's participation and women's roles within them mainly depending on their agendas and objectives the Kurdish guerrilla movement led by the PKK falls into the category of domestically oriented guerrilla organizations that women undertake a variety of roles from sympathizers to warriors and leadership as will be indicated in the following analysis.

This research discusses the women's participation in Kurdish guerrilla movement in terms of its impact on emergence of Kurdish women's feminist movement and their activism in political arenas, the above-mentioned Latin America guerrilla movements also need to be analyzed from this perspective. There are different views regarding status of women in post-revolutionary period. Many studies focus on women's organizing and demobilization in Latin America (Navarro, 1989; Alvarez, 1990; Jelin, 1990; Radcliffe and Westwood, 1993; Jaquette, 1994a; Friedman, 1998). According to Friedman (1998), Latin America cases present a paradox. Women mobilize politically under even the most repressive forms of authoritarian rule, but in the transition to democracy, they demobilize. Latin American women have played central roles in overthrowing authoritarian regimes in many countries. Yet women's organizational strength and leadership has declined with the advent of democracy. For instance, women held only 8 percent of Latin American ministerial posts in 1994. However, they constituted only 13.6 percent of parliaments in 1997 (UNDP 1995, 62; IPU 1997, 95- 96 mentioned in Friedman, 1998). A trend toward the disarticulation of women's organizations established under dictatorship has further deepened this 'democratic exclusion' (Chuchryk 1994; Feijóo and Nari 1994; Waylen 1996). In her study of the Nicaragua case, With regards to women's marginalization in the transitions to democracy, Friedman (1998) contends that the institutionalization of politics during the transition restrains the forms of organization that women established under the former regimes and their subsequent political incorporation into democracy. More clearly, the political opportunity structure, the ensemble of political institutions and actors influencing social mobilization, of each phase of democratic transition is gendered. That means, it reflects certain gender relations. These gender relations usually represent the traditional division of labour that identifies men with the more socially valued public sphere of work and politics, and women with the less-esteemed private sphere of the home. The indications of gender relations within the political institutions characterizing different regimes, such as parties and the state, generates a peculiar set of opportunities and obstacles that determine women's political participation. These processes help to explain both the substantial roles of women in the struggle against authoritarian rule and their subsequent marginalization in the early stages of democracy.

On the other hand, the study Kampwirth (2004) accounts the rise of feminist movements in the cases Nicaragua, El Salvador and the Mexican state Chiapas, as the unintended consequences of the guerrilla movements in those countries. Based on the experiences of women with the guerrilla organizations who later become feminists, Kampwirth (2004) asserts that there are reasons why revolutionary movements can unintentionally engender feminists and feminist mobilizations. First reason is an ideological one. That is, revolutionary guerrilla groups tend to promote egalitarianism. Kampwirth (2004) clarifies that many of the women she interview remember the time they were guerrillas or members of other revolutionary groups were often the times they received the most equal treatment from men. However, when the struggles ended and their male fellows attempted to return gender relations to their pre-revolutionary inegalitarian 'norms', women revolutionaries were taken aback by this contradiction and in many cases they refused to accept it. The second reason of feminism and feminist mobilization subsequent to revolution is the resources acquired by women revolutionaries during their struggles, namely self-confidence and organization skills. The final reason was the persistence of pre-existing networks which natural served as a feminist infrastructure. These studies concerning women's situation in the post-revolution period of Latin America countries raise significant points that Kurdish women can utilize in advancing their movement. It would not be appropriate to compare the Kurdish guerrilla movement with these above-mentioned cases since the Kurdish struggle still continues yet Kurdish women concern on the post-conflict period as they expressed during field research. In this regard, it is pointed out, the experiences of Latin American women urge Kurdish women to put efforts for strengthening their independent organization and achieving gender equality in the political arenas in order to maintain their power in the post-conflict period.

Kurdish guerrilla movement and women's participation

There are a significant number of studies focusing Kurdish guerrilla movement in Turkey particularly on the basis on the emergence and development of the Kurdish armed struggle which identified with the PKK, and the PKK's role in the mobilization of Kurds as a social and political movement (Gunter, 1997; Romano, 2006, Marcus, 2007; Özcan, 2006; Yeğen, 1998; Kirişci and Winrow, 1997; White, 2000; Jongerden, 2011, Güneş, 2012) and the mobilization of Kurds by the PKK (Romano, 2006; Güneş, 2012). In those studies which focused upon the development of the Kurdish national movement by the PKK as a social and political movement and which studied the role of the PKK in the mobilization of Kurds and its ideological influences, women were mentioned in the sense of how they were mobilized by the PKK and their involvement in legal political areas which mainly refers to ideological influences (Romano, 2006; Marcus, 2007; Güneş, 2012). As I will argue in this thesis, these works are useful in explaining the emergence of Kurdish women's activism and the ideological connections between the Kurdish national movement and the pro-Kurdish political movement, which influenced the Kurdish women's struggle for gender equality.

Furthermore, women's participation and their roles within the guerrilla movement have become significant since the beginning of 1990s. The studies have pointed out oppression due to both their ethnic identity and gender identity lead women to join the PKK. The state oppression toward Kurds and oppression of women within patriarchal family structures, have induced a vast number of university students, high school students from urban as well as young women in rural to participate the guerrilla movement (Özcan, 1999; Marcus, 2007; Flach, 2007; Westrheim, 2008, Wolf 2004). The independent organization of women within the PKK under the name of PAJK (the Party for Freedom of the Women of Kurdistan) enables women to carry on both national and gender based struggle and undertake not only warrior roles but also fulfilling leadership positions. A comprehensive analysis of Kurdish national movement on the basis of its role both in mobilizing Kurds as a whole and Kurdish women in particular in legal political arenas will be carried out in the Chapter 3.

Women and (Kurdish) Politics in Turkey

There is a broad body of literature that study the women and politics, and women's political representation in Turkey. In particular studies concerning the role of women in policy-making have increased in parallel to the increase in women's participation in politics in the 1990s. These studies have mostly focused on the reasons behind women's under representation in politics, characteristics of women's political work, and the activism of Kurdish women and Islamist/conservative women (Tekeli 1981; Arat, 1989; Talaslı 1996; TÜSİAD 2000 Report; Güneş-Ayata, 1990, 1998, 2001; Berktay, 1998; Saktanber, 2002; White, 2002; TÜSİAD and KAGİDER 2008 Report; Çağlayan, 2007; Turam, 2008). In addition, most of these studies have revealed that the primary reason for women's lower political representation is a lack of support from the political parties.[12] They have also explored a strong connection between party ideology and the promotion of women's inclusion in parties. Since women have not been a significant influence on political parties in the sense of forcing them to advance women's political representation, women's agency in transforming party politics has not been a significant matter in these studies. Research has pointed out that left wing political parties are more inclusive than the right wing parties. For instance, Talaslı (1996) noted that among ten parties that were represented in the parliament between 1991 and 1995, right-wing parties had a worse record than left-wing parties in terms of the number of women in positions of power, the inclusion of women in party platforms, and the usage of positive discrimination measures.

Furthermore, there have been several single-case studies, which only analyse women's involvement with Islamist political parties and the Islamist movement and address the role of women's organization in parties (Arat, 2005; Güneş-Ayata, 2001; Saktanber, 2002; White, 2002; Turam, 2008). For instance, Ayşe Saktanber (2002) examined the Ankara Ladies Commission of the Islamist Fazilet Party (FP, Virtue Party) and the study found out that women in the party regarded their activism as a matter of service to God, to their community, and to men. Her study was limited to the case of the FP, and only to its women's organization. Likewise, Yeşim Arat (2005) who has several studies on women and politics in Turkey concentrated on the activities of female commissions of the Islamist Refah Party (RP, Welfare Party) and its successor, the FP.

---

[12] These matters have been also been addressed in the following reports prepared by civil society organizations: TÜSİAD 2000 Report, Walking Towards Equality between Men and Women: Education, Employment and Politics (Kadın-Erkek Eşitliğine Doğru Yürüyüş: Eğitim, Çalışma Yaşamı ve Siyaset). TÜSİAD and KAGİDER's 2008 Report, Gender Inequality in Turkey: Problems, Priorities and Suggestions for Solutions (*Türkiye'de Toplumsal Cinsiyet Eşitsizliği: Sorunlar, Öncelikler ve Çözüm Önerileri*).

However, in comparison to the literature on the Kurdish national movement and women and politics in Turkey, works on pro-Kurdish legal politics and women's involvement in legal politic are less numerous. That is to say, legal political parties and their roles in the Kurdish national movement have not received enough academic attention. The changes that they have made in the political area, in terms representing Kurdish demands, and their influences in Turkish politics have not been sufficiently studied. The first works on pro-Kurdish political parties appeared toward end of 1990s and the beginning of the 2000s.[13] There might be a few reasons for this lack of academic interest, such as the fact that they were perceived as Kurdish ethnic identity-based parties. Such studies concentrated only upon the phenomenon as a Kurdish issue. They were small scale and not influential enough to receive attention; and due to the political conditions of early 1990's, when there was intensive conflict between the PKK and the Turkish State, attention was focused upon the activities of the PKK. When pro-Kurdish political parties started to increase their bases and have success in elections at the end of the 1990s they started to receive attention. Furthermore, changes in the political environment in Turkey and the PKK's objectives allowed for the raising of political parties' roles and brought interest in the pro-Kurdish legal parties. However, in these later studies, which emphasize the transforming role of Kurdish activists within the legal political arenas the gender difference of activists is not specified. In this sense, the works of Nicole Watts (1999, 2006, and 2010) are useful in understanding the influences and roles of the pro-Kurdish political parties in the Kurdish national movement. Watts's works on

---

[13] Nicole F Watts, "Allies and Enemies: Pro-Kurdish Parties in Turkish Politics, 1990-4" *International Journal of Middle East Studies,* Vol. 31, No. 4 (Nov., 1999): 631-656. Watts reminds Barkey's article as the first academic work on pro-Kurdish political parties in Turkey. Henry J. Barkey, "The People's Democracy Party (HADEP): The Travails of a Legal Kurdish Party in Turkey," *Journal of Muslim Minority Affairs* 18, no.1 (1998): 129-138. Aylin Güney, "The People's Democracy Party." *Turkish Studies* 3, no.1 (2002): 122-137.

pro-Kurdish party politics and ethno-political activists highlight their contribution to the Kurdish national movement, its impact in changing state policies towards Kurds and its role in the expression of Kurdish identity and demands. Nevertheless, there is no gender-based differentiation in her analysis of activists and the roles of women in pro-Kurdish party politics and the impacts of party politics on women are not mentioned. Watts's book, *Activists in Office: Kurdish Politics and Protest in Turkey* (2010) and her articles "Activists in Office: Pro-Kurdish Contentious Politics in Turkey" (2006) and "Allies and Enemies: Pro-Kurdish Parties in Turkish Politics, 1990-4" (1999) explore how Kurdish activists have made themselves matter and how they have impressed their ideas and agendas on a repressive state through using electoral politics. Her focus is on Kurdish activists in and from Turkey who have sought to use electoral politics and the institutions of the state to change state policies, challenge the state oppression and obtain Kurdish demands through operating within the political realm. Watt's works contribute to this research in terms of contextualizing pro-Kurdish politics since 1990, which is necessary in order to situate women's engagement in politics.

As mentioned above, while there have been some academic studies about the political experiences of women in general in Turkey, there is much less academic research concerning Kurdish women and their political activism. Moreover, while there are resources available which are relevant to the Kurdish national movement, there are only very limited empirical resources and researches which directly focus on Kurdish women or on the gender issues of the Kurdish nationalist movement and pro-Kurdish politics in Turkey. Apparently, the gender issues have been ignored in the dominant literature concerning Kurdish question and Kurdish national movement. The number of academic studies focusing on Kurdish women remains low when one considers the size of Kurdish population[14] and half of them as women, in Turkey in particular in the Middle East in general. Furthermore, Kurdish women who are more generally ignored in the literature are dealt as the women of Turkey, Iran, Iraq or Syria. The literature, which actually treats Kurdish women as such, is limited in both quantity and quality, and is mostly related to the status of the Kurds as a stateless nation.

Despite the increasing political activism of Kurdish women in the post-1980[15] and the emergence of Kurdish feminism in 1990s primarily through establishment of various women organizations and publication of a number of journals named Roza, Jujîn, Yaşamda Özgür Kadın and Jin û Jiyan, 16 Kurdish women and the specificity of their experiences have been ignored and not been recognized by Turkish feminism and in the dominant literature concerning women in Turkey. To exemplify, in those two primary books, which include a number of articles, concerning women in Turkey there is no mention of Kurdish women: 1980'ler Türkiye'sinde Kadın Bakış Açısından Kadınlar [From a Women's Perspective Women in Turkey in the 1980s] (1995), 20. Yüzyılın Sonunda Kadınlar ve Gelecek [Women and the Future at the End of the 20th Century] (1998), 75 Yılda Kadınlar ve Erkekler [Women and Men in 75 Years] (1998). Rather, they were viewed as "Eastern" and "rural" women (Ertürk, 1995; İlkkaracan and İlkkaracan, 1998; İlkkaracan, 1998) or as tribal women (Yalçın-Heckmann, 1995) but not as 'Kurdish women' in feminist studies. It is only in the

---

[14] Kurds are the largest ethnic group in Turkey after ethnic Turks. It is estimated that they make up anywhere from 15 to 20 percent of the population of Turkey which is currently stated as 76 million. The other three countries that Kurds are divided are Iran, Iraq and Syria.

[15] For a detailed analysis of Kurdish women's political activism in Turkey in the post-1980, see Handan Çağlayan (2007), *Analar, Yoldaşlar, Tanrıçalar: Kürt Hareketinde Kadınlar ve Kadın Kimliğinin Oluşması*, İstanbul: İletişim. Also see L. Yalçın-Heckmann and P. van Gelder (2000), "90'larda Türkiye'de Siyasal Söylemin Dönüşümü Çerçevesinde Kürt Kadınlarının İmajı: Bazı Eleştirel Değerlendirmeler", *in* A. G. Altınay (ed.), *Vatan, Millet, Kadınlar*, İstanbul: İletişim, pp. 308–338.

[16] For a content and comparative study of these journals, *see* Necla Açık (2002), "Ulusal Mücadele, Kadın Mitosu ve Kadınların Harekete Geçirilmesi: Türkiye'deki Çagdaş Kürt Kadın Dergilerinin Bir Analizi" in *90'larda Türkiye'de Feminizm*, A. Bora and A. Günal (eds.), İstanbul: İletişim, pp. 279–306.

work of Yalçın-Heckmann and van Gelder (2000) Kurdish women are referred to; yet it cannot be included into the Turkish feminist studies because the research was not carried by Turkish feminist circles. Besides, in this research Kurdish women are addressed on the basis of nationalist discourses. Their experiences are received less attention in comparison to the roles ascribed to them by the Kurdish nationalist movement.

In those studies which address Kurdish women as women in the East (Kurdish region) the situation of the women is found to be much worse than in other regions of the country with regard to almost all indicators of women's status that are used. Actually, in comparison to the western of Turkey where mostly Turkish people populated, the Kurdish populated areas, which mainly include Eastern and South-eastern regions, and Kurdish people are more impoverished and deprived in terms of socio-economic indicators such as income, educational level and occupational status. Kurds are materially and non-materially are in an environment of insecurity and Kurdish women are insecure twice as much compared to Kurdish men (İçduygu et al., 1999). Similarly, Kurdish women are poorer and more disadvantaged compared to Kurdish men as well as non-Kurdish women in the sense of socio-economic indicators (Gündüz-Hoşgör and Smits, 2002). The studies explore women in the Eastern regions experience poverty, illiteracy, polygamy, and unemployment as well as extremes of oppression and gender-based violence (İlkkaracan, 1998; İçduygu et al., 1999; Smits and Gündüz-Hoşgör, 2003 & 2006). In this regard, this research will illuminate how Kurdish women have taken significant steps in terms of promoting gender equality in political arena despite their poor socio-economic conditions as above studies explored.

As has been pointed out there is a lack of academic scholarship addressing Kurdish women and so their political activism too. The studies of Bayrak (2002), Mojab (2005), and Çağlayan (2007) are some of the exceptional works focusing on Kurdish women but few of them require attention with regard to further analysis.

One of the major works on Kurdish women is the book which is entitled *Women of A Non-State Nation: The Kurds* edited by Shahrzad Mojab (2001). This book includes noteworthy articles written by different academics and refers to the historical, political, legal, social, cultural and linguistic perspectives concerning Kurdish women. Some of these articles, which throw light on gender and women's issues in Kurdish society, are worth mentioning in detail. Mojab has two chapters in this book which are, "Introduction: The solitude of the stateless-Kurdish women at the margins of feminist knowledge" and "Women and Nationalism in the Kurdish Republic of 1946" respectively. The first article raises questions about feminism and nationalism as two different ideological positions, which influence the role and status of Kurdish women; it is therefore worthwhile highlighting some of the important points of this piece of work. In this study, Mojab underlines the fact that Kurds in general and Kurdish women in particular have been subject of repressive policies in four countries: Turkey, Iran, Iraq and Syria, among which they have been divided after the First World War. In this regard, she puts forward important critiques of Turkish feminism[17] because of Turkish feminists' prioritizing national identity in their relation with Kurdish women which divide women along ethnic lines and Kurdish nationalism[18] because of its influence in maintaining traditional gender roles and

---

[17] S. Mojab (2001), "Introduction: The Solitude of the Stateless: Kurdish Women at the Margins of Feminist Knowledge", in Mojab (ed.), *Women of a Non-State Nation: The Kurds*, pp.5–6.

[18] Ibid., pp.8–9.

norms in the Kurdish national movement. Further, she does not just criticise Kurdish nationalism, she underlines that nationalism and feminism are two contradicting ideological standpoints.[19]

There are some other significant articles in the book edited by Mojab, which are not directly related to this research but worth mentioning in order to give an idea about gender relations in Kurdish society historically. One of which is Hassanpour's article[20], which raises the debate in the domain of language. Amir Hassanpour claims that the unequal distribution of gender power is obviously recorded in the Kurdish language. He proves the patriarchal reproduction of power relations in the Kurdish language by presenting several pieces of linguistic evidence. Another article is Rohat Alakom's, which makes a significant contribution by revealing the existence of a Kurdish women's society in İstanbul in 1919. It was called the Society for the Advancement of Kurdish Women [Kürd Kadınları Teali Cemiyeti].[21]

In his work, Martin van Bruinessen made an analysis of the most significant and well-known cases of Kurdish women who played great political roles in Kurdish history[22]. In this context, he throws light upon Adela Khanum of Halabja[23], Kara Fatima Khanum[24] and Leyla Zana, the former Member of Parliament in Turkey, who

---

[19] Ibid., p.6. See also S. Mojab (2001), "Women and Nationalism in the Kurdish Republic of 1946", in Mojab (ed.), *Women of a Non-State Nation: The Kurds*, pp.71, 88.

[20] A. Hassanpour, (2001) "The (Re)production of Patriarchy in the Kurdish Language", in Mojab (ed.), *Women of a Non-State Nation: The Kurds*, pp.227–63.

[21] R. Alakom (2001), "Kurdish Women in Constantinople at the Beginning of the Twentieth Century", in Mojab (ed.), *Women of a Non-State Nation: The Kurds*, p.60.

[22] M. van Bruinessen (2001), "From Adela Khanum to Leyla Zana: Women as Political Leaders in Kurdish History", in Mojab (ed.), *Women of a Non-State Nation: The Kurds*, p.95.

[23] M. van Bruinessen (2001), "From Adela Khanum to Leyla Zana: Women as Political Leaders in Kurdish History", in Mojab (ed.), *Women of a Non-State Nation: The Kurds*, pp. 96-8.

[24] M. van Bruinessen (2001), "From Adela Khanum to Leyla Zana: Women as Political

has been in jail for her support of Kurdish rights[25]. The most substantial point about Van Bruinessen's piece is that, 'Kurdish society is highly male-dominated and has been for all of its known history'.[26] Emphasizing the achievements of these women, past and present, he argues that the evidence does not support the claim to gender equality in Kurdish society. These remarks represent a contradiction to the Kurdish nationalist discourse, which claims that Kurdish women enjoy equality with Kurdish men.

The works mentioned above raise two problems. While one points out the damaging effects of the Turkish state discourse on the Kurds, the other highlights the influence of the Kurdish nationalist discourse. The common point is that these two issues represent distinct articulations of the same ideological stance, that of nationalism. Furthermore, while these studies provide a general perspective regarding the situation and role of Kurdish women in Kurdish society, none of them is related to the political activism of Kurdish women. In this sense, Handan Çağlayan's work which examines the construction of Kurdish women's identity under the influence of Kurdish national movement and Kurdish nationalism, is particular relevant for this study.

Çağlayan's book (2007), entitled *Analar, Yoldaşlar, Tanrıçalar: Kürt Hareketinde Kadınlar ve Kadın Kimliğinin Oluşumu* [Mothers, Comrades and Goddesses: Women in the Kurdish Movement and The Construction of Women's Identity], is a pioneering study with a strong theoretical framework and rich empirical data on Kurdish women's political activism in Turkey. This study that applies a historical analysis to illuminate the ways in which Kurdish women's identity has been constructed after the 1980s examines the role of the Kurdish national movement and

---

Leaders in Kurdish History", in Mojab (ed.), *Women of a Non-State Nation: The Kurds*, p.99.
[25] Ibid., pp.106–7.
[26] Ibid., p.95.

the pro-Kurdish parties since the 1990s. She attempts to explicate the processes by which Kurdish women become political actors through exploring their experiences. Using social movement theory, it focuses on the changes in the Kurdish movement's gender ideology and the role of women in the movement between the early 1990s and 2003. She argued that although the parties had a limited emphasis on women in the early 1990s, they gave special attention to women's participation and a gender perspective in the early 2000s as part of their mobilization strategy and as a result of the claim making, struggle, and resistance of Kurdish women.

Çağlayan's study provides important insights for this research. The complexity and multi-dimensionality of the political movement of Kurdish women is well explained in Çağlayan's work which provides a basis upon which to contextualize today's visible growth and the activism of Kurdish women within the pro-Kurdish party in relation to feminizing politics. However, it has certain drawbacks, which will be dealt with in this thesis. There is a brief reference to the role of the political leadership in the political activism of Kurdish women. Another point is that since the analysis only covers a period up to 2003 the outcomes of women's increasing role in the political arena and their growth in representation are not included in the analysis. Thus, this research represents a further step which is specifically interested in analyzing and investigating the outcomes of growth in the activism of Kurdish women in politics and the evolution of pro-Kurdish party politics in terms of its gender ideology and policies, issues which have not been of previous academic concern.

Other studies, which refer to Kurdish women, are the master thesis of Metin Yüksel[27] and Zeynep Kutluata.[28] Basically, there are three focal points in Yüksel's

---

[27] Metin Yüksel. (2003). *Diversifying Feminism in Turkey in the 1990s.* (Unpublished MA Thesis). Ankara: Bilkent University.

work. The first point is to explore Kurdish women's relation with feminism and the feminist movements in Turkey. The second point concerns their relationship with nationalism and the Kurdish nationalist movement. The third point concerns the specificity/difference of Kurdish womanhood experience. As has been mentioned, nationalism and feminism are two fundamental theoretical approaches, which characterize these studies. As with Yüksel's study, in the work of Kutluata ethnic identity plays an essential role in shaping the experiences of Kurdish women. Kutluata highlights the importance of Kurdish women's activism after the 1990s in the context of their ethnic and gender identities as a means for discussing the issue of difference with regard to cases of language and birth control. Undoubtedly, each of them contributes to my research; some of their points are particularly useful in structuring a historical background of Kurdish women's visibility in the political arena since the 1990s. However, my research more specifically deals with the increasing political involvement of Kurdish women and its potential to transform pro-Kurdish party politics.

With the exception of Çağlayan's study, the scholarly works concerning Kurdish women mentioned above do not address Kurdish women's political involvement in pro-Kurdish politics in Turkey. Therefore, the increasing involvement of Kurdish women in pro-Kurdish politics, their increasing political representation, and their role in changing gender policies of the pro-Kurdish political parties have not been well researched. This thesis, in treating such an under-researched phenomenon, constitutes a significant contribution to the scholarship concerning women and political representation.

---

[28] Zeynep Kutluata. (2003). *The Politics of Difference within the Feminist Movement in Turkey as Manifested in the Case of Kurdish Woman/Feminist Journals* (Unpublished MA Thesis). İstanbul: Boğaziçi University.

CHAPTER THREE

The Actors Promoting Feminization in Pro-Kurdish Politics

Introduction: Feminization of pro-Kurdish Politics as a Multifaceted Process

This chapter explores actors and factors that contribute to the feminization of pro-Kurdish party politics since 1990. This examination reveals that *feminizing* politics in Kurdish case is a multifaceted process that includes a number of actors, different factors, multiple arguments and motives. The empirical research points out that there are three significant actors that have played an influential role in the feminization of pro-Kurdish party politics: the Kurdish national movement led by the PKK since end of 1970s, the pro-Kurdish political party and female political activists. These three actors, which are interlinked, have contributed to feminization of pro-Kurdish politics in different ways. The Kurdish national movement led by PKK (*Partiya Karkerên Kurdistan/ Kurdistan Workers Party*), an armed organization formally founded in 1978 to fight for Kurdish rights in Turkey, has become a major actor in mobilizing Kurdish people for the Kurdish national cause. Kurdish women have been increasingly mobilized under the influence of the PKK and especially from the beginning of 1990s when the party was institutionalised; a high number of women began to join the PKK as guerrilla fighters. Thus, the ideological discourses of the movement and its mobilization strategies have played a role in shaping gender discourses and organizational structure of the pro-Kurdish political parties (Çağlayan, 2007:126) as well as in the construction of the political identities of activists.

The following section analyses the identities of both the political party and female political activists taking into consideration the movement's ideology, program and discourses. The statements of female political activists who were interviewed during the field research reveal ideological connections between women's political activism, the pro-Kurdish political party and the Kurdish national movement with regards to gender inequality and women's emancipation. For instance, the vast majority of interviewees repeatedly stated that "People whose women are not free cannot be free" which is the statement of the PKK leader Abdullah Öcalan in addressing the significance of emancipation of women as necessary for liberation of Kurdish people. This perspective influences female political activists' activities and objectives, which target to eliminate the traditional patriarchal structures in society. Furthermore, pro-Kurdish political parties' ideological ties to the national movement which will be analysed through a study of their program and statutes in the following sections are utilized by female political activists in order to open a space for women in the political arena.

In this chapter, women's arguments for gender equality and the party's response to their demands are explained by referring to the argument of equal representation. There are basically three main arguments in the feminist literature dealing with the representation of women in bodies of representative democracy (Lovenduski 2000: 87ff.; Voet 1998: 100; Phillips 1995: 229-238), these are *justice*, *pragmatic*, and *difference* which are taken into account in the interest of explaining the feminization process in the Kurdish case. From this standpoint, arguments of equal representation (*justice, pragmatic and difference*) are employed to find out in what context women make their arguments and in what context the party encourages gender equity in politics. Thus, utilizing these concepts to evaluate the feminization process in Kurdish context will provide answers for the question of why pro-Kurdish party politics has been feminized.

The *Justice* argument contends that it is not fair for men to monopolize representation, particularly in a country that regards itself as democratic. Anne Phillips states that: "There is no argument from justice that can defend the current state of affairs; and there *is* an argument from justice for parity between women and men" (1995: 65). That is to say, unequal representation of women is unfair and undemocratic.

The *pragmatic* argument suggests that women have particular interests and these can only be represented and understood by them (Squires 1999: 205). Similarly Phillipps asserts that "(W) omen have a distinct and separate interest as women; that is this interest cannot be adequately represented by men; and that the election of women ensures its representation" (Phillipps 1998: 234). Furthermore, the *pragmatic* argument claims that women have experiences and interests that political parties must address by supporting more women politicians if they are to achieve and maintain power (and, in particular, if they want to win women's votes).

The *difference* argument claims that women have particular experiences and qualities (female morals, ethics, new political style), which should be integrated in politics to change male-centred institutions and policies. Women can revitalize democracy; women could be a remedy against political annoyance and the representational crisis. Shortly, this argument suggests that women will create a different style and approach to politics which will contribute to change it for the better, towards an outcome of benefit to all (Lovenduski 2005: 24).

This chapter examines these three actors in terms of their roles in transforming pro-Kurdish politics to include women in the decision-making process. First, it focuses on the PKK's ideology and discourses in order to explore their influence in the mobilization of Kurdish women and their role in the emergence of women's political activism. Besides, the role of women in PKK is investigated with regards to their impacts on female political activists in the legal political areas. Secondly, pro-Kurdish political parties are addressed to find out how their gender approach has changed since 1990 through examining its written documents exploring the connections and interactions with the national movement regarding gender ideology and political objectives. Thirdly, it concentrates on female political activists and their agency in raising the question of women's underrepresentation and their arguments and claims for equal representation. All these actors are addressed in the interests of exploring their roles in feminization of pro-Kurdish politics as seen below analysis.

The Role of Kurdish National Movement

The Kurdish national movement in Turkey is identified with the PKK, which has carried on an armed struggle against Turkish state since 1984. PKK has not acted only as a military organization claiming for freedom of Kurds. It has also acted as a political organization, which plays a role of social engineering aimed to re-create the Kurdish society on the basis of its ideology[29]. Its ideologies and discourses, which obviously challenge the existing society structures, are mostly framed by its leader Abdullah Öcalan through documents written by him or about him. A historical analysis of the PKK with particular focus on its ideology and objectives will demonstrate that women have received a significant interest through time which influences their increasing participation in the movement. More importantly, the

---

[29] For a detailed analysis of Kurdish national movement regarding its ideology see Romano (2006), Marcus. (2007) and Güneş (2012). Besides, for the role of the movement's ideology on emergence of Kurdish women movement and construction of Kurdish women identity see Çağlayan (2007).

primary contribution of the national movement to women's activism is to create awareness among Kurdish women that they are twice oppressed due to both their ethnic and gender identities which have shaped their activism since 1990s.

One of the major points to highlight is that the gender ideology and discourses of the PKK have led to the emergence of gender identity-based women's activism in Turkey at a significant level since 1990s. In addition, views and political identities of both pro-Kurdish political organizations and individual activists have been shaped by the PKK's ideologies and discourses. Although there are claims that pro-Kurdish political parties are the extensions of the PKK, it is important to take into consideration the relation between the PKK and pro-Kurdish political parties on the ideological level.[30]

The research conducted with female political activists revealed how they perceived and responded to the gender discourses and ideology of the PKK to define their roles and demands within the pro-Kurdish party politics. In this regard, women activists employed gender ideology and discourses of the national movement as tools to open space and make arguments for gender equality in the political areas.

In order to make a further analysis regarding the impact of the PKK in legal political areas as an armed political organization, a historical analysis is carried out in order to identify the ways in which its gender ideology and political objectives have changed since end of 1970s. This process will illuminate how women have been mobilized by the PKK and how their mobilization has been a determinant factor in the emergence of women's political activism.

---

[30] N. Watts (2006 and 2010) and H. Çağlayan (2007) also in their works consider the relation between PKK and pro-Kurdish political parties as ideological.

A Brief History of the PKK

The PKK is not only an armed organization. The PKK is one of the most important secular insurgent political movements in Kurdistan and the Middle East (Jongerden and Akkaya, 2011: 124). The establishment of PKK in 1978 as a leftist Marxist movement represents a crucial turning point in Kurdish struggle in Turkey. It was formally founded in the Fis village (Lice, Diyarbakir) in Kurdistan in the southeast of Turkey in November 1978 after a two-year planning period (Gunter 1990, 1997; McDowall, 2000; White 2000; Özcan, 2006; Marcus 2007). The PKK started as an illegal party planning for an independent Kurdish state and freedom for all Kurds living in Iraq, Iran, Turkey and Syria (Marcus, 2007: 9). The seventies and the early eighties could be described as the "revolutionary" era in Turkey. Many Kurds were involved in these "revolutionary" organizations, which were regarded to be Marxist-Leninist, Stalinist or Maoist. Despite the persecution, the PKK emerged from this situation. It survived the repression following the 1980 coup, and launched its first attack against Turkish military targets in 1984 with a small group of guerrilla. The PKK is differentiated from other Kurdish political parties by its social base, which includes a considerable number of peasants. It advocates both socialism and independence for greater Kurdistan, and put a priority on armed struggle. Furthermore, in the context of emergence of Kurdish nationalism with the leadership of PKK in the 1980s Mango notes that:

> The PKK produced its first programme, in which it defined itself as a national democratic revolutionary movement based on an alliance of workers, peasants and intellectuals, aiming at destroying 'colonialism' and creating 'a democratic and united Kurdistan' which would eventually be based on Marxist –Leninist principles (Mango, 1994: 988).

The PKK has expanded immensely in a short period of time despite opposition from some Kurdish tribes and elites. In this respect Romano states that at the beginning the PKK appeared as a radical group of students led by Abdullah Öcalan who began his career as a student of political science at the Ankara University. From a group of six, Öcalan's group would, in less than 20 years, recruit tens of thousands of guerrillas, establish camps and offices in dozens of countries attract the full attention of the Turkish state and gather support from Kurdish masses in Turkey and diaspora societies. Early in Kurdish history, elites who followed tribal lines fronted the revolts. In contrast to this, the PKK stands out as a movement that was built up from nothing (Romano, 2006: 70-71). The PKK's resistance against Turkish military power gradually turned the PKK into a political force (White, 2000). Özcan (2006: 19) claims that the PKK-led insurgence, which developed from a small group of university students in the early seventies, came to be the biggest challenge to the Turkish state in the twentieth century.

The PKK has not only focused on armed struggle and its struggle was not only, against Turkish state, especially at the beginning. It has also carried out a struggle against Kurdish feudal/tribal structures. In addition, the PKK is regarded as a political organization, which intends to re-create Kurdish identity and transform the Kurdish society. In this sense, PKK has concerned about educational issues in order to develop Kurdish identity among Kurds. The PKK's messages were primarily targeting young population and women (van Bruinessen, 1988: 42). Its aim was to develop a conscious Kurdish identity, which had been repressed and shaped by the coloniser. It aimed to enable people to have a 'new personality', to develop their culture and moral values. Thus, the PKK has slowly become a significant agent for the political, social and cultural change in the Kurdish area, "Kurdistan". There are two reasons behind the PKK to take on these roles and carry out these activities: The PKK considers itself as a nation-building party with a modernization agenda. In this regard, the PKK is not only an armed and political organization fighting for Kurdish national rights it can also be regarded as an agent for transforming the living conditions in the Kurdish regions.

Consequently, the emergence of PKK and its struggle has opened up spaces for Kurds in Turkey. It has played a crucial role in raising the Kurdish political consciousness, establishing a web of networks in and outside Turkey to recruit militants and mobilizing the Kurdish people. It has undermined the religious-tribal structures in the Kurdish region by presenting new opportunities for the middle class, the rural and urbanized Kurdish youth particularly since the 1980s. Furthermore, the PKK has played a significant role in terms of being the first nation-building organization to address women's issues and to take the position that women as human beings have equalled rights to men. This is also very much related to the growth in participation of women in PKK since 1980s. Kurdish women firstly mobilized around Kurdish cause with the influence of PKK and its discourses addressing women. Especially, the PKK leader, Abdullah Öcalan has become an important figure in the sense of its discourses concerning women's emancipation, which are presented in detail below. In this regard, the role of women in PKK is examined for the purpose of demonstrating the interactions between women in PKK and female activists in legal politics in the following.

PKK, Öcalan and Women: Shift in Ideology and Discourses

Since 1980s there have been shift in PKK's ideology and objectives due to political changes in Turkey and globally[31]. This study focuses on the changes in gender ideology and discourse of the PKK and its leader, which I argue encourages

---

[31] For a detailed analysis regarding transformations in PKK's ideology and political objectives see Akkaya and Jongerden (2012).

women's participation in both PKK and legal politics and create gender awareness among women.

Based on empirical research conducted with women political activists and analysis of the party related factors (ideology, manifesto) this study asserts that, as other works concerning PKK's ideological transformations in 2000s (Akkaya and Jongerden, 2012) and the roles of political parties in national struggle (Watts, 2010) the political objectives, ideology and discourses of the pro-Kurdish political party and political activists are directly and/or indirectly influenced by the developments and changes in Kurdish national movement.

The founder of PKK, Abdullah Öcalan is the key figure of the Kurdish liberation movement in terms of shaping ideology, political objectives and political projects of the movement.[32] Thus, the changes in the discourse of Öcalan, which also refer to changes in PKK discourses, have the potential to influence the gender structures in the Kurdish society. In particular, Öcalan's insertion of the idea of a new masculinity and femininity (or New Man and New Woman)[33] into the ideological framework of the PKK influenced Kurdish organizations and contributed to politicise women as well as men.

In 1990s Öcalan saw women as active agents in the nationalistic discourse. In his view, they were mothers and fighters in the guerrilla and their support was fundamental for keeping Kurdish national unity and protecting their homeland.[34] In this respect, Öcalan talks about two main, interdependent concepts, love and

---

[32] The significance of the role of Abdullah Öcalan in determining ideology and objectives of the movement is emphasized in many works concerning Kurdish national movement. For this see White (2000), Özcan(2006), Romano (2006), Marcus (2007), Güneş (2012) and Akkaya and Jongerden (2012).

[33] For the PKK ideology on building the "New Man" (and New Woman) sees White (2010) and Çağlayan (2007).

[34] See Çağlayan (2007) regarding the role of Kurdish national movement in constructing gender identity of Kurdish women since 1980s.

beauty, indispensable in anyone engaged in armed struggle. In his speeches Öcalan (1992) emphasized that the real beauty consists in being aware of Kurdistan's reality. It is a new concept created by PKK that calls for direct women participation through slogan like this *"Woman is becoming free through struggle, a free woman is becoming beautiful, the beautiful woman is loved,"*[35] very popular in the 1990s. In this slogan, love does not mean a romantic relation between men and women. According to Öcalan a male guerrilla and a female guerrilla can love each other only if the objective is achieved.[36] In other words, Öcalan states the way of the love relationship between men and women and he tells how it can be tolerated. He also says that, however this process has not been realized yet. In his view, women are encouraged to fight for freedom but it is the freedom of their people and their homeland. There is no mention of any gender related issues.

Öcalan emphasizes the necessity of developing a *new masculinity* and *femininity* that is different from their traditional understanding of masculinity and femininity. At this process, the major responsibility is imposed to women. Women have to break themselves from internalizing values of traditional family life, which assigns them the status of an object or a slave. Öcalan expresses that despite these conditions, many young girls and women have participated in the Kurdish nationalist movement. The motivation of these women, especially young and unmarried ones, is to be committed to their homeland with pure love and the desire to liberate their homeland from exploitation, feudal values and patriarchy. It has been expressed that not only women, also men have to change themselves (Yalçın-Heckmann and van Gelder, 2000: 316). It can be said at this time that the PKK carried out an intensive

---

[35] In Turkish it is "Kadın savaştıkça özgürleşir; özgürleşen kadın güzelleşir; güzelleşen kadın sevilir."

[36] The objective is what PKK has fought for against Turkish state. That is freedom of Kurds in their homeland "Kurdistan".

armed struggle against the Turkish state forces and therefore the movement needed more recruitment. That is why, Öcalan's discourses called women to fight for their homeland, a role in the 1990's considered instrumental to the movement.

As in most national liberation or anti-colonial movements the discourses of "women's emancipation" and "national liberation" have been used by the Kurdish movement. The discourses of women's emancipation have been constantly emphasized by the PKK's leader. The earliest text concerning the emancipation of Kurdish women in the writings of Abdullah Öcalan came along in 1986.[37] However, it was during the 1990s and particularly after his arrest by the Turkish security forces in 1999 when Öcalan concentrates on an historical examination towards development of human society in the construction of his ideological perspectives regarding women. In this connection, he found that in the Neolithic period society was mainly organized in accordance with an agricultural, matriarchal system, which presented women in a sacred position as the creative source of life. "Natural society" was formed around the identity "woman-mother", in keeping with nature and agricultural activity. In contrast to a culture of violence and war dominated by men, female governance was based on peace and the rejecting violence. The domestic system "wife-mother" was the first victim of the hierarchical society established by the patriarchy. This is the beginning of an historical "counterrevolution" causing the deprivation of women in their personality and identity. Öcalan contended that capitalism should be regarded as the maintenance of female gender slavery. The slavery system was enforced on women in early history and then transferred to men. Women are excluded from the public sphere in order to institutionalize the male domination on politics, economy and society. Thus, the hegemony of man extends

---

[37] The new reflections of Öcalan about the man-woman relationship are interpreted as the result of ten years of tension between him and his wife Kesire Yıldırım herself a member of the PKK's central committee until the third congress in 1986.

its bounds from the family to the state (Öcalan, 2004). In the discourse of Öcalan, women's liberation is a precondition for the liberation of Kurdistan. According to him, "the woman's issue is the source of all other issues. The resolution of woman's freedom in general would mean that a solution has been found for the freedom struggle in society in general."[38] As understood from these statements he gives priority to women's freedom. The way he suggests women for obtaining their freedom is the political struggle. He states that:

> It is really important that woman takes her place in the political struggle. This is where woman's struggle gains a lot more importance. A liberated woman, but not alone, should also involve man and they should fight against the male dominated mentality and power together. There is a need to end this rape culture, which has continued for thousands of years. One should overcome the rape culture in order to be able to create the liberated woman.[39]

Until 1990s women were considered as "weak people whom cannot be trusted" (Çağlayan, 2007: 108-109) while men were main actors in the movement. Nevertheless, as the participation of the women increased under the effect of the discourse of Öcalan the PKK started to stress the role of women while criticising the traditional, 'feudal' masculinity of Kurdish men (Çağlayan, 2007). However, this does not indicate that patriarchal structures have been removed in the society.

Despite women's involvement, until after 2000s it can be claimed that female activists are part of a history determined mostly by men. While the Kurdish national movement positions itself as the guarantor of women's liberation, on the other hand, it attempts to decide the scope and content of this liberation and prevents women from constructing their female identity independently. However, it is important to underline that female political activists are not totally confined to the national

---

[38] Abdullah Öcalan "We are concerned with the Democratic Organization and Administration of Society", 07January 2011, http://www.pkkonline.com/en/index.php?sys=article&artID=97 (Accessed on 17 April 2012).

[39] Ibid.

movement discourse. There is diversity among women in terms of their approach towards national movement discourses or the political party's discourse and policies. A great majority of activists are highly motivated to challenge the perspectives that disregard the women's agency. The developments in the political area are mostly results of those activists' efforts that are highly conscious and motivated in the sense of gender identity to question and challenge the perspectives that underestimate the women's agency.

The influence of the Kurdish national movement can be felt from the statements of female activists who were interviewed as part of this research. All the political activists emphasized the importance of political struggle in order to undermine male dominance and obtain equal position in the society. But this process requires mentality change both among men and women. For instance, one of female mayors[40] highlighted the need to create "new men" while they carry out their struggle. She states:

> We (women) want to be free. We don't belong to anybody (men). But, not all women are aware of this. They cannot question men's domination. We struggle to raise consciousness among women about their rights and create awareness that they are equal to men. Besides, men also have to change. They have to extricate themselves from their traditional masculine mentality (Personal interview, Diyarbakir, August 2009).

These statements clearly overlap the Öcalan's theoretical formulation of the need for constructing *new femininity* and *new masculinity* as mentioned above. In addition, another female political activist[41] states that:

> The party has an ideology. Kurdish liberation movement has an ideology. There is a perspective has been produced by the leader (Önderlik)[42] and has

---

[40] This female mayor was elected in March 29, 2009 elections interviewed both during elections campaigns in March 2009 and after being elected in August 2009 in Diyarbakır.
[41] She was on an administration position during the field research in April 2010 when I interviewed her. Currently she is an MP elected in June 2011 national elections.

been presented to us. The society would not be liberated as long as women were liberated. That is very true; the society cannot be liberated without the liberation of women. It does not mean if Kurds obtain their rights and emancipation this will over (she meant women's struggle by this). Supposing that Kurds get their right and emancipation but still there will be conflict continue between sexes (Personal interview, Diyarbakır, April 2010)

These statements denote that they are obviously affected by the national movement, but also they underline that their activism is not limited to what the movement's leaders expressed. Both parties' written documents (programs, guidelines, brochures) and party members and political activists' discourses and explanations demonstrate strong connections between pro-Kurdish political parties and the PKK. At this regard it is obvious that the PKK and its leader Öcalan have had considerable influence on pro-Kurdish legal politics and activists' political ideologies and activities which are very observable in the gender ideology and policies of the political parties.

The PKK leader, Öcalan has shaped the pro-Kurdish politics especially with the political projects and model that he has developed for the solution of Kurdish issue in the Middle East in general and in Turkey in particular after his capture in 1999.

Öcalan's Political Project: Democratic Confederalism

Although Öcalan asserts his views for political solution of Kurdish question in Turkey go back to the first half of 1990s (1999:7; 2011), his proposed political projects have shaped both the national movement and pro-Kurdish political movement to the end of 1990s after he was arrested on February 15, 1999.

It is observed that Öcalan had a political evolution in his views after his capture. The shift in Öcalan's views is exposed with his call for the implementation of a 'true' democracy to solve the Kurdish problem within the existing borders of a

---

[42] Önderlik, which means the leader or leadership, is used for Abdullah Öcalan.

unitary Turkey (Akkaya and Jongerden, 2012). In this regard, political projects like *Democratic Confederalism, Democratic Republic, and Democratic Autonomy*[43] reflected the ideological changes that PKK underwent after the arrest of its leader Abdullah Öcalan in 1999 and represented the opinions and tools through which Kurdish political demands are (re)defined and (re)organized. The idea of *Democratic Confederalism* was defined as a model for 'democratic self-government'. The *Democratic Confederalism* was suggested by Öcalan as an alternative to the nation-state and as a model to solve the problems in the Middle East in general and for the Kurdish question in particular. It is the expression for the democratic unity of the Kurds who are spread in four countries and scattered throughout the world. "This project", Öcalan argues, "builds on the self-government of local communities and is organized in the form of open councils, town councils, local parliaments and larger congresses. The citizens themselves are agents of this kind of self-government, not state-based authorities" (Öcalan 2008: 32 quoted by Akkaya and Jongerden 2012). *Democratic Cofederalism* as the model of organizing the people beyond the state requires defining its relationship with the existing state or official authority. Thus, first the concept of *democratic republic was put forth* which suggests a reform of the Republic of Turkey as the form of government through which the Kurdish question can be solved and then the concept of *democratic autonomy* was developed by Öcalan as a form of relationship with the state and in turn with its jurisdiction. It was presented as the option for a democratic political solution to the Kurdish question in Turkey.

The significance of *Democratic Confederalism* from a gender perspective means equality of sexes as its most significant feature. Women are encouraged to

---

[43] For a detailed analysis of these political projects in the context of radical democracy see Akkaya and Jongerden (2012).

set up their own democratic organizations and to participate in establishing democratic self-government system in a democratic society. The reflections on the change in the discourse of the PKK leader would soon be observed in the political objectives and projects of the legal movement too. A 'transitory period' which was experienced between the moderation of Öcalan and the establishment of the DTP (2005) corresponded to the period of a succession of parties within the movement, in particular the HADEP and DEHAP which will be examined below. According to Akkaya and Jongerden (2012) pro-Kurdish party- DTP (2005-2009) established as a result of organizational restructuring of all PKK-affiliated organizations within the framework of the idea of *Democratic Confederalism*. From this standpoint, it can be stated these political projects have determined the political activities of pro-Kurdish political parties as will be seen in the analysis below. Regarding this research which focuses on pro-Kurdish legal politics these political projects are addressed in terms of their influences on pro-Kurdish political parties objectives and projects in general and women's political participation and representation in particular in the following.

The section follows focuses on the women's participation in the PKK in order to explain their influence on the women's activism in political arena.

Women in the PKK

As we saw earlier, the PKK has not limited its mission to obtain Kurds political freedom; it has also acted as a national organization with the purpose of modernizing Kurdish society through eliminating traditional structures. Thus, PKK has not only become a challenge to the Turkish authorities, it has also challenged Kurdish traditionalists who wanted to perpetuate the gender structures within the Kurdish society ruled by landlords and chieftains. The PKK has struggled against traditional power structures and it never allowed landlords and chieftains to take place in its leadership (Alinia, 2004; McDowall 2000; White 2000).

In time, the PKK has become aware of that in order to be a mass movement it has to influence ordinary people, including women. According to Marcus (2007) the participation of women increased after 1989, when the PKK infiltrated into universities and urban centres. Moreover, thanks to its propaganda and political actions in the 1990s the PKK received the support of many women. Besides, women were forced to take political action when many Kurdish men were arrested during the military coup in 1980. Marcus mentions the example of Leyla Zana[44], one of the most prominent Kurdish politicians. Until recently she was the only woman who has been elected in Parliament from a pro-Kurdish party[45]. She did not have formal education and she did not speak Turkish. After her husband's (Mehdi Zana) detention on September 24, just after the September 12, 1980 coup she started to participate in demonstrations and educate herself. She has become a role model for thousands of Kurdish women encouraging them to participate in politics. According to Alinia, during the last two decades the PKK involved women in the guerrilla and in organized political activities (Alinia, 2004: 65). In fact, the PKK, which has the largest number of female guerrillas in the world has become a revolutionary organization in the course of time which stresses women's rights and liberation within the guerrilla and in civil life.

Although it is not the aim of this study to explore women's specific reasons for joining the PKK, an examination of their participation in it would help to explain their

---

[44] Leyla Zana was born in 1961 in the small village of Silvan, which is a town of Diyarbakır in the Kurdish region (south-eastern) of Turkey, as the second child in a traditional Kurdish family. She married Mehdi Zana when she was at age of fifteen. Her husband Mehdi Zana who was a Kurdish political activist was elected as mayor of Diyarbakır in 1977.

[45] Leyla Zana was elected as a deputy in 1991 from HEP (People's Labour Party- Halkın Emek Partisi)

political activism. The fact is that the involvement of women into the PKK is highly complex and needs to be examined thoroughly but this study primarily focuses on this in terms of its effects on the legal and political area. Although a great number of women from urban areas who were students politicized through student organizations, there are a vast number of women who have joined the PKK in rural areas especially since 1990s due to oppression they suffered in their own families. In addition, the state oppression, which had reached its peak in 1990s, also had a role in driving women into participating in the national movement. Flach pointed out that several girls aged 12-14, due to the situation of females within the family, had fled their households in order to join the PKK in the mountains (Flach, 2007: 63-64 quoted in Westrheim, 2008: 28), starting a trend continued in the next generation.

There are a variety of views regarding the reasons why women joined the PKK. In Wolf's view, the most common reason was the general oppression of all Kurds, male and female. The oppression of women within patriarchal Kurdish family structures seems to be a secondary, but strong underlying reason (Wolf, 2004: 197-198 quoted in Westrheim, 2008: 29). In Flach' view, the women who joined the PKK in the 1970s and 1980s were university or high school students. They were driven by a growing awareness of the oppression of the Kurds in Turkey, searching for a Kurdish identity and a socialist life model. Women fled from unprivileged positions or forced marriages. Many, who wanted revenge, joined the PKK because relatives and friends had been killed or mistreated. A significant number of women were recruited for this reason (Flach, 2007: 61 quoted in Westrheim, 2008: 29). In the 1990s when the PKK struggle was better organized, a huge number of politically conscious and educated women, also from Europe, attended the guerrilla. Following the capture of

Öcalan in 1999, thousands of women joined the PKK[46]. The majority wished to support the new political course of the PKK, but primarily they attended in order to fight for the rights of the women in line with the policy of the PKK/PAJK (Partiya Azadiya Jin a Kurdistan / the Freedom Party of Women of Kurdistan). The way female members have managed to organize themselves independently of their male comrades, had a crucial impact on their opportunity to organize both civic and politically. PAJK gradually took over the co-ordination of the ideology, education of members, focusing on gender issues as part of the overall education program (Flach, 2007: 53 mentioned in Westrheim, 2008: 29). As it has been seen, women who have joined the PKK for different reasons have constituted an influential power in the organization questioning unequal gender relations. This has become one of factors that has changed the gender ideology of the movement. Besides the views, which mention the PKK's influential role in mobilizing women to join its ranks, there are some critics of its gender strategy. For instance, Mojab raises a critique about traditional gender relations that continue within the organization. She states that:

> The PKK, which prided itself on recruiting large numbers of women into the nationalist struggle, often entertained traditional gender relations. For example, guerrilla camps in the mountains were segregated along gender lines. Males and females were not allowed to enter intimate relationships, or to marry even according to traditional norms (Mojab, 2001: 9).

In addition, van Bruinessen addresses the inconsistency of discourses and practices regarding the women's position in the PKK. According to van Bruinessen,

---

[46] According to Flach (2007), the first organization for women was initiated in 1992 by Öcalan. In 1993 a women's organization started in Botan area counting about 2300 guerrillas. Through TAJK (The Liberation Movement of the Women of Kurdistan) and YAJK (Association of Liberated Women of Kurdistan) Kurdish women found their expression. In the mid-1990s, the women's army had educated their own independent military leadership. From 1999, the PKK went through structural changes, in order to develop a more democratic organization form. From then women's organizations were so well organized that they became independent of the PKK body. PAJK (the Party for Freedom of the Women of Kurdistan), took over the co-ordination of the ideology and cadre education, focusing on gender issues as part of the overall education program (2007: 53 mentioned in Westrheim, 2008: 29).

the PKK may differentiate itself from earlier nationalist organizations concerning its attitudes towards women, but the actual role patterns do not change in reality because women in PKK enter a new set of unequal relations (2001; 105-106). The armed branch of the PKK, the ARGK (Arteşa Rizgarî ya Gele Kurdistan / People's Liberation Army of Kurdistan)[47], boasts a large number of young female guerrilla fighters and appears to be taking equality between the sexes seriously, at least at this level. Party propaganda celebrates a number of women among its martyrs, some of whom were killed in battle, while others immolated themselves as a form of political protest. Most recently, there have been a few suicide bombings of military targets by PKK women. Women's liberation has begun to figure prominently in the party's public discourse. The leader of PKK, Abdullah Öcalan, has repeatedly compared the oppression of women in Kurdish society to the national oppression of the Kurds and called for double liberation[48]. His views on the status of women are undeniably having an impact among the rank and file of the party. However, this shows more clearly in words than in practice. Both men and women in the PKK have become more aware of traditional gender inequalities and frequently speak of women's liberation and equal rights, but the actual role patterns do not change that easily. There are as yet few, if any, women in commanding positions in the ARGK. For a young woman, joining the guerrillas represents an alternative to marriage and the traditional serving and subjected role, but at the same time she enters a new set of unequal relations and a new stereotyped role (van Bruinessen, 2001: 105-6).

---

[47] The People's Liberation Army of Kurdistan was established in 1985 as the military wing of the Kurdistan Workers' Party (PKK), a leftist Kurdish nationalist organization.

[48] A collection of Öcalan's writings and/or speeches on the position of women and women's Liberation In Kurdish society has been published (Öcalan, 1992).

Despite criticisms against the PKK, the testimonies gathered during the fieldwork, which will be mentioned in the following analysis revealed that female political activists have been greatly influenced from the ideology and organization of the PKK and women's involvement in it. Women's emancipation ideology, their contribution to the party and the roles of female guerrillas and in its administration are mentioned by many female political activists who recognise their strong ties with the PKK's as explained in the sections below.

The Pro-Kurdish Political Parties since 1990s and their Gender Approach

The Kurdish political movement in Turkey began to institutionalize with the establishment of the first pro-Kurdish political party in 1990[49] and this represented one of the turning points for Kurdish national struggle. As a consequence the Kurdish modes of resistance could operate within the organizational ground of the state itself. There are two important roles that pro-Kurdish parties have played since 1990s. First of all, carrying struggle for Kurdish national rights through political channels has led to the mobilization of Kurds in general opening spaces for negotiation and awareness within a legal frame. Secondly, they have provided space for women by encouraging them to engage in politics. As a result, the mobilization of Kurds in general and women in particular through political parties' activities

---

[49] For a detailed analysis regarding pro-Kurdish political parties see:
Nicole F. Watts (2010) *Activists in Office: Kurdish Politics and Protest in Turkey.* United States of America, Seattle, WA: University of Washington Press.

Ibid. "Activists in Office: Pro-Kurdish Contentious Politics in Turkey" *Ethnopolitics,* Vol. 5, No.2, 125-144, June 2006.

Ibid. "Pro-Kurdish Mayors in As-If Democracy: Symbolic Politics in Diyarbakır", World Congress of Kurdish Studies Irbil, 6-9 September 2006,
http://www.institutkurde.org/en/conferences/kurdish_studies_irbil_2006/Nicole+F+WATTS.htl. (Accessed on 15 January 2010).

contributed to the struggle for Kurds' cultural identity as well as to the change of women's status in politics.

The first pro-Kurdish parties were not simply cells for the PKK but emerged from the Turkish political system itself (Bozarslan, 1996; Barkey, 1998; Watts, 1999). A Kurdish deputy who proposed to an intergovernmental committee that Turkey's Kurdish problem could be solved through an autonomy arrangement, was expelled by the leaders of its own party, centre-left Sosyal Demokrat Halk Partisi (Social Democratic People's Party - SHP) in 1989. In addition, expulsions of seven other Kurdish members of the party due to participating at a conference in Paris initiated a series of events which contributed to the formation of the first legal political party, the Halkın Emek Partisi (People's Labour Party- HEP) in June 1990 explicitly committed to the advancement of Kurdish political and cultural rights (Somer, 2004; Watts, 1999; Güney, 2002; Demir, 2005). The party formed electoral alliance with the SHP for October 1991 national elections and 22 Kurdish deputies were elected. However, HEP was closed by the Turkish Constitutional Court in July 1993. Pro-Kurdish partisans established a succession of new Kurdish parties: the Demokrasi Partisi (Democracy Party-DEP) in 1993 (closed by the court in 1994); the Halkın Demokrasi Partisi (People's Democracy Party-HADEP), founded in 1994 and closed by the court in 2003; and the Demokratik Halk Partisi (Democratic People's Party-DEHAP), founded in 1997 and voluntarily replaced by the Demokratik Toplum Partisi (Democratic Society Party-DTP) in late 2005 (Watts, 2006: 134) and DTP which was closed by the court in December 2009 replaced by the Barış ve Demokrasi Partisi (Peace and Democracy Party- BDP).

This picture of pro-Kurdish political parties proved that while Turkey's application for full membership of the European Union in 1987 has had influence on its democratization process and provided an opportunity for their legalization, however, democratic developments were not sufficient to prevent branches of the Turkish state from closing them. Besides, pro-Kurdish activists, parliamentary deputies and intellectuals have been arrested and harassed in various ways.[50] Pro-Kurdish activists who did not engage in armed resistance have been treated as 'terrorists' suffered violence from the Turkish officials and elites and this created an obstacle for their involvement in political activities. This issue will be addressed in Chapter 3 as an obstacle created by the state authorities to discourage women's participation in pro-Kurdish politics.

Despite various obstacles encountered from the state authorities the pro-Kurdish political parties since 1990s have become legal while the PKK is regarded as an "illegal" organization. They opened branches in Kurdish regions and engaged in grass roots activities. Some female political activists who engaged in pro-Kurdish politics in 1990s mentioned about their organization activities at that time to encourage people to join political parties in various Kurdish cities. As testimonies of female political activists clarified those who joined political parties were predominantly sympathizers of the national movement, family members of political prisoners and the PKK fighters and those who were affected from the conflict between the state forces and the PKK. The political conditions of 1990s when there were massive on-going clashes between the PKK militants and Turkish state forces led political parties to undertake the role as representative of Kurdish people. From 1990s, political parties have become a primary point of reference for Kurds who, forced to evacuate their villages, had lost their family members in conflict and were imprisoned due to accusations of supporting the "terrorist" organization and those

---

[50] For more information about coercive measures that pro-Kurdish parties and their members were encountered between 1990 and 2008 see Watts (2010).

claiming their national rights. Most of interviewees confirmed these points based on their experiences and observations during their political engagement in 1990s.

Despite the difficult conditions, in the 1990s pro-Kurdish political parties contributed to increase the parties' base, which enabled them to engage in electoral politics in order to represent the Kurds and defend their national rights on the national political stage by working within the state legal framework. Since 1990, pro-Kurdish political parties have entered all local and national elections except March 1994 local elections from which they withdrew in protest for the repression against the party candidates (Çağlayan, 2007: 142). In the general elections, the candidates of these parties have run as independents or made coalitions with leftist parties in order to surpass the 10 percent threshold to secure nation-wide representation since the percentage of votes they received has always been under 10% until now. After 1991 national elections when which pro-Kurdish party-HEP made alliance with the SHP and 18 pro-Kurdish deputies were elected, they hadn't been able to enter the parliament until 2007 national elections when 22 pro-Kurdish deputies were finally elected. Following this, 34 deputies were elected in 2011 national elections. In local politics, since 1999 local elections a significant number of municipalities have been run by pro-Kurdish party. 37 municipalities were won in 1999 municipality elections; in 2004 municipality elections pro-Kurdish party- DEHAP entered elections with other left-wing parties under the name "Democratic Union of Power" (Demokratik Güç Birliği) and they won 36 municipalities and in 2009 municipality elections the number rose to 99.[51]

---

[51] "Yerel Seçimlerde Partiler ve Kazandıkları Belediye Başkanlıkları" 30 March 2009, http://bianet.org/bianet/bianet/113476-yerel-secimlerde-partiler-ve-kazandiklari belediybaskanliklari, (Accessed 16 November 2011).
"1990'dan Bugüne, HEP'ten DTP'ye Kürtlerin Zorlu Siyaset Mücadelesi", 12 December 2009, http://www.bianet.org/bianet/siyaset/117387-1990-dan-bugune-hep-ten-dtp-ye-kurtlerin-zorlusiyasemucadelesi (Accessed on 16 November 2011).

Pro-Kurdish political parties have been able to elect their own representatives in both local and national elections since end of 1990s. Even with the considerable restrictions on pro-Kurdish political institutions and activists' activities, pro-Kurdish mayors' holding in local office and MPs in the parliament have served a number of important functions. While on national level MPs contribute to raise public attention on Kurdish issue and influence the political agenda local representatives have more opportunities to do more concrete works. For instance, Watts (2006) specifies four functions of local politics. First, holding local office gave the movement's leading representatives new material resources such as control over budgets, infrastructure, and hiring. Second, election to local office has "officialised" the Kurdish movement elite, providing its elected representatives with opportunities to develop extensive personal and institutional relationships at the domestic and international levels. These in turn provide greater access to funds, technical expertise, and more opportunities for information politics and the normalization of a pro-Kurdish platform. Third, holding local office has allowed the Kurdish movement to produce a new 'governmentality' (Foucault 1991 quoted by Watts, 2006 & 2010: 13) as it begins to use the tools of local government to systematically map, survey, educate, and regulate local Kurdish populations. Fourth, election to local office facilitated movement use of symbolic politics. On the other hand, if gender identity of those holds positions in local politics is considered it can be seen that electoral politics has not only made changes in Kurdish rights struggle in general but it has contributed to improve women's status as well.

While pro-Kurdish parties 'representative contention' challenging state policies against Kurds they also have promoted and strengthened the national movement by providing pro-Kurdish activists with new arenas and opportunities to form alliance;

incorporating Kurdish political claims in mainstream domestic and international arenas; building a grass roots and organizational infrastructure. Besides, they have played a role of a 'transmitter' in the context of transferring ideology of the national movement into the legal politics. That is to say, pro-Kurdish political parties enable to disseminate Kurdish national movement's ideology to its supporters and political activists. Whereas pro-Kurdish parties represent the ideology of PKK in the legal arena, they also found spaces of reproducing and redefining the PKK's ideology and implementing its political projects through their programs, statutes and policies. In particular, the national movement's political models such as Democratic Autonomy as a democratic self-government model which enables Kurds to have their political, cultural and linguistic rights is promoting by political parties since mid-2000s. In this regard my research indicates that PKK's ideology and its projects concerning Kurdish self-government and Kurdish society are advocated and have been put into practice especially since they have been able to elect their representatives to the parliament and won considerable number of municipalities in the Kurdish region.

Since 1990s when the first pro-Kurdish political party appeared on the political arena and its successors, in order to carry out a struggle for Kurdish political and cultural rights they also favour the active participation of women in politics and the political parties. However, women's participation in politics and their roles in the political arena have dramatically changed since the beginning of 2000s. In this regard, the following section will focus on women's participation in pro-Kurdish political parties since 1990s in order find out reasons behind their participation.

Women's Participation in pro-Kurdish Political Parties

Women have increasingly participated in pro-Kurdish politics since the beginning of 1990s (Çağlayan, 2007). In this regard, this study will focus on the factors behind their participation in pro-Kurdish political parties and in the different the profile of women political activists in 1990s and in 2000s and their impacts in the feminization of pro-Kurdish politics.

Women who joined pro-Kurdish political parties at the beginning of 1990s had mobilized under the influence of the Kurdish national movement. Although in small number still there were women active in the Kurdish national movement before the pro-Kurdish political party (HEP) was established (Çağlayan, 2007). Some interviewees mentioned their experiences in various leftist political organizations, non-governmental organizations such as labour unions and human rights associations and then they joined political the party when it opened in 1990. Leyla Zana, the first Kurdish female MP elected in 1991, was one of women who became active after her husband Mehdi Zana was arrested in 1980. Similarly, a few interviewees expressed that they became involved due to their male relatives' arrest and detention during 1980s. In addition, women's participation in pro-Kurdish political parties in 1990s was mostly the result of Kurdish national movement's discourses towards women, which encouraged them to join the national struggle for both their emancipation and national liberation (Çağlayan, 2007). Kurdish women gained national consciousness in pro-Kurdish political parties since the establishment of HEP in 1990. However, the number of women significantly increased from mid-1990s during the period HADEP (1994-2003), which influenced women's organization within the party positively by establishing women's units and changing policies of the parties such as inclusion of 'positive discrimination principle' in the party's statutes in 2000. For instance, it was estimated that women constituted 40% of pro-Kurdish party, HADEP's members between 1994 and 2003 (Çağlayan, 2007: 128).[52] Even though this change may not be explained with one factor, according to the interviewees the ideological discourse of the Kurdish national movement and its mobilization strategies along with the parties' grass roots' organization activities have had a significant impact on the number of women involved.

From the female political activists' testimonies it is clear that two are the reasons behind their involvement in politics also as mentioned by Çağlayan (2007: 157). These are "identity rights" and "women's emancipation".[53] While the former reason characterizes their participation during 1990s, from beginning of 2000s female political activists have joined political parties for gender identity concerns as well. Furthermore, the period of 1990s was a process for women where they gained gender awareness within political arenas and started to question male domination in pro-Kurdish politics. As many of interviewees stressed it is mostly because they faced male resistance when they attempted to take part in the decision-making bodies of the party and were treated as secondary by their male fellows; these will be explained in detail in the following chapter where the researcher will talk about the obstacles to the feminization of pro-Kurdish politics.

The research reveals that since 1990s the profile of women activists has changed due the changing political conditions, the expansion of political movement and changing socio-economic conditions in Kurdish society. While during 1990s the majority of women were over middle age, married and primary school graduate, after

---

[52] Despite it was unable to secure precise information about the number of the party members and the proportion of women according to the HADEP's administrators' statements the party had hundred thousand members and forty percent of this was women (Çağlayan, 2007: 128).
[53] Kurdish women established their own associations such as Patriotic Women Foundation (Yurtsever Kadınlar Derneği) and published journals as *Roza* and *Jûjin* from mid-1990s which focused on both women's issues and Kurdish national struggle. Thus they played a role in mobilizing women around both gender and ethnic identities.

2000s in particular active participants were young, single and relatively more educated. Female political activists who first had joined political parties with the purpose of fighting for their national identity rights were mostly relatives of male political activists and prisoners or PKK guerrillas and were influenced from a general conflict between the state forces and the PKK in the Kurdish region. The new active female participants are members of neighbourhood commissions, of district and city woman councils, of district and city administrative boards, of central woman councils and of municipal councils (Çağlayan, 2007: 150-151).

In the following section, political parties' program and statutes will be examined to find out changes in parties' approach and policies towards gender equality and women's issues by taking into consideration the Kurdish national movement's ideological discourses and growth in women's participation. It will be revealed that there is a parallelism with shifts in national movement's gender ideology, political objectives and projects. This analysis demonstrates that the idea of democratization characterizes the process of feminization since the beginning of 2000s in particular.

Changes in Gender Approach of pro-Kurdish Parties

The analysis of pro-Kurdish parties written documents such as parties' programs and statutes will demonstrate that their gender approach has remarkably changed since 1990s. In my view, parallel to this change both descriptive and representation of women have improved in the parties and representation bodies. In this regard, while the analysis of parties' programs and statutes illuminates the changes in parties' gender approach, it also provides answer to why political parties have become advocates of gender of equality.

The research explored some factors that have urged the political parties to promote gender equality and to include in the political decision-making. These are: ideological changes, change of political objectives and projects, electoral concern, integration in international networks and women's growth gender-based activism. While these factors have encouraged the political parties to take further steps in favour of women the justification for improving women's positions can be explained through arguments of equal representation; these are *justice, pragmatic* and *difference* argument.

As legal political organizations of Kurdish national movement seeking for solution for Kurdish issue within the legal framework their ideological leanings and political objectives are shaped by the national movement. In this regard, the findings of some studies, which focused on the relation between political parties' ideology and women's inclusion in political parties, are limited to explain Kurdish case. Several scholars such as Kittilson (Caul; 1999, 2001, 2006, 2010) and Childs (2008) have written explicitly on political parties' relationship with women and questioned conditions under which parties are more likely to include women in their ranks. Most studies have pointed out that party ideology is the major factor determining the party's policies regarding women's representation. Parties that are further left in their political leanings tend to support women's political representation because they embrace more egalitarian ideals than rightist parties do (Caul, 1999; Leyenaar, 2004; Paxton et al., 2007). Accordingly, feminist movements have traditionally felt a greater affinity to left wing and social democratic parties and have allied with them (Ray, 1999). However, some scholars disputed the assumption that there is a strong association between having a left-wing ideology and supporting women's representation (Lovenduski & Norris, 1993; Matland & Studlar, 1996). They suggest instead that the impact of party ideology on women's representation must be examined over time and across parties (Caul, 1999). On the other hand, Paxton and Kunovich (2003) noted that it has generally been expected that political parties of ethnic nationalist and religious movements would espouse conservative gender ideologies and attitudes, and that as a result women will be dramatically underrepresented in those parties.

Pro-Kurdish political parties are left -wing. This might be one of factors that influenced the parties' attitudes toward women, however the research pointed out that pro-Kurdish parties support of women's participation and representation in politics can be influenced by other factors. For example, their gender ideology along with their political objectives and projects which concentrated on developing a democratic solution for Kurdish issue and on the creation of a democratic society since the beginning of 2000s have affected women's inclusion in political decision-making. The parties' programs and statutes provide evidence of these changes.

Party Program and Statutes: Shift in Approach towards Women and Women's Issues

The first pro-Kurdish party, the HEP, which had a significant role in Kurdish rights struggle did not have any woman among its founders in 1990 and women rights were not on its agenda. In fact, there had not been any specific women policy and any significant interest in women issues mentioned in the program and statutes of the first pro-Kurdish political parties until 1994 with the establishment of HADEP. Despite the first female Kurdish MP Leyla Zana was elected from HEP in 1991 HEP and its successor DEP did not have any distinctive women policy.

In the HEP party program of 1992 there is no space dedicated to gender issues. It claims being the party of "workers, unemployed, civil servants, teachers, democrats, social democrats and socialist intellectuals, craftsmen, tradesmen, the masses who were subjected to repression and whoever sides with democracy"[54]. Women's rights were addressed under the title of social policies and after nutrition and housing problem issues. Out of 64 pages party programme one and half page was for nutrition and two and half pages for housing issue however, the party's women rights view was expressed in only one paragraph:

> The education which denies gender equality and excludes women from social life will be prevented; the rules which are against gender equality will be extracted from the laws; the economic, social, cultural and juridical measures which ensure the equality of women with men in all aspects of social life will be taken." (HEP, 1992: 53)

Also as seen from this paragraph, without making any determination about women's problem, the actions, which aim to be implemented in order to ensure gender equality are listed.

In the statutes of the DEP (1993) with the exception the statement "there would not be any discrimination in terms of race, sex, language, religion, sect, family, status, class and occupation for membership" in the section about the membership, no mention can be found regarding women. The successor party, the HADEP founded in 1994 followed the same pattern. In the party program of HADEP (1994) in the section where actions to-do lined for the democratization of state and society, actions to ensure equality between men and women were not included either.[55] In the HADEP's program women policy was taken from the section of social policies to

---

[54] HEP party program (1992)

[55] Same statements, which were placed in the statutes of the HEP as quoted above also taken place in HADEP. In addition, in the HADEP's program it is written, "A particular importance will be given to education activities which will change the society's established customs, that dominated by male ideology, value judgements and beliefs. Maternity institution which is a social and natural duty will be secured."

98

the democratization section. This means that if the titles' order represents prioritisation of issues we can conclude that women issues started to attach more importance in HADEP in comparison to DEP. Moreover, the parties' perspective towards women rights and gender equality can be explained in the context of justice argument, which asserts that inequality between sexes is neither fair nor democratic. Addressing women rights under the title of social policies and aiming to ensure gender equality in every aspect of social life in the HEP's program indicates that the party did not view inequality between sexes as fair. In addition, inclusion of women policy in the section of democratization in the HADEP's program suggests that gender equality is regarded as a requirement for the democratization of state and society. The additional changes were made in the program and statutes of the parties based on this argument.

Political parties' programs and statutes so far have similar features with regards to sections concerning women until end of 1990s. The issue of gender inequality was addressed with some general and surface determinations under the title of social policies. There was not a different approach in the programs and statutes. Even though HEP (1990-1993) had a woman MP it did not have any specific policy of women as well as DEP (1993-1994). Besides, they did not have any influential women units. Women units emerged in the second half of 1990 during the period of HADEP (1994-2003). But these units did not have any specific interest and program in women issues until the end of 1990s. Such a development was going to take place in 2000s.

From mid-1990s and the beginning of 2000s that corresponds to the period of HADEP (1994-2003) there had been some changes in terms of women's participation in pro-Kurdish party politics, which influenced the party's gender policy to a considerable extent. The factors behind progressions in women's participation were the relative decrease of state oppression on pro-Kurdish political parties towards end of 1990s which encouraged people to participate in politics in general, and the organization activities of women branches of HADEP which played an effective role in attracting women to take part in the party activities through mobilizing them on the ground. Whereas there was not a significant number of women within the previous political parties (HEP and DEP) and for instance, there was only one female among thirty HADEP representatives who were selected by the party's founders' committee assembling in May 11th 1994.[56] Moreover, there were a few women who took part in the party council after its first ordinary general assembly (Çağlayan, 2007; 133).

With the growing participation of women and their efforts to take active role in the party, women's concerns started to be taken into account. In the course of time in parallel with women's participation, women's units were institutionalized within the HADEP, and since 1997 they changed significantly the panorama within the party, but the significant change emerged in the congress organized by HADEP in 2000. With this congress, while women and youth branches were acknowledged as autonomous organizations, which have the right of electing their administration, they managed to include the principle of positive discrimination in the party's statutes the principle of positive discrimination (Çağlayan, 2007: 133). The change in the statutes in this congress is significant in terms of representing the party's concern towards women's representation. This clause states:

---

[56] This woman was the elder sister of Mazlum Doğan who was one of the founders of PKK. He committed suicide on the 21st March 1981 with the object of making a protest against the practices in the Diyarbakır prison when he was imprisoned there.

> Positive support must be provided until social obstacles to women's participation in decision-making and administrative organs in ratio of their level of labour and participation. Women should be represented in all administrative and decision-making bodies by ¼. In the absence of this ratio the available number is taken account. The detailed arrangements for the implementation of this rule are determined by regulation (HADEP, 2000: 79-80).

The details of this general rule committed in the statutes were left in the regulation of HADEP women's branches:

> a- Positive discrimination is implementing for candidacy at every level, delegates and the rate of speakers in all meetings. In the election of administration memberships at all levels which is included in the HADEP's statutes, at least one quarter of elected must be women. b- This rule is implemented in the membership of the municipal council, the membership of the provincial council, the deputy candidacy, district, provincial congresses, and convention candidacy; at least one-quarter of member and delegates, parliamentary candidates must be women. There is no upper limit." (HADEP, 2000: 13)

As seen above during the period of HADEP especially in the beginning of 2000s women started to take a more active role in the pro-Kurdish party politics, which is reflected with the amendments in the party's programs and statutes. This period is important because it coincides with the ideological changes in Kurdish national movement after the capture of Öcalan. After Öcalan's arrest, Kurdish movement started to focus on political struggle in order to obtain Kurdish rights within "democratic" borders of Turkish state (Akkaya and Jongerden, 2012). From this standpoint, political organizations become aware of importance of mobilizing society as a whole. Also, "the project of creating democratic, ecologic, gender-egalitarian society"[57] which was formulated by Öcalan in 2002 makes women one of the critical

---

[57] The PKK leader, Abdullah Öcalan who is imprisoned since 1999 specified his ideas that under the name of the *"Democratic, Ecologic, Gender-Egalitarian Society Project"* in 2002 which has leaded to an explicit discursive shift in the ideology of the PKK in the early 2000s, as the PKK accepted discourse of democracy and freedom. This ideological shift affected the Kurdish women's activism not only in the PKK but also in the legal areas. It has opened more space for women than the ethnic nationalist discourse had in the 1990s.
The project of *Democratic Confederalism*, which offers *Democratic Autonomy* as solution for Kurdish question in Turkey is comprehensively analysed by Akkaya and Jongerden (2012).

groups. Therefore, from 2000 onwards in the political area women have become influential actors both related to increasing feminist awareness among female activists and encouragement of national movement and positive discrimination policies of pro-Kurdish parties.

In terms of program and statutes principles, the first most radical regulations concerning 'women's liberation' are observed in DEHAP's (1997-2005) program and statutes. The program and statutes, which were approved with extraordinary congress in 2003, denote a radical differentiation from former pro-Kurdish political parties in terms of both form and content. In terms of form, 'women's liberation' was not near the end as in previous program, it was placed right in the second rank under the heading of 'democratization of state and society.' The program evaluates finding a peaceful solution to Kurdish problem as a primary important issue of democratization while approaching women's liberation as a secondly important issue for democratization.

The main theme that shapes the pro-Kurdish political parties after 2000 is "democratization". It is because the Kurdish movement has abandoned the objective of creating great Kurdistan and started to develop a peaceful solution based on democratizing the Turkish state. Those were in years when Abdullah Öcalan developed his idea of *Democratic Autonomy* as solution for the Kurdish problem in Turkey. In comparison to the previous parties' program it is clear that the equality of gender has become a major concern for the party. Right in the introductory chapter of the program, 'women's liberation' is regarded among the major objectives of the party:

> The political approach which democratizes the state, extends politics to society, is based on human rights and the liberation of women, the protection of ecological balance, social justice and the rule of law is the basic approach of our time. Turkey's democratic reconstruction in this direction in the light of

this program will be provided to power of DEHAP, a democratic mass party of the left (DEHAP, 2003: 7).

According to the new DEHAP program; "In the 20th century the real socialist system that emerged with the ideal of a more equitable society against the inequalities generated by the system could not get rid of collapsing" (DEHAP, 2003: 9). Notwithstanding, "capitalist civilization came to a deadlock and it is far from producing solutions to people's problems and it has become imperative to new solution based on justice, freedom and equality" (DEHAP, 2003: 9). Women will have a significant place in this new departure. According to the party program one of the contradictions that determine the end of the twentieth century is the gender one.

As seen above, the concept of gender contradiction marks all regulations of DEHAP's program. In the party's understanding, the main source of problems, which people struggle in this day and age is the exclusion of women from history which is stated in these statements:

> The inequality between the sexes as a historical and social problem is one of the main problems of our time. This problem does not affect only women; On the basis of being entered 21.century without solving the severe social, political, ecological problems of mankind is, the former inequality that other inequalities are fed to is not being overcome. Male-dominated social structure still maintains a presence (...). Our world today, which is a product of history in which women did not take place, were excluded and silenced, cannot produce a solution for the problems of humanity. An equality, which ignored the half of society, is not the real equality; democracies in which women are not represented with their differences are deficient democracies (DEHAP, 2003: 18-19).

It is clear that DEHAP grounded its opposition against the gender discrimination not as a matter of social policy like previous the ones; it was based on the 'strategic approach' and it addressed sex discrimination as a system problem (DEHAP, 2003: 19). It is also clear that their argument for gender equality refers to the *justice* argument introduced at the beginning of this chapter. In addition, the party's insistence on the representation of women as a necessity to consolidate democracies indicates their approach to both the *pragmatic* and *difference* arguments. This attitude implies that the party recognises the right of women to be different and represent themselves (pragmatic) and that these differences contribute to improve democracies (difference argument). In this sense, the primary application that the party embraced to do is the principle of positive discrimination:

> The DEHAP acts to overcome the barriers to the participation of women in social and political life as a mandatory task. The affirmative action will be applied until there are no conditions that prevent the representation of women in decision-making and implementation processes. The law on political parties will be to organize in this direction (DEHAP: 2003:18-19).

It took responsibility of "struggling against traditional value judgements which count women secondary, weak and contempt". Besides the party aims "to fight against such practices; a young age marriages, dowry, polygamy and *berdel*[58] at all levels which do not recognize the right of women over their own lives" (DEHAP, 2003 18-19). It undertook the mission of ensuring the development of an egalitarian culture and of providing the equality of opportunity in education and employment.

The DEHAP's statutes amendment which was made in the same congress shows parallel characteristics with the program. The first distinction from the previous ones appears in the definition of the party. Along with its similar characteristics to other parties DEHAP is defined as a party which sees "... democratization of society in active participation of women in all areas and the emancipation of women", among its objectives; secondly, it is underlined that the party rejects all forms of discrimination against women and acts upon the principle of that "women are the main subjects of the struggle for the creation of a democratic,

---

[58] "Berdel" has been one of types of marriage in traditional patriarchal Kurdish society. It refers to marriage of girls and boys of the family to the male and female children of another family at the same time mutually. Shortly, it is defined as exchanging of girls for marriage details.

egalitarian and free society" (DEHAP, 2003: 73-74). In the principles section women quota which was set forth ¼ in HADEP increased 35% in DEHAP (DEHAP, 2003: 73-74). The implementation of quota, which has played a significant role in increase of descriptive representation of women will be analysed in detail as a strategy for feminizing politics in the Chapter 4.

The party also cared about the behaviour of its members in their private life. Accordingly, "committing any kinds of violence including domestic and harassment against women" and "making polygamy after being member of the party are subject to the party disciplinary actions" (DEHAP, 2003:137). Based on female political activists' statements it can be said that the party's female activists were influential in raising consciousness about women's issues and enforcing the party to take action. For instance, the issue of polygamy was raised by female members of the party. Some of the participants who were active at the time stated that they put effort in creating awareness in order to prevent polygamous male members from participating in administration and decision-making bodies. They insisted that polygamy should be considered as an obstacle for being delegate, party administrator or electoral candidate. In particular, they obtained the expulsion of polygamous members but just of those who joined the party after this decision was taken. These meant that although the party was willing to take action in favour of women, women activists had to challenge the organisation in order to reach their goals. That is because the party was still dominated by men and the politics was still perceived as a male activity. Therefore, women's issues were assessed from a male perspective. In this regard, the female activists from that period noted that some party administrators believed that domestic violence should be regarded as a private sphere issue therefore they thought it would not be proper to include it into the party statutes. However, women insisted on this point.

A New Period for Pro-Kurdish Politics: Feminization Progressing

The pro-Kurdish political party tradition, which started in 1990, came to a new phase with the DTP (2005-2009). In terms of its political objectives, projects and gender approach the DTP represents a new stage in pro-Kurdish politics. Its efforts to become a democratic mass party in Turkey extended its policy agenda to those issues beyond the Kurdish question. It aims to become a party that defends the rights of any group, not only Kurds and Turks, but also workers with class-based socialist concerns. The inclusion of other oppressed groups cannot be regarded simply as an attempt to extend the number of the party supporters. It aims to draw a picture of the DTP contrary to the constructed image of the party as ethnic party.

The party's attempt to become a democratic mass party influenced its gender approach as well. The DTP's period represented a turning point with regards to women's participation and representation in politics. In terms of its gender approach and policies for instance with the implementation of co-presidency system and 40% quotas which will be explained in detail in Chapter 4 as strategies for feminizing pro-Kurdish party politics, the DTP represents a new stage in pro-Kurdish politics. The political participation of women, regarded as a distinguishing characteristic of the DTP, is encouraged by the party and gender equality and women's issues were addressed in a great extent in the party's program and statutes. It is also because the existence and emphasis of women's participation in the party is an important feature contributing to the party's broader base.

From mid-2000, the DTP started to voice more explicitly its political project, the 'Project for Democratic Autonomy', very much in line with Öcalan's concept of *Democratic Confederalism*. In the 'Democratic Society Congress', which was held in Diyarbakir in October 2007 *'Democratic Autonomy'*, was accepted as a project for Kurdish people in Turkey. This congress report called for radical reforms in Turkey's political and administrative structure in order to ensure democratisation and to develop problem-solving approaches for which the local level should be strengthened. This project proposed regional and local structures, which allow for the expression of cultural differences rather than autonomy based on 'ethnicity' or 'territory' (Akkaya and Jongerden, 2012). In its second congress held in November 2007, the DTP recognized this report officially by the name of 'Democratic Solution to the Kurdish Question - Democratic Autonomy Project'. In the same congress the DTP adopted some important changes in party statutes in accordance to the concept of democratic autonomy aiming at the formation of assemblies at each level of organization. Besides, at local level, a new local government model was developed in accordance to this project. In the light of these developments it can be stated this period started from mid-2000 as a new period in the legal Kurdish politics in which the DTP came to play an important role for the policy of solution whereas the former legal Kurdish parties were confined to a struggle for existence against the policies of denial and annihilation (Akkaya and Jongerden, 2012). Furthermore, the adoption of *Democratic Confederalism* which is defined as a model for 'democratic self-government' enabling Kurdish people to establish their own democracy and system of society promotes a gender egalitarian society. It encourages participation of women in this self-government model as one of significant social groups. Since it seeks the establishment of democracy in all spheres of life of Kurdish society equality of the sexes becomes one of its significant features. Women and youth are encouraged to set up their organizations as two important segments of the society, which enable them to participate in this self-government model. Since the party started to adopt this model its organization structure, its political objectives and policies have changed. Since mid-2005 significant developments have been achieved in favour of women such as the implementation of co-chairship system and 40% gender quotas and the election of women to representation bodies, which prove the feminization of pro-Kurdish politics has progressed.

The DTP is the first party to adopt a co-chairship system in the political life of Turkey, which refers to sharing power between men and women in the administration of the party since 2005. Aysel Tuğluk and Ahmet Türk were elected as co-chairs of the party when co-chairship was implemented for the first time. The DTP had a significant success in election since 1991. After Leyla Zana who was the first Kurdish female deputy elected in 1991 national elections, 8 female MPs entered the Parliament in 2007. In 2007 general elections, the DTP participated in the elections with independent candidates under the name of "candidates of a thousand hopes". 22 deputies were elected among them. It is remarkable that 8 of them were women. In March 29th 2009 local elections, out of 99 municipalities that were won by DTP, female candidates were elected in 14 with 40% quota which was also implemented for the council memberships of municipalities.[59]

The influence of new political project and political objectives on the party's gender approach can be revealed through examining the party's program and

---

[59] Nagihan Akarsel, "Kürt kadınlarının mücadelesi" http://www.yuksekovahaber.com/haber/kurt kadinlarinin-mucadelesi-38948.htm (Accessed on 28 September 2012).

statutes.[60] First of all, women's emancipation and gender equality are addressed to achieve democratization. Secondly, the ways and policies to achieve gender equality in all realms are explained in the party program and statutes below. Especially policies aimed at increasing women's political representation are included in the party's program and statutes. Based on research conducted with female political activists it can be stated that besides the influence of new political project, women in the party have played a role in inclusion of these principles and policies concerning women's issues in general and women's representation in the party's program and statutes.

Examination of the party's program and statutes will reveal the party's perspective on gender equality, its approach towards gender inequality in politics in particular and in other areas and its perspective towards women's issues. It will be pointed out that the party concerns to eliminate gender equality in all areas and its discourses of gender equality are based on the concept of "democratization". The idea is that Kurds would get their rights in a democratic country and in order to be a democratic country and democratic society gender equality has to be achieved. The ideological discourses of the national movement concerning women are clearly recognized in the program of the BDP. Again, the main theme, which is very often uttered especially since end of 1990s, is that women are the main force of democratization, is placed in the program of the BDP. At the beginnings of the program the title of 'women are main dynamics of democratization' represents the perspective of the party apparently on the line of the national movement. Under this title the significant statements address some basic issues of women states that:

---

[60] BDP replaced DTP after its closure in 11 December 2009. The administrators of the party's headquarter in Diyarbakır informed that its guidelines and program were adopted as so. The only change was the name of the party. For that reason the analysis is carried out under the name of BDP.

109

> Gender equality is thus to be a historical, political, economic and cultural issue that need to be resolved as a priority problem. On the basis of being entered 21st Century without solving the serious social, political, ecological problems of mankind is this ancient and widespread inequality that other inequalities are fed. The root of competition, inequality, exploitation, violence, and its transformation into a universal culture, conflict and deepening of the contradictions at the global level is this conflict. Our today's world which is a product of history which does not include women, excluded, silenced cannot produce solutions to the problems of humanity (BDP, 2008: 142).

Considering gender inequality as the primary issue of mankind and source of other inequalities has shaped the party's political projects. As seen in the following, the party's all discourses of democratization indicate equality of gender is major concern for pro-Kurdish politics.

In addition:

> Our party regards gender inequality as one of the fundamental contradictions of our time. Therefore, the party evaluates the problem in the system and determines the strategic approach to opposite it. The party determines to eliminate gender inequality as a challenge of the purification of all areas of life (social, political, cultural, and economic, etc...) from male-dominated character and re-arranging of all these areas of life (BDP, 2008: 142).

In his writings, the leader of national movement, Abdullah Öcalan (1992) mentioned how to create a democratic society and how to remove male domination. The starting point for creating gender equality based society is the family. As seen, the family institution is regarded as core of changing gender relations by the party as well. From this standpoint, BDP emphasizes that the roles of 'masculinity' and 'femininity' begins within the family and that both roles are determinative in all realms of life. For that reason, the party deals with the overcoming gendered roles in the institution of family and democratization of family structure, which has been institutionalised, as an irreconcilable problem. Further, the democratization of politics is underlined through involvement of women. It is stated below:

> As our party approaching the problem of gender inequality as the most severe and widespread discrimination, regards it as fundamental dynamics of the democratization of politics. It knows that democracies, which women cannot attend, are not real democracies. Therefore, it regards a continuous struggle against barriers to the active participation of women in all the political processes that constitute the half of the society, a necessary task... (BDP, 2008: 143-144).

These lines emphasize the importance of women's participation in decision-making processes in the context of democratization. For establishing real democracies supporting women's engagement in politics equally and referring that they are half society indicates that the party makes its argument for gender equality in politics based on justice argument.

The party's official position with respect to women emancipation is included in its section of general principles where it states that 'the emancipation of humanity in the equality of sexes' (BDP, 2008: 3), overlapping the Kurdish national movement's perspective. In addition, the section indicates the ways to reach this goal:

> The party decidedly struggles from the fact that gender liberation is a determining factor in attaining the goal of a democratic society, for the elimination of all obstacles to freedom of gender, particularly will develop women's organization on the basis of women's own will. In accordance to this principle it rejects gender discrimination and all forms of violence against women; in order to create equality between the sexes in all areas of life it provides legal, economic, social, political and cultural measures to be taken. It shall take all steps for the implementation of equality between men and women in the political arena. To provide the highest level of male-female equality it defends co-chairship system and struggles for the institutionalization of it (BDP, 2008: 5-6).

The other measure to achieve gender equality is gender quotas. In this regard, it is stated:

> The party shall take all measures for the implementation positive discrimination in each area of the party life and at the all level in the party including organs and committees of the party. For this purpose it advocates gender quota and struggles for the enactment of it." (BDP, 2008: 6)

Gender quotas, which were included on the basis of the principle of positive discrimination, were not limited to elections. Regarding the implementation of quotas the statement in the part of 'the party's working principles' notes that "40% gender quota is applied in the election of all the party's organs and in determining candidates for national and local elections. Both sexes are taken basis in gender quota." (BDP, 2008: 9) Furthermore, there is a clarification about positive discrimination. It states that "positive discrimination is implemented for women in every area and at all level of the party's life including the party's organs and bodies. If the candidates receive same number of votes the female candidate is considered as elected. Positive discrimination is not under the initiative of any organ or person." (BDP, 2008: 9-10)

The objectives of promoting gender equality and obtaining women's liberation are highlighted in the statements above. The political struggle and the political engagement are the ways to achieve these objectives. For that purpose, the women's organization is encouraged by the party. Also, the party has responsibility to seek for juridical, economic, social, political and cultural measures in order to provide gender equality in all realms of life. Another significant point is that two applications, which are co-chairship and positive discrimination principle are implemented by the party for the concern of advancing women's position in the political realm.

Additionally, two other points that are underlined in the guidelines of the party are about the organization of the women's assemblies and the party's training policy. The statement about central women council states that "central women's council is organized free and autonomous" (BDP, 2008: 73) and provides opportunity for women's council to be influential within the party. In this way, women have become part of the party's training policy. This is stated in the section concerning the party's training schools and academies: "Targeted training is based in the areas of politics, local, women and youth on the level of the academy. Therefore, the decision of the party's council of training, the infrastructure prepared as politics, local governments, woman and youth academies and it is set up as programming " (BDP, 2008: 82). The issue of training became a significant element in the formation of women as political actors in the ideological lines of the party generally and women's assemblies in particular. The opening of schools of politics for women and of women's academies with a particular focus on their role in the feminization of pro-Kurdish party politics will be analysed in the Chapter 4.

In conclusion, in the program, the party's concern for women appears in the section on 'decentralization'. It states: "... our party will encourage women's participation in local government and will take measures to include excluded segments into local process" (BDP, 2008: 152). These expressions about the local government are remarkable considering the increasing number of women in local government. The party's ideological standing towards definition of local governments has played a role in participation and election of women in local politics. The following section will analyse how local governments are very important areas where women can implement policies and develop projects in their favour following the party's goals for the formation of democratic governments.

In its guidelines the party states that "it will struggle to organize the implementation of quota in every aspect of life; landing a job, trade unions, associations, chambers and so on." (BDP, 2008: 144). In the area of education it states that "the curriculum which contains gender inequality to be replaced with a democratic, egalitarian content." (BDP, 2008: 144). Regarding the invisibility of women's labour it says that,

> Male-dominated system renders women's labour invisible in all areas; social, political, cultural, economic and scientific. BDP will ensure the women's labour to be visible in all these areas and will guarantee the rights of women in all social spheres (BDP, 2008: 144-145).

Mentioning the quote directly, the party also states that,

> "In Turkey especially in cities women's participation rate in work force is critically low so women will be given priority in employment. The gradually implementation of the quota shall be 50% of the public employment" (BDP, 2008: 144-145).

Furthermore, the party addresses many issues that influence the life of women by adopting international norms in order to deal with these issues.[61] Regarding women's issues such domestic violence and sexual harassment and the ways the party struggles against these issues it is stated:

> For the elimination domestic violence against women the family will be treated as a continuous and informal area of education. The struggle against all forms of violence against women will be carried; based on international standards women's shelters will be opened where more than fifty thousand inhabitants; support will be provided to victims of violence." (BDP, 2008: 145). "The laws which include sexual abuse and rape crimes against re-arranged, the penalties will be increased..." (BDP, 2008: 145). "Prostitution is the most humiliating form of violence imposed on women by the male-dominated system since ancient times targeted to eliminate completely and brothels are targeted to close..." (BDP, 2008: 146). " Legal arrangements will be made to eliminate all forms of discrimination against women, the requirements of all international conventions, notably CEDAW (Committee on the Elimination of Discrimination against Women) will ensure gender equality, to be met" (BDP, 2008: 146).

An example of how the party standing against issues that are raised by the female activists can be observed in its membership conditions. The issue of

---

[61] It was specified that the party will struggle against traditional value judgements which count women secondary and development of an egalitarian culture will be promoting. An active struggle will be carrying at every level against such practices; early marriage, bride price, polygamy and *berdel* which do not allow women to speak about their life (HADEP, 2008: 145).

polygamy, which was raised by female activists in the previous period, is addressed by the party in the section of membership conditions. In this section, it is stated that "the members who have more than one wife will have their membership cancelled based on the principle of equality between the sexes, in order to protect the women's rights based on from the Civil Code." (BDP, 2008: 11).

The party's approach towards gender equality is clearly identified in its program and statutes. It is shaped by the national movement's ideological discourses and political projects. It is seen the party's concern for achieving gender equality is related to its political agenda, which is democratization. The following statement in the party's program "Women's initiative and freedom will be decisive in the creation of a free and democratic society" (BDP, 2008: 146) explains the party's support for implementing gender equality policies. The strong belief and dedication of to create a democratic society (democratic, ecological and gender egalitarian society) which corresponds the national movement's objective has contributed to make changes first in political areas.

The historical analysis towards pro-Kurdish political parties' guidelines and programs from 1990s have brought out some major points to explain why pro-Kurdish politics has been feminizing. First, the changes have been realized in parallel to the ideological changes in Kurdish national movement. Since the beginning of 2000s Kurdish national movement started to search for solutions for the Kurdish question within the country and political projects developed by Öcalan political parties and political struggle gained in importance. Second, the growing participation of women in politics encouraged women to force the party to change its policies in their favour. In order to achieve their aims to democratize the country in order to obtain Kurdish rights, to create a democratic society and to respond to women's demands the party had to support gender equality.

Women's Arguments and Aims for *Feminizing* Politics

Women's political activism gradually increased within pro-Kurdish politics since the establishment of the first pro-Kurdish party in 1990 presenting a complex picture in its demands and arguments in support for gender equality. Although this study focuses on gender equality in the political arena the statements of female political activists indicate that they claim their right to gender equality in every realm of life. This section shows on the basis of their arguments, which are their claims for gender equality in politics in particular and in the society in general.

In their equality rhetoric, their arguments theoretically reflect the *justice, pragmatic* and *difference* arguments with regard to the equality in politics (Lovenduski 2000 & 2005; Phillips 1995 & 1998); however, it extends to other realms of life. Based on their experiences it can be stated, for instance, the national movement and the party's political project for the creation of a *Democratic Society* is utilized by female activists to justify their arguments and claims. Furthermore, Kurdish women politically as well as socially are very well organized in groups. They fight a very dynamic struggle which involves the participation of other women in Turkey and internationally. This multifaceted picture of Kurdish women's political activism has brought forward diversity of arguments, claims and demands, which have influenced the pro-Kurdish party politics.

The issue of women's interests is very important in women's claim to be equally represented in the decision-making process. In fact, the issue of women's interests is a highly debated issue in feminist literature, in particular the discussion focuses on whether they have universal interests based on their gendered identities or their interests can be differentiated related to their other social identities like ethnicity, race, class, and ideology. It is not only gendered identity that influences women's interests, but their multiple identities (Alvarez 1990; Dahlerup 2006; Goetz and Hassim 2003). In the Kurdish case the issue of women's interests is very complicated in many respects especially due to influence of multiple identities on their activism. Female political activists have been politicized around their ethnic identity. In particular, during 1990s the main concern was to obtain Kurdish national rights. Gender equality was not a priority in women's political involvement (Çağlayan, 2007). Gender identity awareness appeared among women activists towards the end of 1990s and especially since then women activists started to make claims for equal participation and representation in decision-making. The experiences of female political statements indicated that the emergence of gender awareness among women resulted from the gender based discrimination they faced within the party during 1990s. Although they were taking part in all the party's activities like male colleagues they were not treated equally. For instance, they were not appointed in powerful positions and issues related women did not concern the party. Political areas were dominated by men like all other areas and women and their interests were secondary as many female political activists underlined. Therefore, female political activists began to focus on women's rights alongside with Kurdish national rights.

In the context of women's arguments for gender equality the issue of interests urged women to insist on equal participation and representation in the party ranks and decision making organs and representation bodies. The vast majority of women activists involved in this research stated that due to their gender identity women have different experiences and interests than men and they believe that men cannot fully understand women's needs and problems. Because of that, their interests and problems cannot be represented by men. In addition, many female activists underlined that the number of women participating in pro-Kurdish politics is not much less than men and they are active as much as men. Besides, they are electors. In this regard, female activists who were involved in election campaigns in 2009 local elections and female mayor candidates in these elections expressed that many female electors were glad about female candidates because they believe women raise their concerns, demands and interests. In addition, those female activists take part in the party's decision-making and elected representatives underlined that politics that shape the society are dominated by men. Thus, it is necessary that women participate in political decision-making. These statements of female activists identify the arguments on which their demands of equal representation have built upon.

Experiencing similar political mobilization processes shape the female activists' political discourses and their political struggle within the pro-Kurdish politics. Therefore, in debates about why women have to be equal numbers in politics parallel arguments are raised by the female activists. Firstly, one common argument made by female political activists is that if they form the half of the society they should be represented in equal in order to ensure justice and democracy. Female activists' statements apparently correspond to the *justice* argument, which suggests the parity in representation based on the idea that it is not fair if politics is dominated by men. Also, it is necessary in order to have a democratic system and exercise democracy. In this regard, one of female mayors who has been in politics since 1990s and mainly worked in the area of women workings within the party stated:

> We, women in the party started to question many things in 1990s. We know politics shape the society and the society is not only composed of men. We, women are half of the society. Also, there are a huge number of women in our party. So, it is not fair if only men make decision. It is not democratic too. We should be represented in the Parliament, local governments in the same number with men. We should be in the decision making of the party... That is why we have the mission of "More women more democracy"[62] (Personal interview, Diyarbakır, April 2010).

It is important to point out that female political activists' equality rhetoric and discourses, which correspond to the justice argument are mainly based on the national movement's ideological discourses. Regarding their struggle as a liberation movement, the Kurdish national movement and especially its leader- Abdullah Öcalan have used different discourses in order to mobilize Kurdish people and maintain commitment with the supporters of the movement. These discourses have changed from time to time depending on ideological changes and shift in political national and global circumstances. From the statements of the interviewees it is clear that discourses associated to national movement's gender ideology, which have shaped the political parties' gender policies as well are employed by female political activists to justify their demands and to make arguments for gender equality and to strengthen their struggle in the political arena.

The interviews with female activists have revealed that they use some discourses in order to form their demands for gender equality in every area of life. Besides, the female activists' experiences and statements indicate that the ideological discourses of PKK and its leader- Abdullah Öcalan have played a role in forming women's political and ideological standing during their political engagement processes. These discourses are not internalized and used only by women; both

---
[62] In Turkish it refers to "Daha çok kadın daha çok demokrasi".

women and men who take part in political circles and support the Kurdish national movement mention such statements in order to demonstrate both in legal politics and on the 'illegal' level, their support to the equality of sexes. Some of these statements frequently used by female activists are: "BDP is the party of women"[63], "Women are the main dynamic of democratization "[64], "The society cannot be liberated without the liberty of women"[65],"Kurdish movement is the movement of women or Kurdish movement is the movement with women leadership"[66] and PKK is the party of women.[67]

All these statements refer to the central role of women in the national movement in general and in the legal political movement in particular. But these statements address the central role of women in the context of democratization that correspond only to the *justice* argument. In this regard, they present an opportunity for women to construct and justify their political activism. From these interviews it is clear that they employ these discourses, for instance, in cases of facing resistance from male fellows within the political party. They are kind of tools utilized by women in order to gain space in the political area and justify their arguments and claims to have equal status in the political arena.

One of the interviewees who have an administration position within the party says with respect to this:

> The leader of national movement, I mean this is the leader Apo[68] says that, this party is the party of woman. When he says this is the party of woman he does not mean women founded this party or, women are working in this party, rather it means it has an essence to create gender equality within itself. It

---

[63] BDP kadın partisidir.
[64] Kadın demokratikleşmenin temel dinamiğidir.
[65] Kadın özgürleşmeden toplum özgürleşemez.
[66] Kürt hareketi kadın hareketidir veya Kürt hareketi, kadın önderlikli bir harekettir.
[67] PKK kadın partisidir.
[68] Apo is the nickname of Abdullah Öcalan used by the movement's supporters.

implies PKK has such a philosophy. This philosophy influences political organizations as well (Personal interview, Diyarbakır, March 2010).

The equality discourses of the national movement which influence the legal political areas as underlined by the vast majority of female activists involved in this research encourage women to play an active role in politics. The expressions of the interviewees make it clear that they have internalized these ideological discourses. Moreover, the circumstances in which women employ these statements prove their ability to challenge male domination in political organizations. One of the participants who has been within the party ranks since the period of HADEP (1994-2003) denotes that whenever they face any obstacle within the party and in political circles outside it they are reminded of these statements as rules of national movement that all pro-Kurdish political organizations and political activists should follow. She adds that this encouragement keeps them stronger against resistance they face from male fellows toward changes that women want to make for the purpose of empowering their role (Personal interview, Istanbul, September 2010).

Secondly, women activists emphasize the need for female representatives to promote their interests and demands, which they insist are different from men's. Based on these statements, the pragmatic argument which states that women have different interests than men and these interests can be better represented by themselves (Squires, 1999; Phillips 1998) explain why women argue for equality in politics. In addition, pragmatic arguments use difference points in order to claim that women have, and why they have, specific interests, concerns and experiences which can only be understood, sympathized and represented by women (Lovenduski, 2005: 23) which overlap activists' explanations. They underline that as result of patriarchal mentality, which promotes male superiority women have different experiences due to their secondary position in the society. They need to transform existing gender relations and to create equal opportunities in all areas such as politics, economic and education. One of female mayors regarding the need for female representatives stated:

> We (women) know women's needs better than men. As a woman mayor I concern about women's in my district. For example, I am the mayor of the district where women are not visible in public sphere at all. It is a very male-dominated place. For me it is an issue. A male mayor might not care but I want to change this structure. As a female mayor I think of women' needs when providing municipality services. I meet regularly with women in public area to find out their needs and demands. I can see more women outside and come to visit me in municipality (Personal interview, Diyarbakır, July 2010).

Similarly, the vast majority of female mayors who run in small areas raise same issues, which emphasize that women representatives are required to represent women's issues and interests in representational bodies which refer to pragmatic arguments.

Thirdly, female activists believe that women contribute to politics with new political style, morals and ethics. In other words, women have peculiar characteristics and experiences, which should be incorporated into politics to transform male-dominated policies and political institutions. These statements of female activists refer to the *difference* argument, which basically assumes women have distinctive political style and they offer a different approach to politics. This view maintains that women can change politics for the better and the result will be for the benefit of all (Lovenduski 2005: 24).

Overall, female activists present strong advocacy for equality of sexes in politics. They put forward various opinions in order to justify their justice, pragmatic and difference arguments. If they are seen as different from each other at first glance yet, they are actually interconnected. In all these arguments which are essential for the system of democracy in theory at least, these common points come to fore: women are different than men based on their sex. It leads to different experiences and interests. They best represent themselves because they know what they need. In addition, they have different attributes, which enable them to do politics in a "just" way. Although these points need to be questioned, female activists believe women can have an impact in their favour and this urges and motivate them make an effort in order to achieve their goals.

Conclusion: Women as the main dynamics of democratization

In this chapter showed the three actors identified have played a vital role in the feminization of pro-Kurdish party politics. These are Kurdish national movement led by the PKK and pro-Kurdish political parties, and female political activists. This chapter revealed that shifts in ideological discourses and political projects of the national movement and political parties' and the emergence of gender-identity based political activism among women have determined a transformation in pro-Kurdish politics in favour of women from 2000s onwards in particular. This analysis suggests that democratization is the main term that determined efforts and policies towards gender equality in pro-Kurdish politics.

This chapter indicated that the national movement is a significant actor in raising the issue of gender inequality. Kurdish national movement, which has mobilized Kurds to struggle for national emancipation since 1980s in Turkey, has focused on women especially from early 1990s. Kurdish national discourse, which identified women's emancipation with national liberation and addressed to eliminate traditional structures in Kurdish society encouraged women to join the national struggle. Meanwhile women participated in pro-Kurdish political parties due to ethnic identity concerns as well. Therefore, during 1990s the pro-Kurdish parties and their members, including women, were carrying a political agenda predominantly concerning ethnic identity-based demands of Kurds.

The idea of separation from the Turkish state was gradually abandoned from the first half of 1990s when the Kurdish national movement began to consider a democratic solution for the Kurdish question in Turkey. With the abandonment of the objective of creating great Kurdistan, the national movement started to focus more on political struggle than the armed struggle in order to obtain Kurdish rights. However, critical breaks in the Kurdish national movement occurred since end of 1990s after the capture of PKK leader Abdullah Öcalan in 1999. The arrest of Öcalan influenced the movement's political objectives and projects, which shaped legal political areas. In 2000s, the aims and objectives of the movement have evolved towards the goal of national autonomy, and what Öcalan terms *"Democratic Confederalism"*. The *Democratic Confederalism,* which was suggested by Öcalan as an alternative to the nation-state and as a model to solve the problems in the Middle East in general and Kurdish question in particular are based on 'democratic self-government', which enables Kurdish people to establish their own democracy and system of society without a state. Its significance from a gender perspective is that feminism or equality of sexes is one of central pillars of the model. Women are encouraged to set up their own democratic organizations and to participate in establishing democratic self-government system and democratic society. The model of *Democratic Confederalism* was adopted under the name of *Democratic Autonomy* and officially declared in 2007 as a political project offering solutions for political, cultural and linguistic rights of Kurds in Turkey. In this regard, since these political projects started to shape legal political arenas especially from the first half of 2000, significant developments have been made in legal areas, which escalate the feminization of pro-Kurdish politics. Based on female activists' statements and analysis of political parties' documents the concept of democratization characterizes gender approach of the political parties and policies concerning women's status in politics.

This chapter revealed that women and their issues did not receive attention especially in the first period of 1990s. As examination towards political parties' program and guidelines pointed out, women were out of the parties' (HEP, DEP, and HADEP) focus of interest. However, a significant change was made in the party program of HADEP by including women policy into the democratization section. This indicates that concern for women's issues in the context of democratization is back to HADEP's period but this did not reflect practices. Apart from this, during 1990s there was not any specific women policy implemented by the parties. Besides, although there were women units established during the HADEP's period in the second half of 1990s they were not effective to raise women's concerns and to develop a specific women policy. Women's issues have entered the agenda of woman's units in the parties in 2000s with the development of gender awareness among women. Although there were not any influential or concrete developments in terms of women's status in politics, there is an important characteristic of this period started with HADEP. This is the emergence of the idea of looking at gender equality from the perspective of democratization. This has become a major determinant for the further developments regarding women's participation and representation in pro-Kurdish politics in 2000s especially with the development of political projects of *Democratic Confederalism* and *Democratic Autonomy*.

This chapter also revealed significant differences regarding women political activists involved in politics in 1990s and those involved in 2000s. The reasons behind their participation in politics and their profiles, which determine their demands and concerns were different. Whereas women were involved in politics as result of ethnic identity consciousness to struggle for their national rights in 1990s, gender identity consciousness has played a dominant role in their activism in 2000s. The political parties' primary concern to raise Kurdish issue and to ensure recognition of Kurdish identity and national rights influenced women to prioritize their ethnic identity rights in 1990s. However, especially female political activists' experiences in 1990s encouraged them to question male domination in politics. Female political activists started to raise women issues and gender equality through women's units in the party from the beginning of 2000s.

This chapter found an important point regarding to what context gender equality discourses and demands are formed. It is found that the discourses of gender equality and women's emancipation which were also raised in 1990s have put into practice since the models which offer democratic solution for the Kurdish issue are recognized by pro-Kurdish political parties from the first part of 2000 in particular. Thus, the pro-Kurdish political parties' discourses and policies that promote gender equality and women's emancipation are mainly formed in the context of democratization. In this respect, when justice argument primarily explains the political parties' support for equality of sexes in political areas, female political activists' claims and arguments for gender equality in politics are much more diversified. Female political activists argued that as constituting the half of society their exclusion from political decision-making is not fair. They want to take place in decision-making equally, which is required to create a democratic system and society. Arguing for equality of sexes on this basis refers to justice argument. In addition, female political activists make their arguments based on pragmatic argument, which states that they have different issues and interests due to their gender identity and these can be better represented by women themselves. Finally, the argument of fulfilling their political roles from a gender perspective, having distinctive experiences, concerns and moral, which contribute to change gendered political institutions and culture and to offer a different approach for the benefit of all overlap difference argument.

The following chapter focuses on the obstacles, which determine the level of women's political participation and representation in general and Kurdish women's in particular.

CHAPTER FOUR

Obstacles to Feminizing (pro-Kurdish Party) Politics

Introduction

As mentioned in the previous chapters, Kurdish women have been involved in legal politics since the first pro-Kurdish political party (HEP) founded in 1990. Since then, a number of significant developments have been undertaken to include women in decision-making processes. Policies, ideologies and organization style have changed in favour of advancing of women's position in pro-Kurdish legal politics. However, their increasing participation and representation in political decision-making does not prove that they have had easy access to political power or have not confronted any challenges and obstacles in their effort for joining political organizations, taking part in decision making bodies and nominating and electing as political representatives. In fact, women initially faced barriers when they attempted to join political parties; then they encountered challenges and obstacles after they joined political parties and entered the representation bodies such as parliament and local governments. Within the political institutions dominated by men and their norms women face a variety of barriers and difficulties in their attempt to access position of power. The experiences of female political activists in pro-Kurdish politics interviewed during field research indicate that they have faced various challenges and impediments during their political engagement within the political institutions including political, socio-economic and cultural factors and state politics towards female political activists, which has made political arenas insecure for women.

The wide scope of the problem of women's under representation has motivated many scholars into analysing on the factors that led to this under representation. These analyses have displayed the significance of a large number of factors that can be grouped into four categories; political, socio-economic and cultural factors and state politics: pro-Kurdish politics "high risk area" which is specific to Kurdish case.

The political factors mostly focus on the characteristics of the political regime in a country. The structure of the parliament, for instance the number of legislative seats, the party system and the electoral system are included in this category. Among all the political factors, the richest literature has been produced on the impact of electoral system with the broadly accepted conclusion that proportional representation leads to higher percentages of women in parliaments compared to plurality/majority systems (Lovenduski - Hills 1981; Rule 1987, 1994b; Norris 1985, 1997, 2006). Besides, male domination in political arenas, which characterizes the political institutions and political culture, can also be included within the political factors. Many studies pointed out that male domination in politics and political institutions is a major problem that has led to the establishment of the belief that politics is a male activity. (Lovenduski, 2005; Arat, 1985&1989; Talaslı, 1996: 186-187).

Socio-economic factors, which emphasize the significance of socio-economic development level of a society, include basically financial resources and education (Matland, 1998; Arat, 1985 & 1989; Güneş-Ayata, 1995; Koray 1995; Talaslı, 1996). This set of variables that have been revealed influential for female participation and representation in politics indicate the interrelatedness of gender gap in different areas. Socio-economic development of both the society broadly and the women particularly is figured out to be effectual in increasing the supply of female candidates in politics which indicates the connection between socio-economic and political development. Unequal distribution of resources in the society generates severe barriers for women because they do not have much opportunity to succeed in political competitions due to the lack of money and education due to the patriarchal structures dominant in most societies of the world- they encounter (Paxton – Hughes 2007). Therefore, studies focusing on the importance of this set of factors have regarded the average education level of women in the society and women participation in labour market as the candidates for political offices are usually recruited from the upper layers of the society (Matland, 1998).

Cultural factors, which primarily include social norms surrounding women's expected roles, duties and capabilities, are explained as factors that shape the attitudes of both the women and the public in general. The role of culture in shaping social and political phenomena is generally explained through two different indicators; religious affiliation and traditional attitudes. A number of cultural factors have been revealed significant in determining women's political representation. However, the stress has been on religious orientations and views on gender-based social roles (Norris - Inglehart 2001; Paxton 1997; Reynolds 1999; Tremblay 2007; Kirkpatrick, 1974; Currell 1974; Lynn and Flora, 1977; Keskin, 1997; Talaslı, 1996). A number of studies have already suggested that cultural factors are more important than even the political factors. Some of these studies assert that it is these cultural factors that, most of the time, shape the other set of political and socio-economic indicators (Paxton – Kunovich, 2003). Another important point with respect to the significance of cultural factors is their dual impact. The constituents of a political culture influence not only the attitudes of the men or of the power-holders in the society but women themselves are also under the influence of these cultural values. Therefore, if an anti-egalitarian culture is dominant in a society, while the public generally would not prefer female candidates, the women themselves also would not be willing to take place in politics (Norris – Inglehart, 2001).

The last set of obstacles as specific to Kurdish case this chapter focusing is, state politics towards female political activists which include different forms of pressure, oppression and violent acts such as threat, arrest, detention and harass have made political arenas insecure for women; therefore it is considered as an obstacle to women's participation and representation in pro-Kurdish politics.

The field research conducted with female political activists revealed that they think the factors that determine the women's level of political participation and representation are shaped by patriarchy. Regarding this, it is relevant to explain patriarchy for the following analysis. Patriarchy is a social and ideological construct that refers to men is superior to women. It has been conceptualized and analysed by several feminist scholars in different ways. Patriarchy is a fluid and shifting set of social relations in which men oppress women, in which different men exercise varying degrees of power and control, and in which women resist in diverse ways (Collins 1990; hooks 1984; Kandiyoti 1988; Baca Zinn et al., 1986). Sylvia Walby in *Theorising Patriarchy* calls it "a system of social structures and practices in which men dominate, oppress and exploit women" (Walby, 1990). Various feminist writers who have contributed to develop of patriarchal approach such as Simone de Beauvoir (1953), Viola Klein (1971), Kate Millett (1969), Shulamith Firestone (1970), and Zillah Eisenstein (1981) in the twentieth century have a common argument regarding patriarchy. In their perspective, patriarchy is a power structure, which sustains male domination and due to this patriarchal principle, which structures the society women are inferior to men. The "relationship between the sexes is one of dominance and subordination" (Millett, 1969: 25) in all units such as the family, the society, the economy, and the polity which are interconnected patriarchal units (Arat, 1989: 17). In such a system, therefore, women become disadvantageous in terms of involving in politics.

The factors mentioned above have been empirically proved to be important in determining the level of women's political representation. The arguments on the roles played by these sets of factors in terms of determining the level of female participation and representation in pro-Kurdish politics in particular and in Turkey in general are discussed below.

Political Factors

The political factors that influence the level of women's representation in Turkey in general and in pro-Kurdish politics in particular are the political and electoral systems, the party system and the political culture. A determining factor is the political culture, which is shaped by men due to men's being historically dominating political domain and political institutions.

A number of studies on women's political representation have found that the type and features of the political and electoral system influence women's representation. The electoral system of a country introduces rules for how voting is carried out, and how votes are calculated and combined to produce a final result.[69]

---

[69] The types of electoral systems are divided into three categories in general: proportional representation system (PR), plurality-majority system and mixed system. In plurality-majority systems, voters cast a ballot for a single representative, and the candidate who receives the most votes wins (example, the United States and the United Kingdom). In contrast, in many PR electoral systems, political parties put up a list or slate of candidates equal to the number of seats in a district. Independent candidates may also run, and they are listed separately on the ballot as if they were their

Many researches which used cross-national empirical data have revealed that proportional representation systems (PR) are more contributory to women's representation and lead to higher percentages of women in parliaments compared to plurality-majority and mixed electoral systems are[70] (Leyenaar, 2004; Matland & Montgomery, 2003; Matland & Taylor, 1997; Rule, 1987; Rule & Zimmerman, 1994; Lovenduski - Hills 1981; Norris 1985, 1997, 2004, 2006). In this regard, in Turkey who has a multi-party system with two or three strong parties and often a fourth party that is electorally successful; since the election system is based on closed list proportional representation the political and election systems cannot regarded a major political obstacle. On the other hand, in Turkey, to participate in the distribution of seats, a party must obtain at least 10% of the votes cast at the national level. Therefore, although election system is not a reason behind women's under representation in general 10% threshold, which has been in force since 1983 has created some issues for pro-Kurdish politics. As pro-Kurdish political parties have never gained more than 10% percentage of the vote so far and they have had to enter national elections as independent candidates, implementation of this rule was raised as issue by female political activists. A few female political activists mentioned

---

own party. The seats are divided according to the proportion of votes received by the various parties or groups of running candidates. The proportional representation system has two sub-categories: a closed-list system and an open-list system. In a closed-list system, the party fixes the order in which the candidates are listed and elected, and the voter simply casts a vote for the party as a whole. In an open-list system, which most European parties use, voters are presented in unordered or random lists of candidates chosen in party primaries. Voters cannot vote for a party directly but must cast a vote for an individual candidate. This vote counts for the specific candidate as well as for the party. Therefore, the order of the final list completely depends on the number of votes won by each candidate on the list. The most popular candidates rise to the top of the list and have a better chance of being elected. Mixed systems combine majoritarian and proportional elements.

[70] The reason why there is more opportunity for women of being elected in the PR systems compared with other systems is, the PR systems send a larger number of representatives to the national legislature, and political parties need to make a balance in their candidate lists to order to receive votes from different constituents, which urges the political parties to include more women in their lists. On the other hand, the plurality-majority system offers a less opportunity for women to be nominated because political parties nominate a single candidate per district and it is commonly accepted that allocating this place to a female candidate is a politically risky decision.

the negative influence of election threshold on women's representation. One of female political activists stated:

> 10% percentage election threshold is not democratic application. This practice affects women most. Now it not an issue but especially before 2007 (when pro-Kurdish parties began to enter election with independent candidates) men in the party did not want to candidate women because they were thinking people do not vote for women so the party would lose votes and could not make 10% percentage votes (Personal interview, Istanbul, August 2010).

In addition, the scholarship on women's political representation agrees that competitive multi-party electoral systems like Turkey's one are probably to generate greater women's representation than single-party electoral systems do (Bystydzienski, 1995; Leyenaar, 2004; McDonagh, 2009). However, in Turkey where the multi-party system has been exercised since 1945 there have not been any significant changes in the proportion of women elected to representation offices until 2000s. This is evident because mainstream political parties started to nominate women both for local and national elections, which prove the claim that they were influenced by pro-Kurdish political parties' policy towards women. Kurdish political parties have the highest rate of female representatives in office in comparison to the mainstream political parties such as the AKP (Justice and Development Party/ Adalet ve Kalkınma Partisi), the CHP (Republican People's Party/ Cumhuriyet Halk Partisi and the MHP (Nationalist Movement Party/ Milliyetçi Hareket Partisi).

Rather than the political and election systems in Turkey, it is the political party that play a major role in the representation of different groups in society in particular women as well as in shaping the political culture which is fundamental problem due to their patriarchal organization (Arat, 1985&1989). This research shows that politics and political institutions in Turkey are characterized by masculine culture and this is the major political reason behind the exclusion of women from politics.

Instead of focusing on whether women are different, concentrating on how institutions are gendered explains the exclusion of women and their subordination in politics. The argument is that politics itself as an activity is perceived as a male and political institutions such as political parties and parliament through which the activity of politics is exercised are therefore male dominated. Men do politics and men govern the political institutions and critical positions are occupied by men; thus, the decisions and policies are made from a male perspective, which excludes both women's physical precedence and their interests from representative bodies. Succinctly, politics and political institutions are gendered: "the term 'gendered institutions' refers that gender is present in the processes, practices, images and ideologies, and distribution of power in the various sectors of social life" (Acker 1992, 567).[71] Gendered institution is one where power relationships, rules, or other organizations are constructed in a way that systematically reinforces gender differences. Such constructs have traditionally placed women in a subservient position and work, deliberately or by accident. The practices and routines of an institution may sustain or even produce gendered stereotypes (Duerst Lahti and Kelly 1995; Kenney 1996; Hawkesworth 2003). For example, a legislature's plenary debate or committee hearing format may cater to a masculine combative style, making it difficult to work in a consensus-building fashion that women may prefer (Kathlene 1994; Simon Rosenthal 2000). Institutional procedures can advantage the interests of a dominant group and exclude a different or new group from becoming full participants in the institution's activities. If political institutions such as the party and the parliament are gendered institutions, then they may operate in a way that

---

[71] Maria Escobar-Lemmon and Michelle M. Taylor-Robinson (2009) "Getting to the Top: Career Paths of Women in Latin American Cabinets". *Political Research Quarterly* 62 (4): 685-699, p. 685. http://www.jstor.org/discover/10.2307/25594440?uid=3738032&uid=2129&uid=2&uid=70&uid=4&sid=21102486998231 (Accessed on 12 May 2012).

systematically denies women an equal opportunity to participate. This creates tokenism, which limits the opportunities women have to make policy and also limits the extent to which democratic institutions truly claim to represent all citizens. Thus women, beyond the occasional exception become only token participants in politics.

If the parties' approach toward elected women only allows a symbolic role, then the number of women does not make any difference. This raises the difference between descriptive representation and substantive representation and relation between them, which explains improvement in women's representation. Tokenism is an issue in Turkey because although women have been involved in politics since they gained the right to elect and be elected in 1930s, their role has remained symbolic. The increase in women's representation in recent years has not made a huge difference. For instance, even in parties like the CHP with a clear gender equality agenda, women do not dare to break unwritten socio-political boundaries, as the party maintains its own established hierarchies. The male dominated system does not allow women to be extremely vocal participants. Women representatives elected from these mainstream parties who hold political power and enter the Parliament become token participants in politics. In this regard, for instance, Tütüncü and Ayata (2008) contended that the increase in the number of female MPs elected from the AKP ticket has been representative but not substantive: it is mere tokenism because elected women have been loyal to their party and have not supported a specific policy in defence of women's rights.

Political parties are the main gatekeepers for women representatives because they decide how many women are on their lists, who the candidates are, and where the candidates figure on the lists, which are a critical factor for being elected in many political systems (Baldez, 2008; Saint-Germain & Metoyer, 2008; Sanbonmatsu,

2006). In Turkey, despite the implementation of multi-party political and PR electoral systems, which provide more opportunity to women be elected the lower number of female representatives, shows that it is not influential. This addresses the political parties as becoming key agents to influence the gender combination in politics. But political parties in Turkey in routinely exclude women from decision-making positions, resist nominating them as candidates and deny their female candidates adequate campaign support. Even if they are nominated in national elections they are not placed near the top in the list; in local elections they are not nominated for where the party has potential of votes for its candidate to get elected. These common discriminative practices of political parties cannot easily be challenged by female politicians due to established male dominated political culture, gendered institutions and systems even if they have awareness of gender inequity in politics.

The political parties' hierarchical structure traditionally excludes women from its representational bodies. The leadership of political parties has been predominantly constituted by men.[72] The hierarchical structure of parties generates a power struggle among men, which prevent women from an active participation and restrain from accessing position of power. In a hierarchical structure, decisions are

---

[72] Since the establishment of the Republic of Turkey 8 female have been elected as party leader until 2008. Nezihe Muhittin (1923 Kadın Partisi-The Women's Party), Behice Boran (1970-1975 Turkiye İşçi Partisi- Turkey's Labour Party), Rahşan Ecevit (the founding president of DSP Demokratik Sol Parti- Democratic Left Party), Tansu Çiller (DYP Doğru Yol Partisi- True Path Party), Nesrin Nas (ANAP, Anavatan Partisi- Motherland Party), Aysel Tuğluk and Emine Ayna (co-presidents of DTP, Demokratik Toplum Partisi- Democratic Society Party), Filiz Koçali (Sosyalist Demokrasi Partisi- Socialist Democracy party), Sevim Belli (Sosyalist Parti- Socialist Party). Now it is 9 with the Gültan Kışanak co-presidency of BDP (Barış ve Demokrasi Partisi- Peace and Democracy party).

"Cumhuriyet tarihinde 8 kadın genel başkan" 3 December 2008,
http://www.kazete.com.tr/haber_Cumhuriyet-tarihinde-8-kadin-genel-baskan_17301.aspx
(Accessed on 17 August 2012).

Filiz Koçali, "Parti genel başkanı ilk kadın: Behice Boran", 9 April 2003,
http://www.bianet.org/kadin/siyaset/9952-parti-genel-baskani-ilk-kadin-behice-boran
(Accessed on 17 August 2012).

made from above and implemented from the base. None of the political parties seems to acknowledge that women have a place in the decision-making processes and support women to obtain powerful positions. The ruling party AKP has 20 members at the Central Executive Committee (CEC) and only 3 of them are female. One of them is the chairwoman of women branches and the rest are a deputy chairman and a parliamentary group deputy chairman[73]. The main opposition party in the Parliament CHP has 3 female out of 19 at the Central Executive Board (CEB). One of them is general secretary and the rest are deputy chairman[74]. The second opposition party in the Parliament is MHP, which has 3 female out of 75 at the Central Executive Committee (CEB)[75]. In contrast to these three political parties, the pro-Kurdish party BDP, which also has seats in the Parliament, has 8 female out of 19 at the Central Executive Committee (CEB)[76]. Furthermore, the three mainstream political parties in the Parliament have male president and the most critical positions are occupied by male members of these parties. In contrast, the pro-Kurdish party has co-chairship where a man and a woman share administrative responsibilities.

Women join the political parties mostly through the party's women units, and this explains why they are gendered institutions. Political parties incorporate values and practices based on traditional expectations for men and women. Subordination of women is part of the everyday workings of political institutions. The roles attributed to women in political institutions in Turkey, which are mainly based on existing gender roles, reinforce their inferior status rather than challenge unequal gender

---

[73] More information about the party can be found on http://www.akparti.org.tr/

[74] More information about the party can be found on http://www.chp.org.tr/

[75] More information about the party can be found on http://www.mhp.org.tr/mhp_index.php

[76] Detailed information about the party is available on http://www.bdp.org.tr/index.php/tr

relations. On the contrary, in the Kurdish case, separated organization of women under the name of women's assemblies within the party refers different meanings as research indicates. Çavdar's (2006) analysis of women's branches of two political parties (Republican People's Party- CHP and Virtue Party- FP) demonstrates that rather than empowering women in politics, being influential in transforming gendered structure, policies, and culture of the parties women are excluded from the central party organizations and decision making processes through separated women's branches. On one hand, women's branches of the political parties represent women's separate organization to empower them; on the other hand they represent the separation based on sex which leads to continuation of division based on traditional gender roles. In her analysis of women's branches of Republican People's Party (Cumhuriyet Halk Partisi- CHP) and Virtue Party (Fazilet Partisi- FP)[77] as the representatives of two opposite political ideology, secular and Islamic Çavdar (2006) points that activities of women's branches, most of which take place outside of formal institutions through home gatherings, tea parties, private meetings, etc., have been glossed over and considered social but not necessarily political. It contradicts the assumption that political participation takes place within formal and government-oriented institutions. This approach regards the public domain to be the only relevant realm of politics and overlooks the activities that take place in the private domain, regarding them 'apolitical' and therefore irrelevant. Çavdar's findings show that women's branches participated in politics, whether within the secular Republican People's Party (CHP) or the Islamist party (VP), could not make a change in

---

[77] It was an Islamist political party founded as successor to the Welfare Party (Refah Partisi- RP) in December 1998. It was banned in June 2001, for violating the secularist articles of the Constitution by the Constitution Court. After the party's ban, the party MPs established two political parties: reformist Justice and Development Party (Adalet ve Kalkınma Partisi- AKP) and traditionalist Felicity Party (Saadet Partisi- SP).

women's inferior status in politics and create an opportunity for women to be equal citizens in political life. She concluded that both women's branches reinforced the traditional gender division of labour, women's lack of autonomy, and women's exclusion from the decision-making process. Thus, the means of political participation do not allow them to transcend the boundaries in politics (Çavdar, 2006). In addition, despite their ideological polarization those two political parties share common points in terms of intra-party gender hierarchies and lack of democratic practices. While pro-Kurdish political parties share some common points with the general picture in Turkey they have differentiated in some respects. Although the male domination in pro-Kurdish politics and political institutions had been a major issue until the end of 1990s, since then, the data gathered during the fieldwork shows that due to deep ideological changes, pro-Kurdish parties promoted gender equality policies which influenced to change the way Kurdish politics dealt with women's participation.

The first pro-Kurdish party was established in 1990. But women's status did not improve until the beginning of 2000s. If political parties are in fact the gatekeepers of female political participation (Caul, 1999; Dahlerup & Freidenvall, 2005: 30; Paxton & Kunovich, 2003), focusing on pro-Kurdish parties' policies, party rules and party culture based on female activists' experiences will facilitate to uncover obstacles that female political activists have encountered in their effort to access political decision-making positions. Primarily based on data gathered from the field research conducted with female political activists, this study mainly focus on party culture to demonstrate to what extent it has masculinised characteristics and how has it affected the way women negotiate their positions within the party. A point needs to be clarified before analysing pro-Kurdish political parties. On one hand, they represents a challenge to the state's 'unitary nation' with their existence within the Turkish political system due to carrying a 'contentious politics' and searching for a new government model -'*Democratic Autonomy*'- as mentioned in the previous chapter. On the other hand, it is inevitable for them to become influenced from existing political culture since they are located and operating within the same system as other political parties in Turkey.

Ideologically, pro-Kurdish political parties have been welcoming women's participation in pro-Kurdish politics. As mentioned in the previous chapter, this is because they have carried a political struggle for Kurdish national rights and they need to mobilize women in order to be influential for the interest of national struggle. On the other hand, also mentioned in the former chapter, gender equality has increasingly been addressed in the parties' program and statutes. However, the problem arose when female political activists started to claim for equal participation and representation in decision-making bodies.

Based on interviews held over with female political activists it can be argued that women in pro-Kurdish political parties in 1990s in particular operated as 'space invaders' (Puwar, 2004) within a masculinised space that has been created and managed by men, who are largely indifferent to the issue of female political representation. A vast majority of female political activists expressed that the leadership positions being occupied by men, decisions-making bodies were being dominated by men and the dominance of traditional patriarchal political culture were primary obstacles that influenced women's engagement. Female activists' lack of political experiences and gender awareness to question male domination and lower number of women in the party, in the first period of 1990s in particular, are considered as reasons for perpetuating their subordination position in politics during that decade. The female activists' statements point out that even women's involvement in politics was unusual in many areas during that decade. The main reason was probably the perception about politics being regarded as a male activity; there were also other reasons such as political conditions of 1990s which made pro-Kurdish politics as a risky activity along with women's traditional gender roles. One female mayor remembered the reaction that she received from men when she first applied to join the party. She stated:

> HADEP opened office in Cihanbeyli (Konya) in 1994. Then I went to HADEP office and told them I want to join the party. And they ask me a very interesting question: 'Are you sure that you want to join the party because women are not going to the party?' I told them I want to work in the party. It was new founded and they needed to complete the list of members of the board. They included me in the list and then I started to work at the party as a member of the board. (Personal interview, Dersim/Tunceli, August 2009)

These statements specify that while women's involvement in the party was unusual for men; but, on the other hand, women could enter any party organs. However, their presence in a decision-making body did not mean they had power to shape processes in favour of women. First of all, most of the women in pro-Kurdish politics did not have gender consciousness during that time; rather, they joined political parties due to their ethnic identity concerns until end of 1990s particularly. In addition, even if some of them had concern for gender equality and women's issues they were not powerful enough to raise these issues. The fact is the conflicts arose when women started to raise the issue of gender inequality in politics and ask for their interests to be represented.

Many participants mentioned the tension between male and female in male dominated areas where men do not want to share power. In this regard, they also pointed to the contradiction between their discourses and practices regarding their approach towards women and equality of sexes. Two female mayors who have worked in the party since 1990s have experienced male reaction. One of them who joined the party in the beginning of 1990s stated that:

> The involvement of women in politics and exercising power in politics is essentially to step in men's power domains and men are not happy to share this power. They want make all decisions as they do at their home (Personal interview, Ankara, August 2010).

Another female mayor involved in the party activities in the mid-1990s said that:

> Men wanted women to be present but don't touch anything, don't argue against anything. They want to make all decisions and the women's role is to do what they decided. It has not been easy for women to arrive these stages (quota, co-presidency, involving in decision making processes). We have worked hard to make ourselves accepted among men. Women have carried out an uphill struggle against masculine mentality dominated political area (Personal interview, Diyarbakır, July 2009).

The discourses and practices of male members of the party do not confirm female activists' statements. For example, when interviewed, all party members (whether female or male) seem to believe that there is no difference between them in the party as well as in a democratic society. However, the female interviewees noted a difference between their discourses and their behaviours on the ground. One of female political activists made a very interesting comment at this respect:

> In theory and discourses of the movement gender equality in the society and the role of women in creating a democratic and egalitarian society are promoted but it does not mean it is so in practice. In practice we have experienced difficulties. At one point, you have a struggle against the system; you have a struggle for your identity [ethnic]. At another point, you have a struggle against oppression and exclusion you face due to your gender identity. You even are treated with contempt by your male fellows together. You are treated as subordinates. You are not regarded as equal. Anything about women is regarded as unimportant (Personal interview, Diyarbakır, March 2010).

Furthermore, female activists also mention the reasons behind men's attitudes toward women and their reaction against their discriminative attitudes in order to have position in the political arena. In this regard, one of the female mayors who has been mainly involved in women activities in her political engagement within the party expressed that:

> We are living in a patriarchal society. It is not easy for men to get rid of their masculine mentality. It requires transformation of the society as a whole and this takes a long process. In politics [pro-Kurdish politics] we have made men to accept the reality that we take place in decision-making bodies of the party, in the parliament and in local governments. It is very obvious that in our party male domination is decreasing, but still women sometimes facing resistance from men. Sometimes we realize that they do not consider women activities and issues as important (Personal interview, Mardin, July 2010).

Another activist who has been involved in pro-Kurdish politics since the mid of 1990s and initiated very significant policies in favour of women as a mayor stated that:

> Men have not easily accepted our influence in the party and the changing policies in favour of women. Male members in the party said that there is no need for women's separate organization because we all ultimately carry on a national struggle. In addition, their approach to women was very symbolic. For instance, they proposed a commission of 5 people and one of them can be a female in order to show that women also are included. We struggle a lot against men in order to make them accept us as equal. (Personal interview, Diyarbakır, August 2009)

These statements denote that male members of the party use national struggle as an excuse to silent women. When the national movement identified women's emancipation with national liberation, men's resistance to women's claim to have equal power in politics under the name of national struggle suggests that men want to maintain their domination in political domain. Like many others, a very experienced female mayor, stressed the role of state in constructing male dominated system, pointing out that this situation is common in Turkish society as a whole. The role of state in constituting and perpetuating male domination is emphasized by a great majority of political activists. The most used definition by female activists for the state is that the state [some of them emphasized as 'Turkish' state] is patriarchal.

All state institutions such as schools and political institutions re-produce the patriarchal ideology. In this respect the female political activist noted:

> We [women] have faced severe challenges and difficulties. We have carried a struggle against *masculine mentality* from the beginning [she meant since the establishment of the first political party] in the political arena. But it is difficult. The social structure, which has been shaped by the state is masculine-minded. Therefore, it excludes women as a matter of course. The state is male and the state institutions are male institutions. When we look at politics, political system and political institutions they all are dominated by men. It is the male perspective that has shaped these institutions. It is hard to see a woman as a decision maker in the political institutions. It is most difficult barrier that women face when they want to be for instance an administrator in the party, a mayor candidate and deputy candidate in the elections (Personal interview, Istanbul, September 2010)

These experiences and statements of female political activists demonstrate that they have faced several obstacles in their struggle to eliminate gender discrimination in the political arena. However, when they had become influential to enforce parties to change policies in favour of women such as implementing quotas, changing organizational style and applying co-chairship system the male domination in the party has started to diminish. Female activists' experiences showed that transforming politics and political institutions in the way that both sexes are equally represented is a long and difficult process.

In conclusion, this section showed that in Turkey it is not the political system and electoral system that create obstacles to increasing women's participation in politics and women's representation in representation offices. As many researches indicate, proportional representation (PR) electoral system based on the competition among parties often provides new windows of opportunity for women. Despite this, however, there is still a gender gap in politics in Turkey in general. On the other hand, in pro-Kurdish politics although it is not reached a desired level, there have been improvements in women's representation, which enhance the role of political parties. However, the Kurdish case pointed out, despite there is not visible constraints to pretend women's enter into politics and their access to powerful positions, invisible barriers like masculine political culture and gendered practices have been a major obstacle to women's representation in politics. The below section analyses socio-economic factors such as lack of economic resources and lack of education to find out to what extent they become obstacles to feminization of pro-Kurdish politics.

Socio-economic Factors

The social-economic factors, which indicate the importance of socio-economic development level of a society are the most common ones, financial resources and education (Matland, 1998; Arat, 1985 & 1989; Güneş-Ayata, 1995; Koray 1995; Talaslı, 1996). The socio-economic variables that are identified significant for female representation in politics point to the interrelatedness of gender gap in various areas. Socio-economic development of both the society in general and the women in particular is considered to be effectual in increasing the supply of female candidates in politics. Some studies show that if women have access to educational and professional opportunities, they will have the human and financial capital necessary to run for an elected office (Mackay, 2004). Nevertheless, some empirical studies suggest that women's educational attainment and participation in the paid labour force do not always translate into high rates of political participation; in some cases, women's socio-economic resources may have no effect on their political incorporation (Paxton & Hughes, 2007; Paxton & Kunovich, 2003).

As mentioned above, although many researches demonstrate that the social and economic status of women in society has a direct influence on their participation in political institutions and elected bodies. In the Kurdish case, socio-economic conditions take second place in women's participation in politics and women's recruitment to representation bodies. This means that despite the poor socio-economic conditions of Kurdish women, their participation in politics and recruitment to representation bodies has significantly been improving. The analysis of socio-economic conditions of Kurdish women below will explain the reasons for the wider presence of women in pro-Kurdish parties.

In Turkey, candidacy for both parliamentary representation and local governments requires money. Candidates need to have money for their candidacy application and running an effective election campaigns. That means personal economic agency is necessary for an inspiring politician in order to enter competition with each other. This makes it very difficult for women, with little to no existent access to wealth, the participation in an electoral campaign in order to get elected. Women's participation in labour force is very low. This situation causes the exclusion of women from social security mechanism and makes them to be dependent on their male members (husband-father).[78] According to TÜİK, in 2009, 69% of women population does not get involved in workforce. Besides, 8% of the rest of women population who can work is unemployed and 9,3% works in agriculture.[79] In addition, Turkish women hold only 8.7% of the registered property in the country. In the eastern part of Turkey, 93.5% of women have no income. And even in a much wealthier area, the Aegean region, 76.4 percent of women has no income."[80]

---

[78] For women and employment see KEİG (Kadın Emeği ve İstihdamı Girişimi/ Women's Labour and Employment Initiative) reports available at http://www.keig.org/ (Accessed on 22 November 2012).

[79] See TÜİK (Türkiye İstatistik Kurumu / Turkish Statistical Institute) report on women's employment, http://www.tuik.gov.tr/Start.do (Accessed on 22 November 2012).

[80] Jenny White "What About Women and Minorities on March 29?" http://www.kamilpasha.com/2009/03/08/what-about-women-on-march-29/ (Accessed on 15 December 2010).

There are no statistics regarding Kurdish women's economic situation and employment. As Çağlayan remarks, although the data collected by the Turkish Statistical Institute (Turkstat) does not differentiate in terms of ethnic origin, the data suggests that in comparison to either Kurdish men or non-Kurdish women, Kurdish women's participation in labour market is lower: they receive lower salaries, and they work in more unstable conditions. "In the East," she states, "either they do not participate in the paid labour force or they work in precarious and low-paid jobs as unpaid [domestic] workers, seasonal agricultural labourers or textile workers."[81] In addition, women face discrimination both in the private and public arena. Domestic works create an obstacle to women's participation in work force. In this context, "Capitalism benefits from patriarchal control over women," asserts Çağlayan. "Women are marginalized in the production process, and their employment is increasingly informalized."[82] Additionally, Kurdish women are deprived more due to armed conflict, village evacuations and forced migration.[83] Thus, in Kurdish case the war and poverty have been key mobilizing factors influence women to join political organizations.

Being the Eastern part (Kurdish region) one of the poorest areas of Turkey, it is obvious that Kurdish women are economically worse off in comparison to Turkish women. In contrast to general picture in Turkey, the poor economic conditions of Kurdish women have become a mobilizing factor to their involvement in politics. While the lack of economic resources is an obstacle to increasing women's participation and representation in Turkey's politics in general, for women in pro-

---

[81] Kathambi Kinoti. "Kurdish Women: Resilience In The Face Of Double Discrimination", 12 April 2012, http://www.awid.org/News-Analysis/Friday-Files/Kurdish-Women-Resilience-in-the-face-of-double-discrimination. (Accessed on 22 November 2012).

[82] Ibid.

[83] Ibid.

Kurdish politics, the situation is different in the sense that personal economic resources have not been a determinant factor in the pro-Kurdish politics. The profile of female political activists presents that they live in poor economic conditions. For a vast majority it is a kind of unpaid work at the beginning but, in due course, according to as they get experienced to fulfil any position in the party and related organizations they can work as professional which could support them financially.

The general the profile of women involved in pro-Kurdish politics in personal economic resources sense is not encouraging. The number of women doing a work outside the political arena is very low and these are not stable, long-term jobs. Apart from elected representatives (MPs and mayors), the rest works in the party, municipalities run by pro-Kurdish mayors, pro-Kurdish social-cultural organizations, women's associations and Kurdish media. As long as it is not a high profile work and likely well paid, the expressions of female political activists meant that they are economically struggling to cover their life expenses. The economic status of women is closely linked to their formal education level. Since the university degree is primary way to obtain employment, the low number of university graduates (12/45) explains that the vast majority of women involved in pro-Kurdish politics do not have a proper occupation.

The profile of female political activists proves that economic resources are not a primary factor to become involved and be elected as a candidate in the pro-Kurdish party politics, and this fact differentiates them from mainstream political parties in Turkey. Their participation is due to the fact that pro-Kurdish political parties have been carrying a national struggle. Thus, political activists are mainly motivated to contribute to their national right struggle and gender-identity struggle, especially from the beginning of 2000s. This is why within pro-Kurdish party politics candidates are mostly determined according to their personal abilities of representing people or to their political experience.

As for their economic conditions, female political activists' education level is not encouraging; however, it remains a determinant factor in the women's participation in Turkey's politics. The high education levels of female politicians in mainstream political parties show that formal education is strongly associated with political participation. In particular, it becomes a significant factor in nomination of candidates for representative bodies.[84] In addition, education enhances other factors supporting political engagement, such as access to high-income jobs that provide the resources and contacts, and access to non-political associations that can be a recruitment ground for political activity. Therefore, lack of education becomes a barrier for women in search for a political career.

The education level plays a significant role in obtaining positions at the professional level in Turkey in general. Although it is not the only factor, it is one of the main ones that play a role in nominating women as MPs and mayors. Especially in mainstream political parties, those who have higher position and are well known in society, such as academics and journalists, are offered to join parties during elections, which also cause the questioning women's role in politics. For instance, the main opposition party-CHP's current female MPs Sabahat Akkiray (singer), Binnaz Toprak (academic), and Şükran Güldal Mumcu (wife of journalist Uğur Mumcu who was killed in an assassination in January 24, 1993) are only a few

---

[84] The profile of female MPs of mainstream political parties shows that they all are university graduates. For more information regarding the profile of MPs visit Turkish Grand National Assembly (TBMM Türkiye Büyük Millet Meclisi)'s website.
http://www.tbmm.gov.tr/develop/owa/milletvekillerimiz_sd.liste

examples.[85]   On the other hand, when the education background of female politicians is examined it is easy to notice that the profile of pro-Kurdish female activists does not reflect with the general assumptions exposed above.

While it is a fact that women are still less educated than men, in the Kurdish case, it is even worse. The research conducted showed that although the lack of formal education has become one of major challenges that women face in their political engagement, it doesn't prevent them from developing their personal education and knowledge once in the party and reaching top positions.

As mentioned in the previous sections, Kurdish women's involvement in politics started with the founding of the first pro-Kurdish political party (HEP) in 1990. That decade witnessed an intensive violent confrontation between the PKK fighters and the state's military forces; and in this context, Kurdish women who joined the political party were motivated by more immediate social and political concerns and not for pursuing a political career. This has determined the profile of the first activists and is why female political activists present a diversified picture in terms of educational background.

Since 1990s, there have been 20 female MPs and 23 female mayors elected from pro-Kurdish parties. Some of them were re-elected such as Leyla Zana who was the first Kurdish female MP elected in 1991 was re-elected in June 2012 national elections. 6 MPs who were elected in 2007 elections re-elected in 2012. In addition, Leyla Güven became mayor (Küçük Dikili, Seyhan Adana) in 2004 elections and was re-elected as mayor of Viranşehir (Şanlıurfa) in 2009. The education level of those professional politicians together with female political activists who contributed to this study provided some interesting points, which are different from the general

---

[85] The information about female MPs can be obtained on
http://www.tbmm.gov.tr/develop/owa/milletvekillerimiz_sd.liste

profile of women in Turkey's politics. The case of Kurdish women demonstrates that in the pattern of political recruitment, education levels are not a prominent obstacle, but still influences nomination of candidates, especially for MPs, and it is becoming a determinant factor as the number of candidates increase for representative positions.

It is not common to see female MPs and mayor without university degree in Turkey's politics. But in pro-Kurdish politics, there are many examples of female representatives who do not have university education. That is because Kurds have been mobilized through pro-Kurdish political organizations due to facing oppressive state policies. Therefore, both men and women who lacked formal education opportunities have obtained political experiences through their engagement in the party activities. The vast majority of women who did not have school education or had only primary school education have had opportunities to make political career by participating in political activities of the party and political education and training provided by the party.

Female members of pro-Kurdish party have obtained seats in local government in 1999 local elections. Since then 26 female mayors have been elected and 3 of them were elected twice. The education background of female mayors is quite diversified. While the lowest education level among MPs is at high school, for mayors however it is primary school level. According to the research, 6 of them are primary school graduates; 1 is secondary; 6 are high school and 9 are university graduates. In addition, 2 female mayor candidates in 2009 local elections interviewed were university graduates. In terms of education level, it is more of a concern for MPs. Since 7 MPs were elected twice, the actual number becomes 13 for the analysis. It is pointed out that almost half of them are high school graduates (6/13) and the rest have a university degree. In comparison to the members of women's assemblies, female political activists who hold position in the party, like the party's provincial head, district head and members of central executives committee, are highly educated. Most of female activists who are involved in ground level activities are non-educated or less educated. The relation between education and age is inversely proportional. For instance, among female political activists, those who are older are mainly non-educated or less educated than the younger ones. Therefore, it can be concluded that the education level increases among the young activists. Besides, those young female political activists who were not able to have education due to economic and political conditions benefit from institutions like Open University and school in order to get a degree.

The lower formal education level of female activists does not imply that education background is not regarded as a significant qualification in pro-Kurdish politics. This situation is related to the profile of women who have been involved in pro-Kurdish since the beginning of 1990s. The research pointed out that the majority of women who joined the party especially in 1990s were relatives (mother, wife and sister) of male activists involved in armed struggle; who were arrested and imprisoned because of their political actions. The profile of this group of women shows that their social and economic conditions were relatively poor represents a common feature. In addition, being women in a traditional patriarchal society, their roles were only restricted to carry on domestic works until they become politicized following the armed struggle.

Although the profile of female activists has diversified, especially after 2000s, there are still a great number of female members who had not been involved in any activities outside their home until they started to the party branches. In traditional patriarchal society, women are in a subordinate position, which is very much emphasized by activists when it comes to explain about their education. The activists who do not have education or have lower level and who are mainly older generation stated that it is because especially male members of the family did not allow them to go school. Young female political activists mostly raised economic reasons and political conditions in the region hindered them from obtaining an education. The education level has not been a major problem yet, but as the party increases its power and its number of representatives, the education background will become a significant factor in the process of nominating candidates for representative bodies and electing member for the party's decision-making organs.

In conclusion, while economic resources and education level are two interrelated factors that determine women's political participation and representation. In the Kurdish case, they have not been primary determinant factors. Female political activists, despite their poor economic conditions and low level of education, have been able to become political actors by virtue of their personal abilities and experiences such as their political experiences, commitment to their cause and capacity of representing their electors' interests.

The section that follows focuses on a number of cultural factors, which can be regarded as invisible barriers causing exclusion of women from political areas.

Cultural Factors

Cultural factors include general customs and beliefs of a society and social norms and values surrounding women's expected roles, duties and capabilities. These factors create resistance from men, families and society at large to both women attempting to enter politics and for those who already are active in the political arena.

Cultural factors which determine the attitudes and behaviours of both the women and the public in general are shaped by the patriarchal structure. In addition, these factors, which are stemmed from societal expectations and can be described as invisible barriers to increase in women's political participation and representation. A number of cultural factors have been revealed significant in influencing women's political representation. However, the emphasis has been on religious orientations and views on gender-based social roles (Norris - Inglehart 2001; Paxton 1997; Reynolds 1999; Tremblay 2007; Kirkpatrick, 1974; Currell 1974; Lynn and Flora, 1977; Keskin, 1997; Talaslı, 1996). Several studies suggest that cultural factors are more important than even the political factors. Some of these studies assert that it is these cultural factors that, most of the time, shape the other set of political and socio-economic indicators (Paxton - Kunovich 2003). The study shows how cultural factors have influenced women's political participation and representation in a great extent due to the communities to which Kurdish women are attached, Kurdish society in local level and Turkish society in broader level, to be patriarchal. Many other factors that have been examined in the sections above under the titles of political and socio-economic factors are also formed by cultural factors.

As mentioned in the section dedicated to the analysis of political factors, masculine political culture is one of barriers to women's access to decision-making. This political culture has been established under the influence of a wider acceptance of women's roles in the society. Social norms and values as cultural elements of society determine women's roles, duties and capabilities. If the society is patriarchal, to which the Kurdish society subscribes, women are secondary and they are confined to private sphere. The roles and duties that are set by the traditional patriarchal society for women have affected women's struggle to feminize pro-Kurdish politics.

Traditional beliefs and cultural attitudes regarding the role and status of women in society are prevalent in Kurdish society and in Turkey in general. For many women as part of this system, it is difficult to dislocate from this culture and tradition. Women are assigned a secondary place by the existing customs and culture. Despite women's education and entry into the job market, the women's role is typically one of housewife. The man, on the other hand, is the breadwinner, head of household and has a right to public life. Confining women's identity to domestic sphere is one of the barriers to women' entry into politics and politics by its nature pulls one into public life. Generally, cultural attitudes are hostile to women's involvement in politics.[86]

The research conducted with female political activists explored significant points regarding the influence of cultural factors on their political movement to achieve gender equality in politics. These are considered very hard obstacles due to traditional gender roles being historically constructed by patriarchy, but they have to change in order to achieve a substantive women's representation in politics.

While political conditions of 1990s allowed many women to enter politics under the influence of their family's politically active male members, they were

---

[86] For feminist critics regarding public and private dichotomy;
See Carole Pateman (1989), "Feminist Critiques of the Public/Private Dichotomy," *The Disorder of Women*, Stanford: Stanford University Press. p. 118. As Pateman observed in 1983, "the dichotomy between the public and the private. . . is ultimately what the feminist movement is about." (1989; 118).
Pateman focuses on liberal theory in her work. A number of other studies contribute debate on public and private dichotomy. See Susan Moller Okin (1991), "Gender, the Public and the Private," in *Political Theory Today*, ed. David Held. Cambridge: Polity Press.; Jean Bethke Elshtain (1981), *Public Man, Private Woman*, Princeton: Princeton University Press,; Seyla Benhabib (1998), "Models of Public Space: Hannah Arendt, the Liberal Tradition, and Jurgen Habermas," *Feminism, the Public and the Private*. ed. Joan Landes, NY: Oxford University Press,; Joan Landes (1998), "Introduction" *Feminism, the Public and the Private*, ed. Joan B. Landes, NY and Oxford: Oxford University Press,; Mary Ryan (1990). *Women in Public,* Baltimore: The Johns Hopkins Press. ; Linda Imray and Audrey Middleton (1983). "Public and Private: Marking the Boundaries," in *The Public and the Private*, eds. Eva Gamarnikow, David Morgan, Jane Purvis, Daphne Taylorson. London: Heinemann.

subject to gender discrimination by men during that period. Many of them testified that they were doing trivial works, which did not provide them any authority in the party. Their male fellows most of time treated women as the way they treated their female members at home. They were expected to accomplish the tasks given to them by men. Many female political activists who were involved in politics in 1990s mentioned that they experienced such cases their male fellows opposed women's participation in political activities. At this regard, one of female political activists who joined the party at the second half of 1990 stated:

> We (female party members) were very active and we were attending all the party's activities. But some of our male fellows were not happy with our presence in the party. I remember they were saying why you are attending these activities. Go home and o your works! This is the mentality of a patriarchal society. They think women's place is the home (Personal interview, Diyarbakır, April 2010).

In addition, several women noted that there men who were not against women's participation in politics but they were expected women to do works which contribute the party's maintenance like paperwork and to domestic works but not taken part in decision-making processes. To illustrate this, one of female political activists complained about the way they treated them. She stated:

> They were treating us we do not understand anything. We were not asked for opinions most of time when decisions were taken on the party's activities. Because they were thinking we are not capable. We do not understand politics. We have made so much effort to make ourselves accepted among men's world. (Personal interview, Istanbul, August 2010)

Families play a significant role in women' participation in politics depending on to what extent they consider traditional gender roles. Besides, the level of the family's politicization was determinant in most cases. Some female activists mentioned that there were many male members of the party who were quite active but did not allow female members attending any activity and they did not want to female activists to get close them. Not all politicized families or male members did encourage women to join the party. Furthermore, there are many cases that women activists faced strong reaction from their families. A considerable number of female political activists mentioned their family pressure and restrictions on their political activism which pushed them to move away from their family. Especially those who are the party's cadres live in cities different than where their families live, in order to get away from family pressure. Some of them stated when their family members put pressure on them not to get involved in politics; they had to cut off their connection with their families. One of female political activists expressed that her family was not happy about her participating in the party end of 1990s when she was living with them in one of cities in western part of Turkey. She stated:

> They hindered me to go the party and attending the party's activities. Because they wanted to me have a life as many other women; getting married, having children and doing housework. Then, I decided to move to another city in Kurdistan (south-eastern and eastern part of Turkey where political activists called Kurdistan). After months I got in touch with them and visit them. Now, they are fine with what I am doing (Personal interview, Diyarbakır, April 2010).

These statements showed that women's involvement in politics was a challenge to existing gender norms, which impose certain roles for women. When women began to attend political activities, as many of female political activists underlined, they started to question and stand against gender-based roles attributed by their families and society particularly since second half of the 1990s.

Elected women raised the issue and fought to have women in decision-making positions. In a patriarchal society, women are very rarely elected to political representation institutions; and even if they are elected, they are not considered fit to these elected positions by men and they are underestimated most of time. One of female mayor mentioned her experiences with male residents of the district after she was elected in March 2009 election. She stated:

> This district is male dominated. Women are not involved in public life. Men usually do if something needs to be done on the municipality. The mayor of this district was male until I was elected. The municipal employees were predominantly men. After I was elected, men got confused about how to call me. They used to call mayor as "Başkan Bey" (Mr. President) when they see woman they get confused and especially at the beginning they most of the time called me. When I saw outside, in the city centre many men just ignored me. (Personal interview, Diyarbakır, July 2009)

This mayor also mentioned about her experiences during election campaigns and how men in the district treated a female mayor candidate, which well explains how men regard women in a traditional patriarchal society. She asserted:

> When I was meeting with the public during elections I was not welcomed by many male electors. I heard such expressions many times. They were saying: How come! Now we are going to be governed by a woman!
> (Personal interview, Diyarbakır, July 2009)

This treatment of the district's male residences towards their female mayor is related to division of gender roles in society, which has made politics as men's activity. In Turkey, lower rate of women's representation in both national level and local level demonstrate that politics is still regarded as men's activity. Social conventions regarding gender and politics traditionally exclude women and political arena is viewed as a masculine domain. Women have been marginalized because men monopolize the decision-making structure and are in the majority.

Gender-based roles of women in private sphere hinder women to engage in politics. Many female political activists cite domestic responsibilities as one of barriers to women's involving in politics. A few female activists stated that they rarely attend the party's activities and become less active since they have had children. A few others who have grown-up children expressed that due to their passion for their political activism; they raised their children along with their engagement in politics but with great difficulties. As they informed, some of female activists gradually terminated their political participation after having children. Apparently, women's traditional roles, which include carrying out domestic works, such as taking care of children and elderly in the family, restrict women to attend in political activities.

Traditional gender roles also reflect on women's voting behaviour. They tend to vote according to preferences of male members of the family as raised by female political activists who have been involved election campaigns in 2007 national elections and 2011 local elections. They mentioned that during their visits to electors at their homes, especially in rural areas, many of the women electors were led to the husbands-or male members of the family because, as one of female political activists remarked:

> Many women were telling that, male members of the family decide who they are going to for then they vote for that party or person. It is better to meet with men. But we wanted to meet women. When men were there they did not want us to meet women. They were saying no need to talk to women because they do not know parties and candidates. But we did not accept and we meet women most of time. We told them it is right who they voter for. Thanks to women we gained most votes in some rural areas I believe (Personal interview, Diyarbakır, March 2009).

Despite the male dominated, traditional, non-egalitarian culture in Kurdish society, it has shifted in a more egalitarian direction in recent years due to the influence of women's political activism; yet discriminatory cultural and social attitudes and burden of responsibilities in the home, which determine women's participation in politics, are still continuing according to the experiences presented. Still, female political activists receive support from men who seem to be quite supportive in women's struggle for gender equality. One of female political activists who has been involved in politics since the 1990s with all her family members, mentioned about her husband's reaction when they were arguing over a problem. She expressed:

> Although my husband is very active in politics and supportive women's rights during an argument he told me: "Oh madam! Your movement has grown, that you doing something; that is, you come upon us and do you (women activists) see yourself in something different?! These were his statements. You see we think men change, their mentality change. But male mentality never changes (Personal interview, Diyarbakır, April 2010).

These statements demonstrated that despite their struggle, female activists are quite pessimistic regarding eliminating of male domination in political area and in society, which is historically constructed and maintained through many institutions and practices.

The below section examines some obstacles which are specific to the Kurdish case in Turkey. Due to state politics towards pro-Kurdish politics, the barriers that Kurdish women have encountered, such as sexual violence, indicates intersection of gender and ethnic identities which refers they are twice oppressed.

State Politics: pro-Kurdish Politics 'High Risk Area'

Whereas there are common obstacles to women's participation in politics within the political institutions, this research showed that there are barriers and challenges specific to female Kurdish political activists.

Pro-Kurdish political activists, whether male or female, have faced different kinds of pressure, oppression and violent acts because of their political engagement within the pro-Kurdish parties since 1990s. Kurds whether they are sympathizers of Kurdish national movement or not, have faced a variety of violent acts and legal restrictions which reached peak point in the first period of 1990s. Unknown killings, threats, detention, arrest and torture are the most common types of pressure exercised toward Kurdish political activists by the Turkish state. When Kurdish women got increasingly involved in politics, they suffered the same violence and oppressions as men. However, in addition, they have been subjected to sexual violence due to their sexual identity and therefore suffered a kind of double oppression.

The violent actions of the state officials in order to suppress the political activism of women have caused an insecure political environment for political activists. Especially those who have been subjected to sexual violence have had serious issues, which influence both their political and personal life. The experiences and statements of political activists interviewed for this research revealed that coercion mechanisms used by the state authorities suppressing pro-Kurdish politics have had various serious impacts on them. In many cases, the violence perpetrated damaged their physical and psychological health curtailing their organization and political activities, but ultimately failed in its effort to silence and make them give up their political struggle as underlined by many female political activists. The state politics towards pro-Kurdish politics is gendered when it targets female activists, and this causes obstacles for politically active women who carry on a political struggle against 'oppressive' and 'patriarchal' Turkish state.

The main reason for the pressure on female political activists is related to the state authorities' conception about pro-Kurdish political parties. Pro-Kurdish political organizations have been identified as political extensions of the PKK, which is labelled as a terrorist organization aiming to establish an independent Kurdish state, namely 'Kurdistan'. In order to reduce the effectiveness and narrow the flexibility of pro-Kurdish political parties, the state has exercised various forms of coercion. That is why pro-Kurdish parties and political activists have been oppressed by the state authorities since 1990s. Pro-Kurdish parties were closed by the constitutional court with the allegation that they were linked to the PKK and party offices were bombed and their property was confiscated by the state. In addition, party administrators and activists were shot, tortured, prosecuted, imprisoned, beaten, fined and threatened (Watts, 2010: 94).

When the form and impact of such state and state-sponsored coercive campaigns against the parties and activists is examined, it is revealed the nature and levels of state coercion against the parties and activists and how the state-party relations have differentiated over time (Watts, 2010: 94). Watts argues that physical pressure has lessened since 1999, leading to an emphasis on juridical coercion. Considering this subject, the critic divides this moment into two phases: the first phrase is from 1990 to 1998; the second from 1999 to 2008. In the first period, multiple official efforts include using of both formal (legal) mechanisms and extra judicial actors in order to suppress pro-Kurdish parties and activists and their activities. In the second period, the official efforts to suppress pro-Kurdish parties and their activities relied more on the juridical and bureaucratic-political mechanisms of disciplinary or authoritative power (Foucault 1977; Giddens 1984: 33, 258-61; quoted by Watts, 2010; 95) as coercion-repression methods. Even if the methods of coercion have transformed the purpose remained same. It is quite obvious Turkish authorities intend to suppress pro-Kurdish parties as organizations and party members and administrators as individuals through these coercion methods since 1990s (Watts, 2010: 95). This research analysed the second phase.

Female activists were subject of the most severe violent acts whether sexual or not during 1990s. That is because the 1990's were very decisive for the massive entry of women into the Kurdish national movement. The emergence of the Kurdish political party (DEP) and the popular revolts (serhildan)[87] in 1990-93, signalled the origin of a new dynamism in Kurdish society and Kurdish national movement in Turkey which brought the opportunity for women to become significant actors in the movement itself. As a result, female activists were exposed to massive oppression when the Emergency Rule Law (Olağanüstü Hal, or OHAL) came into effect in thirteen provinces mainly populated by Kurds. [88] One definite fact is this heavy coercion-repression both legal and illegal methods put in danger pro-Kurdish activists.

Being involved in pro-Kurdish politics has always been a risk. Thousands of political activists have been detained and arrested accused of having links with the PKK. In particular, after March 2009 elections there have been a mass arrest of Kurdish activists and politicians by the Turkish authorities on charges of belonging to the urban wing of the PKK, the KCK (Association of Communities in Kurdistan-Koma Civakên Kurdistan). The KCK is a societal organization presented as an alternative to the nation-state. The PKK and all-affiliated organizations have been restructured under the name of KCK since 2005 after the model of *Democratic Confederalism,* which was developed and proposed as a democratic self-

---

[87] *Serhildan* is a Kurdish word refers to revolt in English. It is used to describe Kurdish people's revolts mainly in 1990s against the Turkish state oppression.

[88] Emergency Law Rule (Olağanüstü Hal, or OHAL) was replaced martial law in July 1987, which was operated in much of the southeast between the coup of September 12, 1980, and the summer of 1987. OHAL, which was in effect in thirteen provinces (Bingöl, Diyarbakır, Elazığ, Hakkari, Mardin, Siirt, Tunceli, Van, Adıyaman, Bitlis, Batman, Şirnak and Muş) at its height, put these provinces under authority of a regional governor who had exceptional power. The security forces could be authorized by the governor to search homes and party offices without a warrant, order the evacuations of entire villages, and constrain public meetings. In comparison to the other parts of the country the basic legal and political were suspended in these provinces; individual could be detained for much longer time without a trial and wire taps could be placed on phones without a court order (the signature of a prosecutor was enough). It was entirely lifted in all provinces in November 2002 (Watts, 2010; 89).

government model for Kurds by the PKK's imprisoned leader, Abdullah Öcalan in the first part of 2000s (Akkaya & Jongerden, 2011).

According to data released in October 2011, nearly 4,000 people were arrested under the KCK operations.[89] Although there are not official statistics, according to the party administrators and female political activists who I met during research, stated that at least one-third of those have been arrested are women. Female political activists who have been arrested are mayors, other elected municipal officials, employees of local governments, administrators in the party, and members of DÖKH *(Democratik Free Women Movement / Demokratik Özgür Kadın Hareketi)*, women assemblies and youth assemblies of DTP[90]. In this regard, one of female MPs Sebahat Tuncel stated, *"the AKP government makes every effort in order to break the resistance of the Kurdish women movement. Because of its political genocide operations under the name of KCK more than 500 women who are active in politics are in jail. 2 female mayor and 2 MPs are under arrest."*[91] Furthermore, figures regarding the number of arrests in 2012 are 6300.[92]

The pro-Kurdish party is severely restricted in its actions due to continual judicial harassment in the form of hundreds of legal cases against its deputies, mayors and members. These proceedings stem from their political evaluations,

---

[89] "İki buçuk yılda 4000'e yakın tutuklu", 6 October 2011,
http://www.imc-tv.com/haber-iki-bucuk-yilda-4000e-yakin-tutuklu-212.html (Accessed on 5 November 2011).

[90] While this interview was held in August 2009 the pro-Kurdish party was DTP, which was later closed by the constitutional court in December 2009.

[91] Özlem Galip, "Kadinlara olan guven artti", 21 January 2012,
http://www.yeniozgurpolitika.org/index.php?rupel=nuce&id=5894#.TxwKvdPE31I. (Accessed on 21 January 2012).

[92] "KCK'dan Kaç Kişi Tutuklu?", 17 February 2012,
http://www.haberdiyarbakir.com/kckdan-kac-kisi-tutuklu-49489h/ (Accessed on 20 February 2012).

statements and speeches. The BDP's views on the Kurdish issue continually force the party to be confronted with the judicial authorities, who generally open cases against deputies, mayors and members of the party for supposedly making propaganda on behalf of the Kurdistan Workers' Party, or PKK, 'praising crime or criminals,' campaigning in languages other than Turkish and violating laws. The juridical system of the state creates strong difficulties and restricts the political engagement of activists.

The vast majority of activists who participated in this research experienced different degrees of oppression. After the March 2009 elections, female activists interviewed said that a vast number of women have been detained and arrested during what was known as "KCK" operation and that pressure on them has increased. The aim of this chapter is to analyse which kind of political oppression women suffered and which were its consequences in terms of their participation in politics. Considering the reasons behind the oppressive methods of the state authorities and consequences of this pressure many significant points are explored. These following points are addressed in detail: the aim to weaken the increasing political activism of women; the women's awareness of the difficulties and risks of being involved in politics and the consequent violence; the lack of support from their families due mainly to the gendered violent acts toward women such as sexual harassment and rape; the severe psychological and physical harms of the gendered violence by the state authorities.

Violence against women is a widespread problem in Turkey. But the violence that female activists have faced because of their involvement in the pro-Kurdish politics is the result of a deliberate policy of the state authorities in order to discourage them to join political organizations. As statements of female activists who are involved in this research show, female activists have been subjected to sexual violence and physical violence intensively which create serious obstacles to their political engagement. Due to this sexual violence, some female political activists have gave up on their political activism on their own decision, some were forced by their families to leave politics after being exposed to sexual violence; and some due to psychological and physical problems arising from sexual violence have left politics.

Women are a vulnerable target for a largely unaccountable police and army force that operates with wide arbitrary powers. Gender based violence has been used systematically as a weapon of battle by the security forces of the state. In Turkey, commonly reported methods of torture include electroshocks, *falaka* (beating of the soles of the feet), stripping people naked, blind folding, hosing, severe beatings, rape, death threats, sexual assault, and 'Palestinian hangings' (KHRP, 2006). Common forms of sexual torture carried out by the state security forces reported by the victims include vaginal, oral, or anal rape using penis, batons, water hoses or other materials; mass rapes; urinating into the victim's mouth; electroshocks to breast nipples and sexual organs; forced virginity-tests; strip-searching, and stripping during questioning.[93] Female activists interviewed for this research reported a variety of sexual violent acts such as rape, sexual abuse, and sexual harassment which they face during detention, raids on their homes and when they were kidnapped by the security forces. Women participating in this study also reported that women who were detained for any political reason particularly in the

---

[93] NGO Shadow report for the Review of Turkish Government under the UN International Convention Against Torture and Other Cruel, Inhuman or Degrading Treatment or punishment (CAT) Turkey Report- 2002, 29 May 2002, http://bianet.org/english/human-rights/10387-turkey-report---2002. (Accessed on 18 September 2012).

1990s, have been subjected to sexual violence or threatened with rape in the presence of their husbands or other close family members, **obviously as a means of compelling her husband or family member to "confess". Using the idea of "honour" as a weapon to degrade her family and her community.**

As female political activists informed since they started to organize in political areas and the women's movement has gradually increased its power with participations of women since the middle of the 1990s, women have started campaigning to raise the issue of sexualised violence at the hands of security forces to a wider public. Under favour of the support of women's and human rights organisations, victims of violence have found the strength and courage to report this tabooed form of violence. In 1997, the *Legal Support Office Against Sexual Abuse and Rape in Custody* (LAPASAR)[94] was established in Istanbul with the intention to support victims of sexual violence at the hands of state forces. **By the end of 2001, 147 women, 112 of them Kurds, had asked for help from this legal aid in order to bring the perpetrators to justice. Fifty-one of the women alleged they had been raped and the rest reported other forms of sexual torture. The suspected perpetrators were overwhelmingly police officers, although allegations were also made against gendarmes, soldiers and village guards. Only one was convicted.**[95] Furthermore, in their interviews with over 100 female prisoners in Diyarbakır, Muş, Mardin, Batman and Midyat, the Diyarbakir Bar Women's Commission found that almost all of the women had been subjected to "virginity testing", and nearly all had experienced

---

[94] Later, it also opened a branch in Berlin so that refugee women could also apply for help after their migration.

[95] Turkey Report – 2002. 29 May 2002, http://bianet.org/english/human-rights/10387-turkey-report---2002. (Accessed on 18 September 2012).

some form of sexual abuse, either verbal or physical, when in police custody.[96] In March 2005, the lawyers Eren Keskin and Fatma Karakaş reported that two hundred and eleven women had applied for legal support with their office within nine years. They also gave the following figures: the majority of the perpetrators, in total one hundred and sixty-three, were policemen, followed by gendarmes, soldiers, prison guards, and village guards. The majority of women attacked were Kurdish, in total one hundred and sixty-seven. The majority of women, in total one hundred and eighty-eight, cited political or war related reasons as causes for their arrests (Keskin & Karakaş, 2005). When agents of the state are the perpetrators, they reinforce a culture of violence and discrimination that places all women at risk. State agents may be resorting to torture in the form of rape and sexual assault in the knowledge that victims are unlikely to want to report their experiences. In this situation, women are at high risk of exposure to violence and humiliation.

Women's Experiences of Gendered Violence

Almost all of the activists interviewed during the fieldwork have faced various kinds of violent acts from the state forces such as threat, harassment, detention and torture. It is an on-going process. Although the methods and intensity from period to period since 1990s have changed, female political activists involved in pro-Kurdish politics have faced life damaging coercion from the state forces. The oppressive mechanisms particularly sexual violence towards politically active women caused them both physical and psychological damage. Each individual raised several issues. Reflecting the common thinking among women, this sort of violence derives

---

[96] "AI: Sexual Violence of Women in Detention", 26 February 2003,
http://bianet.org/english/women/16923-ai-sexual-violence-of-women-in-detention,
(Accessed 18 September 2012).

from the patriarchal mentality that pervades the entire Turkish society. In effect, women face double discrimination when facing the state authorities and perceive them as representing the both nationalist ideology and patriarchal mentality. With this in mind, it is important to present the female activists' views and experiences in order to understand the reasons behind the growing pressure over female activists and detention and incarceration of a large number of women. One of female mayors (Diyarbakır, July 2009) mentioned the operations toward political activists, especially those who took part in election campaign activities for March 2009 local elections. She underlined that female activists were specifically targeted because of their intensive political involvement much visible during elections. She informed that many female activists actively worked during election campaigns and this effort contributed a lot to obtain good results. Another female mayor expressed her views about incarceration of activists after the elections stating that,

> It is aimed to discourage women to participate in politics. But this does not affect our works. Especially women assemblies as one of the bodies of party easily gather strength (Personal interview, Mardin, August 2009).

Similarly, one of the female activists who has an administration position in the party underlined that the following:

> We know this is not only against a woman; this is also against Kurdish women's movement. It is against the women's liberation struggle. It is aimed to suppress the acquisitions of Kurdish women through employing these methods. They want to intimidate and discourage women to involve in politics. This aims to make inroads on our campaign of 'we are not honour of anyone; our honour is our freedom'[97]. The cases of sexual harassment and rape toward women reflect male mentality to control women's body. They use their male power over woman body. We [female activists] think they do this intended (Personal interview, Diyarbakır, August 2009).

---

[97] In Turkish it is "Biz kimsenin namusu değiliz; namusumuz özgürlüğümüzdür."

Even if legal restrictions and violent acts prevented some women from joining the party, the activists interviewed agreed in saying that they do not think that violence and oppression will be able to destroy their political activism.

Cases of violence are mostly mentioned by other female activists rather than victims themselves. One of the female mayors, for instance, mentioned several cases. She said that very recently, about 15-20 days before the interview (July 2009), the houses of 3 activists of DÖKH were raided by the police within a week. Two of them were taken to security directorate but they were not arrested. However, these female activists were exposed to violence, harassment and torture. Then, they were threatened and forced to spy for their captors or they would have never seen the party again. Another female activist was taken to a police car and was interrogated for hours inside it. She was subjected to violence as well without any legal action taken against her. In addition, she informed about another case happened very recently in a house raided while a member of DÖKH was there. Even she was not the person they were looking for, but she was not allowed to go and she said, she was exposed to sexual harassment by four policemen. The police used different devices during sexual harassment. [Actually she was trying to tell that she was raped. But it seemed too hard for her to tell the word of "rape" loudly]. She added that:

> The victim has been through a trauma. Due to fear of being arrested by the police again she changed her place many times. She threw out her dresses. She tried to forget everything she lived. She did not tell anybody immediately when she faced this horrible thing. 5 days later she decided to tell her terrible case. Then she went to IHD (Human Rights Association) to complain about what she has experienced and she got help to make allegation against the police who abused to her. IHD filed a criminal complaint against the police. Now she is receiving a treatment under psychologist control (Personal interview, Diyarbakır, July 2009).

As this case, in many other cases female political activists who had been exposed such violence had to leave politics.

Due to heavy pressure, the party's weakness, exercising the state of emergency law in many of Kurdish cities, low number of female activists and the weak organization of women in 1990s, the sexual violent acts that women faced were not known as it happens today. Currently, these are not kept silent but they are publicized by female activists through such as press statements and demonstrations.

These examples of both sexual and non-sexual violence demonstrate that female activists have become the target of the state forces and their involvement in pro-Kurdish politics has become dangerous for them. Certainly, the pressure and oppressive methods that have been carried out by the state authorities have created obstacles to women's political engagement and expansion of their political activism. Since female political activists could able extend their power in political and make their claims for gender equality they need a strong women's gender-identity based activism. However, state authorities' policy toward female political activists which aim to discourage women to join pro-Kurdish party politics in order to weaken Kurdish political movement, which leads to the weakening of women's political activism. And this is a major threat for the women's future objectives in politics.

Conclusion

This chapter attempted to find out what are the obstacles to the feminization of pro-Kurdish party politics in Turkey. The obstacles to increasing women's political participation and political representation in pro-Kurdish politics were revealed based on women political activists' experiences and literature concerning women's under-representation in Turkey with a particular focus on Kurdish women. Their experiences were analysed, taking into consideration political, socio-economic, and cultural factors within the specific Kurdish case and the violence perpetrated against them by the state.

Despite the point that each of these factors addressed different issues, challenges and barriers, this study showed that the main reason behind all these obstacles is the patriarchal system where decision making powers are in the hands of males and women are not included. Especially, cultural factors point patriarchy as major barrier due to determining social norms and values that determine women's roles. Traditional gender roles attributed women creates obstacles for women's entry into politics as well as for female activists in political arenas.

This study also showed that although socio-economic conditions of Kurdish women are not encouraging, they were not a deterrent for their participation and representation in pro-Kurdish politics.

The following chapter will identify a number of strategies to overcome these obstacles and analyse what women can do and how the party can be supportive to advance both women's descriptive and substantive representation.

CHAPTER FIVE

Strategies and Opportunities for Feminizing pro-Kurdish Party Politics

Introduction

The research conducted with female political activists and the analysis of pro-Kurdish political parties' characteristics and their gender policies and practices showed that the strategies that willingly or unwillingly both the party and female political activists have implemented facilitated the feminization of pro-Kurdish politics particularly since the beginning of 2000s. This chapter aims to explore what strategies have been used by both in order to transform the pro-Kurdish party politics, enabling equally involvement and representation of women in politics and removing male domination in the political arena.

The issue of how to achieve equality of women's political representation has been debated among feminists. Feminists have different opinions with regards to the best ways to achieve equal political representation. The division among feminists is over the question of whether or not to work within (or inside) the system; it refers to the use of insider and outsider strategies. According to Lovenduski, for the feminization of politics sustained and substantial increases in the numbers of women representatives' insider strategies are essential. However, according to her, insider strategies work better when there is an autonomous women's movement in the system (2005: 88).

Lovenduski asserts that effective organization is necessary but not sufficient. Historically, feminists adopted institutional strategies, working within parties and accepting existing rules of the game. She gave two contrasting examples to explain how different strategies employed by women's advocates to achieve women's equal political representation. The example of Scotland demonstrates how important it is for feminists to be mobilized ahead of decisions about change. The Scottish example shows that the best opportunities to influence decisions come at the point of the establishment of political institutions. Feminists were involved in at the every stage of constitution making process in Scotland in 1970s which has contributed to the increase of women's political representation, as Lovenduski pointed out (2005:84-88). On the contrary, in the United States, after many years of campaigns for equal representation, women's presence was comparatively low. Nevertheless, by the beginning of the twentieth century, women's advocates had been active in the main American political parties. Women's advocates employed two basic strategies: getting women into party committees and creating special political clubs for women. The history of the struggle for accomplishing women's equal representation in the United States is marked by generational shifts, major debates and substantial achievements. The U.S example presents an instance of how the feminization of politics depends on the nature of the parties, the opportunity structure of the times and the surrounding women's movement (Lovenduski, 2005: 88-89).

Lovenduski defines the adoption of strategies to enhance women's political representation as a process in which the ideas about justice are invoked as the basis for political equality. The process is not necessarily linear in the short term, but it is possible to observe some progression over time. Lovenduski specifies the actors in this process as advocacy organizations, political parties and social movements which interact and may correspond, as the claims of advocates in all three become more assertive (2005: 88-89)

In general, Lovenduski (2005: 90-91) introduces three strategies, which contribute to increase women's political representation. These are equality rhetoric, equality promotion (or positive action) and equality guarantees (or positive discrimination). Equality rhetoric is the public approval of women's claims. It is presented in party political discourse, party campaign platforms, the speeches and writings of political leaders. Equality rhetoric specifies words and arguments are spoken and written that may well have an effect on attitudes and beliefs. Equality promotion aims to bring women into political competition by providing specific training and financial support and setting targets for women's presence and other measures to enable women to come forward. Equality promotion seeks to bring more women into politics through encouragement and advancing their ability to compete in diverse ways. It is directed primarily at the supply of potential representatives. Equality guarantees or positive discrimination addresses the demand for women representatives. In such strategies places are reserved for women on electoral slates and representative bodies. Quotas are examples of equality guarantees (Lovenduski, 2005: 90-91).

These findings of Lovenduski regarding strategies have remained limited to explaining the strategies that have contributed to increasing women's political representation in pro-Kurdish politics. Lovenduski's findings mainly contribute to conceptualizing the strategies that are implemented in the Kurdish case. As will be seen below, some of strategies used in the Kurdish case, for example training through school of politics for women, as well as equality promotion and quotas are included in equality guarantees in Lovenduski's terms. Lovenduski examines quotas as an equality strategy both at a global level and in the British context, as will be seen later in the chapter. In addition, they help to classify insider and outsider strategies during the analysis.

The strategies which are examined in this chapter are the change of form of Intra-party Women's Organizations (commissions, branches and assemblies), the expansion of autonomous women's organization: DÖKH, the implementation of the quotas; equal participation in leadership positions (co-chairship), training (the School of Politics for Women) and networking activities.

The Change of Form of Intra-party Women's Organizations: Commissions Branches- Assemblies

There are various discussions regarding the role of women's organizations in improving women's political representation. Case studies of political parties suggest that women party activists at the grassroots level and parties' women's organizations advance women's representation (Caul, 1999). European parties historically have had women's organizations (sections, branches) which support the party, raise funds, recruit women as members, mobilize women in election campaigns, and lobby for women's representation in the leadership bodies. These women's organizations act at the local, regional, and national levels. They often have neither autonomous decision-making power nor representation in the party's main decision-making bodies. They are considered subsidiary, auxiliary organizations and, sometimes, advisory bodies (Kittilson, 2010; Lovenduski & Norris, 2003).

In Turkey, women's organizations in mainstream political parties do not have an influence in improving women's political representation. They lack autonomy, are excluded from the decision-making process and considered as subsidiary organizations (Arat, 2005; Çavdar, 2006; Güneş-Ayata, 2001; Saktanber, 2002). In contrast, women's organizations in pro-Kurdish parties have gradually increased their power within the parties through gaining an authority of making their own decisions and changing their organization form since the beginning of the 1990s (Çağlayan, 2007). In this regard, women's organizations of pro-Kurdish parties are examined as an example of how they are employed as an insider strategy by female political activists to increase women's political representation. In this regard, considering that organizational structures play a significant role in the inclusion of women in political parties, it is important to analyse the organizational form of women within the pro-Kurdish party in order to find out to what extent it has been influential in the increase of women's political representation since it has been adopted as an insider strategy by female political activists. The organization form of female political activists within the parties has been changed since 1990s in the direction of strengthening women's status within it. While, generally speaking, the expansion of the party has played a vital role in the development of its organization, however, it is also true that part of the changes are due to the increasing number of women and the emergence of womanhood-consciousness among women in politics as many female political activists emphasized during field research. Çağlayan (2007) also underlines the influence of women's increasing numbers and their concern for gender issue since the end of the 1990s. The changes in the organizational form make women's organizations more functional and effective and this contributes to the expansion of both the party's political activities and women-based ones. Women have become stronger in the party because the development in the organizational form in that direction has opened space for women to work and make their own decisions. More importantly they gain power to influence the decision-making processes within the party.

Historically women's organizations within the party first were in the form of commissions during the mid-1990s, then they turned into branches in 2000 and finally into assemblies in 2005. This is not simply about changing names. It is more about the growth in the number and influence of women in the party, expanding of political role and influence, increasing importance of electoral politics in Kurdish national struggles, which pushed the party to restructure itself in accordance with women's requirements. On the matter of women's organizations, this transformation reflects women's independence process from the party. As a group which has distinctive interests they have gained power both to make decision internally, and to influence the decision-making mechanisms. An examination of presenting the differences among these forms of organization indicates that women have become more independent and influential in the change from commissions to branches and then to assemblies.

First, women joined the party and engaged in political activities through commissions during the 1990s. The HEP (1990-1993) and the DEP (1993-1994) formed women commissions, in order to mobilize women for the party's organization and propaganda activities. They consisted of a small number of women activists and they were not institutionalized. Women's commissions, which were founded as affiliated to local branches of the party, emerged initially to serve administrative pragmatic needs. The organisers of propaganda activities were predominantly men who were in need of women's work in mobilization activities in order to access all segments of the society. Women's commissions mainly served the purpose of organizing women and directing them to the party's activities. Moreover, the group of women who joined the party and took part in political activities mostly consisted of those whose family members were imprisoned, those who faced human rights violations and who had lost their family members therefore they joined the political party due to national concerns (Çağlayan, 2007: 138).

While in the headquarters of the party there were a few professional women who were well educated, and who had a position thanks to the prominence of their family or their specific personal qualifications, women's commissions in the provincial and district areas were founded by women who predominantly came from a rural area. These were uneducated but they were radicalised during their political engagement within the party; most of them were middle aged women or older. In these cases, the woman's identity that came to the forefront in the party in 1990s was the identity of "mother". This was because at that time women who joined the party were mothers, sisters and wives of those who were imprisoned, or of guerrillas or who had died (Çağlayan, 2007: 138). This identity facilitated women's involvement in the political parties, which were traditionally regarded as male environments. Women's participation in politics with the identity of mother did not pose any threat to gendered hierarchical structure of the political parties and position of male administrators. On the contrary, they strengthened the male-dominated structure of the political parties. Nevertheless, these traditional structures changed when gender awareness emerged among female political activists with influence of their experiences in political parties (Çağlayan, 138-139). Women started to question the gendered structure of politics and political parties and their secondary position within them. As female political activists many women among the party activists started to think that their labour was invisible. Women activists started to question their presence in comparison to men in the party. A few female activists mentioned that, in that period, women's role was limited to the work assigned to them; they were mainly involved in mobilization activities on the ground. Although they were very active and contributed to the parties expanding their branches in the Kurdish region particularly they were treated as uneducated and inexperienced expecting to do whatever was decided by male administrators. Thus, women activists started to question their absence in decision-making processes as men were taking part in the administration positions and were making decisions about the works in the parties.

Furthermore, the awareness and questioning process contributed to change with the evolution of the female activists' profile. As mentioned in the previous chapter, during the 1990s due to the violent environment and the pressure over the party's activities, women who themselves and their family members were victims of state violence and oppression would find the courage to join the parties to defend their rights against the state in the 1990s. In 1999 the decrease of armed fighting between the PKK and the state forces due to the PKK's unilateral ceasefire (1999-2004) and the relatively peaceful moment that followed, contributed to the increase of women's participation, a legacy which would distinguish pro-Kurdish parties from the others. Towards the end of the 1990s, a new category of female party members claiming for the rights and identity of women has emerged (Çağlayan, 2007: 139). These women were in part influenced by insurgent women but, at the same time, they did not see themselves exclusively as "mothers and sisters", on the contrary most of them were young, urbanized and educated. These women were also aware that the Kurdish movement addressed them as women who are assigned the responsibility of changing society and women who have the potential of fulfilling this responsibility.

Through media organs and publications, which were ideologically close to the movement, women were encouraged to participate in all activities. This encouragement was received in response among young female activists. These women made the effort of including women's activities within the party structure towards the end of 1990s. In this sense, the HADEP's first Women Conference, which was organized in 1997 in Istanbul, constituted a first step. Despite the criticism towards local administrators' attitudes, in practice, conference presentations reflected a gender discourse of the Kurdish national movement, which assigned heavy responsibility to women. The slogan of "liberated woman is the liberated homeland"[98], the key slogan of the conference, indicates the strong link between the emancipation of women and the emancipation of the homeland. The theme that was committed in the Kurdish national movement in the beginning of 1990s had taken place in the conference text. It was as follows: "The family/society which is degraded; woman of this family/society is also degraded and enslaving" (Çağlayan, 2007: 139-140).[99] It implies that in order to emancipate herself from the situation that she is in, she has to emancipate the society as well (Çağlayan, 2007: 140). Woman was considered as "liberator".

When the activities of the party in all areas are taken into account it is clear that women had gradually assumed an important role. Although there was a development process in women's position in the party, it is fair to say that their position was not secured yet. Women's commission activities presented a spontaneous and a disorganized situation and, therefore, they struggled to institutionalise their activities within the organisations. In the interviews, female activists who experienced this period explained how women engaged in activities through the commissions. For example, one of the female political activists[100] who

---

[98] It is "Özgürleşen Kadın Özgürleşen Vatandır" in Turkish.
[99] The documents relating to the conference were obtained from the journal of Yaşamda Özgür Kadın (1998, 1st Issue) (Çağlayan, 2007: 140).

[100] She stated that she started to work for *Azadiya Welat* newspaper in Aydın in 1999 when she was 16. She opened *Azadiya Welat* office first in Aydın and she was the newspaper's representative and

started to get involved in the Kurdish movement when working for *Azadiya Welat* newspaper in Aydın in 1999, mentioned significant points about women's organization within the political party. She explained how they organized women through branches during the period of HADEP (1994-2003). She added:

> During our time in *Azadiya Welat* we did not have a specific structure devoted to women. It was not only *Azadiya Welat*; in general in other institutions there was not any structure concerning women. In that period of time we set up HADEP women's branches, which before were in the form of commissions. Then we carried on our activities organised into branches. We did our work throughout Kurdistan[101] and in every province and city we visited; we worked together with women in the political party. Women's branches became autonomous[102] in HADEP's 2000 Annual Convention. In 2004, women decided to change their organizational form from branches to assemblies. Now we carry on our activities in the form of assemblies (Personal interview, Diyarbakır, August 2010).

The HADEP's first women's conference for the first time addressed the need to reorganize women and their growing role by replacing the existing branches with commissions. These commissions, together with the youth ones became autonomous in HADEP's 4th Annual Convention in November 26, 2000 where a new regulation came into force declaring their independence from men (men's authority). It brought a different status to their activities and with it women were able to make decisions and organize activities without the control of the party's central decision-making bodies. According to the new regulations, the heads of branches could attend meetings of town, district and city governments. It has been observed that in comparison to the commissions which were dependent on administration and worked according to its directives, branches gave women an opportunity to found

---

correspondent as well in Aydın region for 2 years. She went back to Kurdistan region (of Turkey) in 2001 and worked in various Kurdish cities (Batman, Muş, Ağrı, Kars). She is currently a member of DÖKH and working for KURDİ-DER (Amed/Diyarbakır).

[101] It mainly refers to the East and Southeast part of Turkey.

[102] That means they were able to take decisions and organize activities without the control of the party's central decision making bodies.

units in which they had power. Women themselves started to select their administrators through organizing their own congress. In such processes of delegate selection and candidate nomination, women's branches have automatically become determinative as an organized power of women within the party. They started to be influential in the administration of the party through their influence on female delegates. On the other hand, the increasing influence of women through branches was not accepted easily by all men in the party as some female activists noted and these created barriers to women's access to political power within the party as mentioned at the previous chapter.

As mentioned above, there is a clear correlation between the organization form of women from commissions to branches and women's increasing power in the party. As women become influential in the party they force it to make changes in its organizational structures and policies to support their inclusion. However, just saying that a mere regulation in support of branches could provoke such a significant change in the party's structure, would not give the whole picture. Branch organizations can also serve the party's male administrators' purposes of organizing and mobilizing women. It is not expected from HADEP as a party, especially in contrast to its leftist discourses, whose minor executives and members were predominantly under the influence of feudal culture and had masculine mentality that regarded women as subordinate, a formal regulation could create a major shift of a change. As women activists' experiences show, the branch organization in HADEP's period, even though men were uncomfortable with that, took form in parallel to activism of women within the party.

During the period of DTP (2005-2009) with its congress in November 8, 2007 and the change in the guidelines,[103] the assembly form of organization[104] was implemented. The growing power of women in the political arena organized under the name of DÖKH that since 2003 influenced the DTP to make institutional changes in favour of women in addition to the political party's restructuring itself under the influence of political projects of national movement as mentioned in Chapter 2. More autonomous and free assemblies, which were established at village-districts, city and region levels, refer to the organisation of the whole society starting from the bottom-up; thus they can recruit more members, have access to more women and organize more activities. Therefore, they can become very influential to negotiate for improving women's position in the party. Female activists, who regard this progression in women's units as a requirement, underline that women are the driving force behind these developments. However, it can be stated that changing the organizational form of women's organizations from branches to assemblies is mostly related to the adoption by the DTP of the national movement's political project of *Democratic Confederalism* and *Democratic Autonomy* in the first half of 2000s (Akkaya and Jongerden, 2012). Therefore, women activists had a limited role in changing the organizational form of women organizations; they played a role in implementing this new organization style which contributes to increase their political power as many female political activists underlined during the interviews. In this

---

[103] "İşte 'suç' sayılan DTP tüzüğü", 19 April 2009, http://www.keditor.org/haber_3742.html. (Accessed on 15 September 2011).

[104] The assembly style of organization is adopted as a requirement of the DTP's new organization model. DTP's new model is a bottom-up organization design in the form of assembly. This new model which is a bottom up organization is based to establish assemblies as neighbourhood assemblies, district assemblies and city assemblies. For instance, neighbourhood assembly puts the neighbourhood issues on its agenda and finds solutions for these issues with neighbourhood residents. That is to say, it is the neighbourhood assembly that responds to problems at neighbourhood at first hand, not the party. But the neighbourhood assembly decisions have to be compatible with district and city assemblies.

regard, one of the female activists who hold an administrator position in women assemblies of the party highlighted the differences between branches and commissions organizational forms as indication of the expansion of women political movement in pro-Kurdish politics. She explained:

> These organizational forms manifest the progression of women's presence in the party and in politics. For instance, a commission included 4 to 5 people and a provincial head. At that time there was no system of co-chairship and co-spokesperson. Only one female activist from the administration and one from the youth unit were members of the commission. In total a commission could count on a total of 4 or 5 people with a maximum of 10, which made things less efficient. Since women are present in every realm of life, the way they get organised is pivotal. It was only when we started to work through assemblies that we gained access to more women involving them in our activities. I think women gain power through organisation (Personal interview, Diyarbakır, April 2010).

As seen, female political activists consider the assembly form of organisation more advantageous as it allows them to include more women into the organization. Another female political activist who has been involved in politics since HADEP's period (1994-2003) and still has an active position in the party stated, regarding the differences between branches and assemblies:

> In the form of branches women depended on the party where men were dominant. Women did not take part in the decision-making processes. Decisions were made by men and the role of women was limited to fulfil their decisions. They just did routine work. Even if these decisions contradicted their views they accepted them. But assembly form of organization makes women more influential. It gives women independence. We hold our meetings; we make our decisions; we implement our decisions. And also we make our decisions to be binding. We do all these independently. That is to say, if we make a decision it is a binding one and everybody in the party included men must accept it (Personal interview, Istanbul, September 2010).

Women's growing and developing political activism urged them to force the party to accept the changes in organizational form, expanding women's activism, increasing women's numbers and visibility through their organizational units within the party provided the party a competitive advantage in the electoral market.

Alongside the party's ideological transformations in the tendency of supporting women's inclusion into politics the party benefited from having large numbers of active female members who could influence the constituencies.

In terms of their contribution to the advancement of women's representation, women's organizations of the parties have given them the opportunity to gain the political experiences since the 1990s. This also enabled them to stand for election for representative bodies. For instance, a number of female representatives such as MPs Fatma Kurtulan and Sebahat Tuncel, who were elected in the 2007 national elections, and women mayors Leyla Güven and Ayse Gökkan who were elected in the 2009 local elections, had gained political experiences mainly through their work in the parties' women's branches. In addition, these elected women with the political experiences of women branches advocate for the inclusion of more women into political decision-making and carry out work concerning improving women's status in their representative bodies which will be examined in the following chapters and in doing so they support the enhancement of women's political representation and improve their lives.

The female activists within the party clearly have advanced their positions with the changes in women's organizational form since the 1990s, but they are still dependent on the party rules. However, women's activism was not limited to the political arena. As one of the activists stated, at the beginning of the 2000s, when she was an active member of the party, female activists in the party, women's associations and other pro- Kurdish organizations started to discuss how to work effectively with Kurdish women activists from different areas. In addition, she mentioned that women were blamed for the lower election results in the 2002 national elections by men because of gender quotas, which were implemented for the first time also pushed them to establish an independent structure. In the 1999 national election, the HADEP implemented a thirty-five women quota, which mandated that women candidates be placed in electable positions on the candidate lists. She stated that many party members reacted strongly when women were placed in the highest slots on the candidate lists in some electoral districts. In addition, in the 2002 national elections, because of the 10% election threshold, the HADEP couldn't get the number of votes required to enter parliament. However, the presence of women in the highest ranks of the HADEP's candidate lists was regarded by the male members as the reason for the party's failure. Interviewees informed that after these discussions, the party's female activists in collaboration with women in various areas came up with the idea of organising independently under the name of DÖKH (Democratic Free Woman Movement- Demokratik Özgür Kadın Hareketi). In the following section, the role of DÖKH in enhancing women's status in pro-Kurdish politics is examined.

The Expansion of 'Autonomous'[105] Women's Organization: DÖKH (Democratic Free Women Movement / Demokratik Özgür Kadın Hareketi)

When the facts that the Kurdish women's movement in general has emerged within the Kurdish national movement, and that their activism in politics has arisen in the pro-Kurdish political parties, are taken into account, the establishment of an independent women's organization under the umbrella of DÖKH as an outsider strategy appears as a turning point in the women's rights struggle. Despite some transformations (ideological, discourses and practices) in support of women, the

---

[105] Being autonomous refers to being independent from any political establishment especially political parties which female political activists believe restrict decisions and work concerning the achievement of gender equality in every realm of life.

Kurdish national movement and its structures and pro-Kurdish political organizations are still challenged by women in order to remove male domination completely. As female activists underlined, for an effective struggle, women should organize themselves outside of these structures. The DÖKH as an autonomous organization of women is assessed as a strategy that generates transformations in the pro-Kurdish party politics for feminization.

DÖKH is an umbrella organization established by Kurdish women activists on 17 September 2003 in order to link together Kurdish women in different areas such as the political party's women's organizations, Kurdish women's associations and women who hold positions in public offices. The aim of DÖKH as a feminist organisation is to address both common gender issues and specific problems that Kurdish women have. The declaration of the DÖKH clarifies many points about this new formation:

> As members of DÖKH we refuse that the history of women's resistance against inequalities along with the history of societies is written as 'the history of those who are locked in the home'. For that reason, as Kurdish women, we started with combining our experiences with the experiences and knowledge and practices of women's movements in the world and acknowledging that the origin of all kinds of inequalities is the inequality between men and women. The dominant systems, which attempt to silence women by force lack the competence to develop solution for the problems of humankind. In this century women will overturn the mechanisms of dominant, racist, nationalist and militarist ideologies which oppress them, through enhancing democracy, equality, freedom, peace and justice. In this respect, since 2003 we intended to organize our objectives and principles via incorporating our energy with women from joint foundations, independent women's associations and women from every segment of the society.[106]

The following analysis will focus on the main objectives and principles of DÖKH, in particular the idea of an independent women's movement with the mission

---

[106] "Demokratik Özgür Kadın Hareketi Kuruluş Amacı", http://ozgurlesenkadin.com/index.php?option=com_content&view=article&id=1&Itemid=8. (Accessed on 10 March 2011).

of struggling for women's interests. This analysis revealed DÖKH's ideological connections with the national movement. Apparently, there is some basic ideological standing shared by the party, the national movement and women's organizations. That is because they represent different struggle areas in the Kurdish movement. It is inevitable that they have common ideological positions, discourse and projects. That is why some of the objectives and principles of DÖKH, which are mentioned below correspond to gender ideology of the national movement and the political party. The objectives and principles regarding unequal position of women and how to struggle and obtain women's rights announced by the DÖKH are:

- Resisting racism, nationalism, sexism, destruction of nature and exploitation of labour; first of all, there should be resistance against male domination over women; this is required given that gender conflict is a primary conflict of the 21st century.

- DÖKH creates a new alternative style specific to women through freeing it from men's mentality, organization models and relation style while the struggle is carried out against a male dominant system.

- DÖKH approaches women's struggle strategically; it views the solution of social problems in the women's emancipation ideology; woman regards free woman's identity and independent women's organization as premises of women's emancipation struggle.

- DÖKH is against state-hierarchy structures. It prefers democratic ecological society, and an emancipatory paradigm. It aims to bring the democratic will of the people into the open. It embarks on organizing the basis of democratic communal values. It aims to make transformation through creating independent women's organization within the democratic confederation.

- DÖKH adopts a democratic struggle line against all kinds of attacks, violence and violations of right towards woman and it exercises the right of self-defence.

- From this point of view, DÖKH expresses the interests of women who come from different regions, class, nationality, religion, sexual orientation and ethnic origin. In order to ensure social equality against ideologies, which produce sexism, nationalism, inequality, hierarchy and violence appear in the male dominant system DÖKH conducts a struggle in the every area such as the social, political, juridical, economic and cultural.

- DÖKH embraces the struggle values of the world feminist women's movement, which has been continuing for centuries. It acts with solidarity in order to carry out a joint struggle with the women's movements.

- It deals with the women's issues, which have resulted from being part of an oppressed gender, nation, class and race due to the mentality which masculinises nations, classes and races, by women's emancipation struggle.[107].

DÖKH built up its organization in line with a set of principles; some of them are highlighted in order to demonstrate the distinctness and specificity of its organizational form. First of all, its organizational model is defined as "In contrast to

---

[107] "Demokratik Özgür Kadın Hareketi Kuruluş Amacı",
http://ozgurlesenkadin.com/index.php?option=com_content&view=article&id=1&Itemid=8 (Accessed on 10 March 2011).

the organization model which categorizes, and polarizes, which is *status quo*, egocentric, vertical and hierarchical, it embraces the organization model which attaches importance to diversities, and addresses the individual who is responsible and asks for freedom, which is labour-based, flexible and horizontal. It regards principles of volunteering, democratic participation and governance as bases."[108] Furthermore, DÖKH has a structure that aims to bring together women's associations and female activists from different organizations, regarding its principle of membership, which does not require formal procedure. Secondly, it emphasizes that those (all institutions, structures and individuals) who believe women's emancipation ideology and accept the program of the movement are the members of DÖKH. They have the right to participate in all activities of the movement, contributing to create decisions of DÖKH and obtaining information about its activities. Thirdly, it specifies that DÖKH organizes itself according to different core working areas, and in the form of assemblies.

The core working areas that movement members carry on are ideological, political or social activities, young women's affairs, and city women assemblies. Among these, the areas of political and young women and city women assemblies are very relevant and have to be explained in detail. The political area consists of women councils of the political party and women committees of local governments. The responsibility of the field is to establish coordination in itself and follow political agenda concerning women and, when required, take a stand. It plays a transforming role in reconstructing politics based on democratic gender equality rules. For this, it aims to develop a free local administration understanding in the line of democratic

---

[108] "Demokratik Özgür Kadın Hareketi Kuruluş Amacı",
http://ozgurlesenkadin.com/index.php?option=com_content&view=article&id=1&Itemid=8 (Accessed on 10 March 2011).

ecological society paradigm (see Chapter 2). In addition, it develops and implements projects to solve women's problems at the local level.

As it is understood from the name, the area of young women aims to encourage young women's participation in the movement. That's why it is present in the organisation of the *Patriot Youth Movement (Yurtsever Gençlik Hareketi)* and in the establishment of its assemblies. It is responsible for providing self-organization of young women through organizing in the areas of society, politics and ideology, praising out their dynamism and will. In addition, it is in charge of enhancing organization, struggle, consciousness and capacity of young women in the line of women's emancipation ideology.

City women's assemblies represent the organizational sense of DÖKH in the confederation system, which refers to the political project of *Democratic Confederalism,* which proposes to organize with assembly form (Akkaya and Jongerden, 2012). It consists of delegates who were elected from the local level of the social field, the political field and young women's field, and local activist women. At first, city women's executives are formed and then on the basis of this, city women's assemblies are established. It is a self-organized power of DÖKH, which produces solutions for women's and children's problems, takes common decisions, provides assembly organization and plans and implements activities on the local level.

While introducing DÖKH's organisation and principles, its members also define its areas of intervention. The areas where DÖKH carries out the struggle are violence, poverty, law, representation, media, struggle for peace, education and training, health. Among these areas it is relevant to emphasize what the movement aims to achieve in respect with the political representation of women: 1) the effective participation of women in decision-making mechanisms, increasing representation of women and implementing gender quotas in all mechanisms based on the idea that democracies would not be true democracy as long as women's representation is not obtained; 2) the principle of positive discrimination as an essential principle until the equality of women and men will be obtained and it encourages women to set their will through struggling against all backwardness which constitutes an impediment to their own independence; 3) the struggle for the principle of positive discrimination to gain legal status in the political arena at first and put it into practice in order to make politics to become socialized.[109]

This makes clear the political and ideological background of the DÖKH. While it presents a picture of a feminist establishment concerned with women's issues and interests, predominantly Kurdish women, it also takes part in the Kurdish identity struggle as can be observed in its activities and discourses. However, the significant role of the DÖKH is to transmit women's activism into the civil society in order to change gender relations as a whole.

Furthermore, the formation process of DÖKH and its aims is well explained through experiences of female activists who were actively involved in debates before it was established in 2003. In this sense, the statements of one of the female political activists[110] about the process of the creation of the DÖKH are a testimonial of one of the turning points in the expansion of the Kurdish women's movement. She said:

---

[109] It means involvement of masses; in Turkey politicians are not in touch with the public. They have distance from public which causes politics being out of touch with the public both in perception and in practice. One outcome is that it becomes the men's affair. Therefore, women are excluded. So, it's becoming socialized also means involvement of each sections of the society.

[110] She is currently a member of DÖKH and working for *KURDÎ-DER* (Amed/Diyarbakır). *KURDÎ-DER* is one of institution belongs to TZP-Kurdî *(Tevgera Ziman û Perwerdehiya / Kürt Eğitim ve Dil Hareketi)*. TZP- Kurdî aims to stop assimilation and auto-assimilation of the Kurdish language. Its aim is to organize the Kurdish language case\action and the protection of Kurdish as a movement among public. In addition, it is in a practical struggle for teaching Kurdish language, raising consciousness about Kurdish language, and carrying out a struggle for education in Kurdish language. They want to

> As a result of discussions in the matter of enhancing women's position in every area, politically active women, together with the women who worked in different institutions such as women's associations and media organisations, wanted to create an independent women's movement.[111] More precisely, women from different organizations needed to create an umbrella organization that included all women. During that period, we worked with women working in the media. At the time there were a few journals and newspapers: *Özgür Kadının Sesi, Özgür Halk, Azadiya Welat* and *Yurtsever Gençlik*.[112] We [politically active women] established coordination with women who work in these press associations and this coordination group elected their delegates to join DÖKH. Since then women have organized in this way in politics (Personal interview,, Diyarbakır, September 2010).

These statements demonstrate that the concern towards gender equality increased among women activists in the beginning of the 2000s and they began to take actions in order to achieve gender equality and this mainly has happened in political areas.

As mentioned above, the objectives behind the establishment of the DÖKH were announced by its members. The principles and its work style are explained in detail. But how all these come to practice still needed to be defined. The explanations of female activists clarify these matters. In addition, regarding the relation with the women's movement or DÖKH, most of female activists addressed the principles and organizational style of the formation. They emphasized the importance of implementing the principles of the formation while they carry on their work. In this regard, one of female activists who works for *KURDİ-DER (Kurdish*

---

form and create a mass that demands education in Kurdish language from primary school to university. (Kürt Dil Hareketi http://www.bydigi.net/candi-gisti/17430-tzp-kurdi.html) (Accessed on 18 August 2011).

[111] She mentioned about the establishment of DÖKH.

[112] *Özgür Kadinin Sesi* (The Voice of Free Woman) is a monthly women journal, which was issued in 1998 under the name of *Özgür Kadın (Free Woman)*, and then it was changed to *Kadının Sesi (The Voice of Woman)* and finally *Özgür Kadının Sesi*. *Özgür Halk* is a monthly political-cultural pro-Kurdish journal. *Özgür Gündem* was a daily basis newspaper, was started to publish on 30 May 1992 and dissolved by order of the court on 14 April 1994. *Özgür Ülke (Free Country)* has been launched on 28 April 1994 replacing it. It was re-started to publish on 4 April 2011.

Language Research and Development Association- Kürt Dilini Araştırma ve Geliştirme Derneği)[113] stated:

> I am a member of DÖKH. It is a movement, which has many constituents. I, as a woman, am a member of this movement. I am also a delegate and I joined the Kurdish Language and Education Movement with quota by the women's movement.[114] (...) We have an agreement with activists of the movement. All our activities are generally carried out jointly. (..) KURDI-DER is a foundation that deals with language. On the other side, there is DÖKH, an ideological organization. It has a number of constituents in the party, non-governmental organizations, women's associations, cultural institutions and so on. As a woman who works in the KURDI-DER I also belong to the women's movement with which we have an agreement. If there is a case of account and calling to account about our activities we do this to the movement. It is not only me bearing this responsibility. Women in other institutions also bear this responsibility. Those who consider their woman identity have commitment to the women's movement at first. Then, they have accountability to the institution they work in (Personal interview, Diyarbakır, September 2010).

The female activist's statements meant a commitment to the principles of DÖKH.

She continued:

> Despite the fact that we (women employees of KURDİ-DER) are not officially appointed to the TZP-Kurdî, we are however part of the women's movement. Thus, in carrying our activities, we do consider ourselves as a member or representative of the women's movement. I mean we regard the principles of the DÖKH, which protect women rights and care about women interests (Personal, Diyarbakır, September 2010).

These statements indicate that there is no official implementation in the organization.

But female members of TZP-Kurdî who are also members of DÖKH put into practice

---

[113] It is one of the institutions, which belongs to *TZP-Kurdî (Tevgera Ziman û Perwerdehiya / Kürt Eğitim ve Dil Hareketi)*. TZP- Kurdî aims to stop assimilation and auto-assimilation of Kurdish language. Its aim is to organize the Kurdish language case\action and the protection of Kurdish as a movement among public. In addition, it is in a practical struggle for teaching Kurdish language, raising consciousness about Kurdish language, carrying out a struggle for education in Kurdish language. They want to form and create a mass that demands education in Kurdish language from primary school to university. "Kürt Dil Hareketi", http://www.bydigi.net/candi-gisti/17430-tzp-kurdi.html (Accessed 18 August 2011).

[114] The Kurdish women's movement, which is led by DÖKH, enforces all pro-Kurdish organizations to implement gender quota. This means female political activists are not only concerned with gender equality in political arenas; they are concerned with achieving gender equality in all areas of life and all institutions in the society.

the principles of DÖKH in the organization. Besides, association as part of the Kurdish national movement requires approving these implementations. Her words make clear that any individual or institution that accepts the principles of DÖKH should act in accordance with them. In addition, regarding the criteria they consider at their work places as members of the women's movement she added:

> Now, we carry out our distinctive works[115] in TZP-Kurdî. We started this year. Until now we had taken part as individual in the movement (DÖKH). But in the last year we have carried out projects concerning women in TZP-Kurdî. We have our distinctive TZP-Kurdî commissions in every city. We have distinctive coordination on the central level. We have women's commissions and women's assemblies. For instance, in some places such as Batman, Van and Yüksekova (Hakkari) we have women's assemblies. There are distinctive women's assemblies within TZP-Kurdî. In certain places as Istanbul, Izmir and Ankara we have women's commissions. Moreover, within TZP-Kurdî in almost all commissions gender quota is implemented (Personal interview, Diyarbakır, September 2010).

At this point, another relevant issue comes up, that is the role of DÖKH in the implementation of quotas in other institutions apart from the political party. Besides, these statements are very significant because they demonstrate the presence and strength of women from DÖKH. The women's movement affected the change of gender combination in pro-Kurdish organizations. As seen above, DÖKH declared that its aims are carrying out a struggle against the mechanisms of sovereign, racist, nationalist and militarist ideologies that oppress women. Women activists of the DÖKH mostly work in diverse civil society organizations and party organizations. Women activists, acting with the support of an organized and independent organisation like DÖKH, are able to negotiate with pro-Kurdish political parties and organizations in order to change policies in favour of women.

---

[115] In Turkish "özgün çalışmalar" refers to carrying out work concerning women.

The member of the DÖKH work towards the establishment of organizations which are called women's assemblies in which women activists come together to approach problems in the cities where they live. Together they organize campaigns, which address women's issues and rights. One of these campaigns entitled "women's honour belongs to women" took place in 2009. The women activists of the DÖKH organized conferences and meetings to inform both women and men about domestic and state's violence against women. Besides, these activities were organized by the activists of the DÖKH to raise consciousness concerning gender's issues and provide information regarding the ways to deal with them. They also provide opportunity to the party representatives to reach the electorates. Consequently, Kurdish women who have been active in the political area since the 1990s were able to raise gender issues more assertively and negotiate their presence and representation in the pro-Kurdish particularly since they started to organize under the name of DÖKH.

In the following section, this study will analyse the implementation of gender quotas as one of the strategies that facilitated the feminizing process of pro-Kurdish parties.

The Implementation of the Quotas

With the increase in the implementation of gender quotas, which Lovenduski examined as equality guarantees or positive discrimination strategies (2005: 91), there has been a great deal of research on gender quotas in the past decade (Dahlerup, 2006; Krook, 2006, 2010; Norris & Lovenduski, 1995). More than a hundred countries around the world have implemented a type of quotas[116] for the selection of female candidates in the past two decades. A vast number of cross-national studies (Benstead, 2010; Krook, 2006, 2009) and single case studies (Baldez, 2004; Bush & Jamal, 2011; Gray, 2003; Opello, 2006) have been carried out to analyse the role of gender quotas in increasing women's representation. Notwithstanding this expanding literature on gender quotas, there are a few studies that focus on the role of political parties in the introduction and implementation of quotas as well as their influence on political parties. In this regard, Murray (2010) specified that political parties are the critical factors that determine whether quotas will be introduced, employed thoroughly, and achieved success in enhancing women's representation. Further, quotas also influence party practices such as candidate selection, the party's relations with its members, and the party's gender composition in representation offices.

The quota system is regarded as a means to achieve an increase in women's participation in politics in order to equalize women's descriptive representation. The core idea behind quota systems is to recruit women into political positions and to ensure that women are not only symbols in political life. Quotas for women entail that women must constitute a certain number or percentage of the members of a body, whether it is a candidate list, a parliamentary assembly, a committee, or a government. While it is regarded as an effective method to increase women's presence in politics it also raises serious questions and, in some cases, strong resistance. In feminizing process of pro-Kurdish party politics quota has become one

---

[116] There are mainly three types of gender quotas: statutory quota, voluntary party quotas, and reserved seats. Statutory (legislative) quotas require that women make up at least a minimal proportion of the legislature or of parliamentary candidates. In voluntary party quotas, one or more political parties in a country voluntarily adopt gender quotas. In reserved seats quotas, a specific number of seats in the legislature are reserved for women, and selected women fill those positions after the election.

of the influential strategies, and currently 40% has been implemented since 2002. For the application of this affirmation action strategy the party's willing to promote gender equality is certainly a determinative factor, but that female activists demand and struggle for equal political participation and representation is as much a significant one. Thus, these debates and processes concerning the introduction and implementation of quotas in the case of pro-Kurdish party politics and how they are employed as effective strategy, which have led to change the balance in favour of women in politics are based on the activists' experiences.

Regarding the application of quotas as one of the most effective strategies facilitating the feminization of pro-Kurdish party politics, it is important to analyse why pro-Kurdish political parties implement quotas, which were the debates before and during the implementation of quotas and what are the arguments behind the application of quotas within the party and in the selection of candidates? Women activists who questioned women's under representation in pro-Kurdish parties advocated the introduction of anti-discrimination measures and gender quotas towards the end of the 1990s. Under the influence of women activists, the pro-Kurdish political party (HADEP) adopted the first voluntary quota in Turkey in 1999. The Kurdish example demonstrates the interplay of the activists' agency and the institutions in the decision to use quotas.

Why did quotas appear in pro-Kurdish politics?

Quotas, which contribute to increase descriptive political representation of women have been implemented in many countries such as the United Kingdom, France and Argentina (Lovenduski, 2005), but they are unusual in Turkey, so it is surprising and significant that they appeared in Kurdish politics. From the experiences of the female activists, it appears that the political party has introduced quotas with the support of women activists. Emergence of quotas in pro-Kurdish politics makes pro-Kurdish party, which has been considered as the legal extension of the Kurdish national movement as a specific case in Turkey's politics. Therefore, quotas in Kurdish politics did not emerge out of a typical historical pattern (industrialization, urbanization, the entrance of women into the formal wage-earning sector). So, where did the impetus for quotas come from? Some have argued that the pro-Kurdish political parties, who approved amendments in party program, were motivated by noble intentions; they wanted to strengthen the position of women within politics. However, as research conducted with female activists pointed out, the pro-Kurdish political parties' support in favour of quotas for women is due to the fact that men did not consider quotas as a threat. Instead, they assumed that women would take on a passive, subdued role in the formal political sector which enables parties to easily dominate female representatives and forward their own agendas through them. However, the process has developed in favour of women through the interplay of multiple factors. These are: the growing argument of women, global dimension, and ideological shifts in Kurdish struggle and enforced by the party, change in gender perspective of the party, and democratization under the influence of Turkey's EU accession. Nevertheless, among these factors, the strong will of female activists to change the established system was the most determinative. That is to say, experiences of female activists prove that emergence of womanhood consciousness among female activists has encouraged women to organize and pushed the political party to make policies in favour of women, including the quota.

When the women's representation was dramatically low in many political parties in Turkey in the 1990s, there was almost no discussion regarding the gender quotas among Turkish feminists who began to be active at that time. In contrast, Kurdish feminists, for instance, through women's journals such as *Roza* and *Jiyan* (Life) questioned the issue of women's under representation in pro-Kurdish political parties. They advocated the introduction of anti-discrimination measures and gender quotas.[117] These discussions among women activists, which mostly took place during the second part of the 1990s were taken into consideration in 1999 by the Pro-Kurdish HADEP which adopted the first voluntary quota in Turkey. Following women's lobbying efforts and the support of Abdullah Öcalan, activists from the HADEP were able to obtain anti- discrimination measures and a twenty-five percent voluntary party quota was accepted at the party's 2000 Annual Convention (Çağlayan, 2007). HADEP was the first political party in Turkey, which adopted a voluntary women's quota. The voluntary quota has been implemented by later pro-Kurdish political parties with an increasing percentage. During the DTP period (2005-2010) the gender quota was increased from 30% to 40% for both national and local candidate lists in 2005. The implementation of quota by the parties has contributed to the institutionalization of women's role in political parties. Besides, it differentiates the pro-Kurdish political parties from other parties where women rarely exercise political power.

Relevant to the Kurdish female activists' demand for quota in order to have equal political representation, Sun-uk (1995) asserts that the need for a quota system stems from the lack of opportunities for women to perform their potential capabilities. If women do have the capabilities and the power to choose, a quota system is not needed. In favour of a quota scheme implementation are arguments such as the belief that it is the most effective way of translating legal equality

---

[117] News which focused on women's underrepresentation were published in the Kurdish feminist journal Roza in 1995 and in the journal of Jiyan for instance a columnist with the pseudo name (Zelal) also raised this issue in her page published in 1997.

between men and women into de facto equality by guaranteeing women's presence in leadership in the immediate term (Htun, 1998). It has also been considered as a starting point that could balance women's participation in various fields because women leaders also function as role models for other women, and serve as evidence that society is inclusive and egalitarian (Sun-uk, 1995).

The most widely used argument for quotas is that they are effective. They make political institutions responsible for ensuring the representation of women, and used over a period of time, normalize women's presence. They reduce the pressure on incoming women who benefit from being part of a larger group. Many of their supporters argue that quotas are a necessary compensation for systems that have deprived women of a presence in politics. This argument draws on the theoretical cases (justice and difference arguments) for women's representation and justifies quotas as the only means to ensure it. As mentioned in Chapter 2 in the analysis of the parties' program and statutes pro-Kurdish parties that support gender equality based on mainly justice argument presented the implementation of quotas to achieve gender equality in politics. Institutionalists argue that quotas are part of a process that brings women into all parts of the political system and sets in motion further processes that will ensure that their presence continues. There are many motivations that affect supporters of quotas. Some advocates are motivated by their beliefs that gender-balance in decision-making is justified at any price. Electoral considerations are also a strong motivator. International pressures may require elites to speed up their processes of integrating women. For example, prospective entrants to the European Union may wish to increase women's representation in an effort to display their democratic credentials. (Htun and Jones 2002; Krook 2003 mentioned in Lovenduski, 2005: 96). When the arguments for the implementation of quotas by the pro-Kurdish party are explored it is seen that female activists regard quotas as a necessary strategy to open space within the gendered political system and political organizations, which coincides with the views of the advocates of quotas. The implementation of quotas enables the overcoming of the obstacles to increasing women's descriptive representation. In Turkey, Kurdish women are a disadvantaged group in many aspects such as lack of education, economic resources, oppression and violence, due to the on-going conflict between the state and the Kurdish forces and to social pressures, which have restricted their political roles. Notably, existing political culture, institutions and system and the conditions that women live in create obstacles to women to have equal opportunities in politics. In addition, when the male domination in politics is taken into account affirmative action policies remain important, and one of these maybe a quota requirement in order to open space for women in politics.

Besides, due to the lack of opportunities and historical domination of men in politics the question of representation of women's interests assumes importance. In their arguments for quota they refer to interest differentiation based on gender. Female activists who believe women's interests and issues could well be represented by women themselves therefore regard quota as a necessary strategy to obtain gender balance. The vast number of female activists shares similar opinions regarding why they are advocates of a quota system. The opinion of one of the activists who hold an administrative position in women's assemblies summarizes all these views:

> Our experiences have taught us if there is not an official decision or rule it is impossible to do anything in favour of women. That is to say, if we want to apply some policies in support gender equality it has to take place in the party's program and guidelines. So it would be possible to ask for the implementation of the rule, so that everybody has to obey it. Additionally, the status of women can only be changed through positive discrimination policies;

because women have been disadvantaged for centuries. Just saying that you respect gender equality as many men do, is not enough by itself. This outlook has to be changed into practice. In this sense, we do believe that quota is essential to provide transformations in politics and in other areas and to eliminate discrimination against women. When the number of women increases in representative bodies and in administrative positions men will get used to working with women. In Kurdish politics, women are not symbolic tokens, but on the contrary are concerned with women's interests and issues because they have experienced them within the women's movement (Personal interview, Diyarbakır, August 2010).

This quote raises a few points. First, female activists consider the quotas as necessary to make change in gender combination in politics. Women are disadvantaged to overcome obstacles therefore affirmative actions such as quotas are required according to the activists. Female political activists' advocacy for quotas is based on the difference arguments. Another point is the response to the opponents of quotas who are sceptical about the ability of female representatives elected through quotas to represent women's interests. In the Kurdish case, the requirements for candidacy such as having experiences within women's movements assure that female representatives act for women's interests.

There are also opponents of quotas, who include both men and women, who argue that they are discriminatory and that they will elevate under-qualified women to power, stigmatize beneficiaries, and that above all, they are unnecessary. There are also fears that the introduction of women's quotas will prompt other groups –ethnic minorities, homosexuals, farmers, etc. to demand their own quota (Htun, 1998). Moreover, probably the strongest argument against quotas is that they risk essentialism. According to critics quotas invoke the essential category of women and marginalize other differences. Liberal theories of representation support arguments that quotas are unfair to men, who should not be excluded on the ground of sex. Another argument that has resonance with feminists is that concentration on quotas may obscure larger questions of political transformation. This argument suggests that quotas are a way of working within the existing system of political institutions that fails to challenge the effects of institutions on gender identity (Lovenduski, 2005: 97). Regarding these opposing arguments towards the quotas in pro-Kurdish politics it has been pointed out that the discussions about quotas are mostly divided as male members represent opposition; female activists enforce the party to implement quotas increasingly in percentage in all levels. As female activists are aware, the opposition is essentially based on men's wish not to lose their power in the party and in politics in general. Many activists evaluated the critics of opponents of quota as reflection of traditional male mentality, which considers the politics as male activity as underlined in Chapter 3. At a national level, discussions about quotas are especially raised during elections. While female activists and women's associations ask for high numbers of female candidates which could be possible with quotas from political parties they face reactions which match the opposing views mentioned above. One of the strongest reactions against quotas was made by the Prime Minister. The Prime Minister Recep Tayyip Erdoğan who rejected the demand from women branches of his party, AKP about the including the principle of woman quota in the party guidelines, said: "I consider the implementation quota as insult toward women."[118] "The application of quotas makes women obliged to the goodwill of men. In other words, men do a favour; then women enter the Parliament. Nothing of the kind may happen."[119] Concerning these statements of the Prime Minister, the

---

[118] Devlet Arık, "Başbakan Erdoğan: 'Kota Uygulamasını Kadınlara Hakaret olarak Görüyorum'" 6 April 2004, http://www.habervitrini.com/haber.asp?id=125372 (Accessed on 17 August 2011).

[119] Emine Özcan, "Başbakan Kotayı Bilmiyor, Cahil Konuşuyor", *Bianet,* 28 November 2008, http://ww.bianet.org/bianet/bianet/111151-basbakan-kotayi-bilmiyor-cahil-konusuyor (Accessed on 17 August 2011).
"Kota kadına saygısızlıktır", *Yenişafak,* 28 November 2008,
http://yenisafak.com.tr/Politika/?t=28.11.2008&i=152883 (Accessed on 17 August 2011).

secretary-general of KA-DER, Aysun Sayın observed, "We refer to gender quotas. 30% gender quotas include both women and men. It connotes quotas for men as well. There is a historical discrimination. Ignoring this is ignorance."[120] In this regard, the pro-Kurdish party has a distinctive role in the sense of being the only political party in Turkey's politics implementing gender quotas.

In general, quotas for women are intended to give women more power in politics and to include women in political decision-making through increasing descriptive representation; however, to introduce quotas against severe resistance 'requires that women have already gained some power' (Dahlerup 1998). A number of issues are raised by the politics of quotas, many of which are parallel or derive from debates about women's presence. First, there is the question of why male-dominated institutions and parties should implement quotas. Second, there is the issue of 'quota women'. Who are they, and are they distinguishable from other elected women, or are they subject to some stigmatization and what parts of their experiences are temporary and transitional, and what parts are more lasting? Third, there is the relationship of quotas to the social structure. Feminist advocates have anticipated that their increased representation of would somehow lead to increased representation by other groups. Fourth, the institutional design is significant. To be effective a quota must be suited to the system in which it is installed (Lovenduski, 2005: 101-102).

Other anti-quota arguments are that they risk a backlash by otherwise supportive male incumbent and hopeful; they risk recruiting unqualified women just because they are women, which will deprive electors of adequate representation;

---

[120] Emine Özcan, "Başbakan Kotayı Bilmiyor, Cahil Konuşuyor", *Bianet*, 28 November 2008, http://ww.bianet.org/bianet/bianet/111151-basbakan-kotayi-bilmiyor-cahil-konusuyor (Accessed on 17 August 2011).

women thus selected may be stigmatized and therefore less powerful and effective in the legislature; the men responsible for political recruitment will nominate women who are more compliant. Finally, politics may become polarized on gender lines. As Lovenduski notes, these are reasonable arguments. However, with the exception of the last point, they are no more than possible temporary effects that will disappear as women's political presence is normalized and as the process of representation continues. Moreover, the arguments that guarantee women's presence polarizes politics on gender lines may actually be a case for quotas, as it suggests that there are gendered interests to be presented. (Lovenduski, 2005: 98) If the quota application in Kurdish politics is assessed in consideration of these anti-quota arguments, some specificities of the Kurdish case appear and these specificities invalidate these criticisms. Firstly, the nomination of female candidates for both national and local elections is predominantly determined by women themselves, themselves organized under the name of DÖKH since 2003. Besides, the candidates are mainly selected among those who are capable enough to represent women and their interests and have experiences in the women's movement. These are determinant factors that make female representatives responsible in terms of representing women's interests. Thus, being nominated by quotas does not make Kurdish women obedient to men. On the contrary, they represent a challenge to men who do not want to share their political power. Secondly, women's experiences have pointed out that they have different concerns, interests and expectations from men. From the beginning, the quota system has been regarded as one of the most effective ways to create opportunities for women by women activists as underlined by many of them in the interviews. It is meant to be implemented until women's position is strengthened and their number is equal to men. On the other hand, they think the equilibrium could change in the future. In other words, men might need quotas due to the growing of women politicians. Even now, in some places, there are more women than men. Therefore, the view they take is that the quota is implemented as a gender quota, which includes both sexes. If it is needed it can be applied for men as well. Regarding the change from women quota to gender quota one of female activists stated:

> We [women activists] have implemented the quota but lately we have decided to make a change in the name of this policy, from women quota [kadın kotası] before it became gender quota [cinsiyet kotası]. We think it should be gender quota instead of quota or women quota because in some cities and districts we cannot find male administrators. Generally men do not want to take position in big cities.[121] For instance, all administrators in Köşk, which is a province of Aydın are women. That is to say, the quota is not always needed for women. It can be needed to provide men's involvement as well (Personal interview, Diyarbakır, August 2010).

In Turkey quotas and equal representation primarily remain an internal party matter. Historically, none of mainland political parties have used quotas of candidates and internal quotas. Despite the low level of women's representation there has not been any quota implementation in Turkey. In Turkey, which offers proportional electoral system, key decisions are made by political parties. That means political parties have a determinative role in making policies in favour of women. Among all political parties in Turkey, Kurdish political parties illustrate well

---

[121] Especially in the 1990s when there was a very intensive conflict between the state forces and Kurdish fighters involving in legal Kurdish politics was highly risky. Therefore, it was quite hard to mobilize people. She also mentioned about reasons why men do not prefer to join the administration rank of the party. A few activists referred to the same points as well. She noted that there are plenty of reasons such as the pressure and violence that have been exercised toward people by the state authorities, incuriosity and laziness. She said that sometimes they feel disqualified and sometimes they are not courageous enough because it is not easy and safe to be a political activist in pro-Kurdish politics and join the pro-Kurdish organizations. There are some costs of this due the state oppression. Compared to men, women's willingness to participate in politics and to take role in administration position despite the risks can be explained by the benefits that they get. This is an opportunity to make change in their life while struggling for national rights. On the other side, she informed, *"a new system 'democratic confederation' is aimed to set in among people, which offers a new life style or a new model of living. In this system, men cannot maintain male mentality, which has been dominant for 5 thousand years in the confederation system. Therefore, they do not want to take responsibility"* (Personal interview, Diyarbakır, August 2010). These statements introduce that women activists have benefits in participation in politics.

the politics of adopting and using quotas in the Turkish political system. As it has been figured out this policy has brought out considerable changes in politics for the benefit of women. Despite the critics against quota, in Kurdish case due to active role of women in all processes of quota implementation, it became one of the most effective strategies for the growth number of women in politics. As mentioned in the first chapter, descriptive representation is one of necessary components of feminization. Therefore, the quotas, which contribute to the increase of female representatives' number, play a significant role in the process of feminization of pro-Kurdish party politics, by developing the descriptive representation of women. Obviously, if there were no other policies and applications changing the gendered structure of politics and political institutions quotas would not be influential that much. In this regard, examining the co-chairship system, which enables equal participation in the core positions of the party makes it understandable how different strategies make different contributions to the feminization of pro-Kurdish party politics. Co-presidency system contributes to increase both descriptive representation and substantive representation of women in pro-Kurdish politics.

Equal Participation in Leadership Positions: Co-chairship

Institutional changes aiming to increase women's representation in the party advanced during the DTP's period (2005-2010). They were advocated by elected women and female political activists, despite men's accusations that these women were seeking power rather than serving Kurdish cause, as female activists interviewed for this research underlined. One of these advancements was the introduction of co-chair positions in which a male and a female chair lead the party simultaneously. The system of co-chairship as an insider strategy has been in force since 2007. Similarly, co-coordinatorship was implemented in the local administration: this strategy provides for a female vice mayor if the mayor is a man and vice versa. Despite the fact that it is not legitimated according to the law on political parties in Turkey, the implementation of co-chairship system has become an influential strategy for the transformation of gendered structure of the political party, and for the decrease of male domination in the party. As it has been pointed out, the co-chairship system has contributed to the empowerment of women by enabling them to exercise power in leadership positions and involving them in decision-making, thereby limiting the traditional male domination.

There are a few points that need to be questioned: what and who plays a role in implementing this policy? What arguments have been put forward by women? Apparently, the party and female activists are two major actors. Furthermore, there are a number of crucial outcomes of this policy. As a positive discrimination policy, the co-chairship system, which allocates role for women in decision-making processes, represents many meanings and brings forward consequential developments for women in politics. It destroys prejudices against women. It allows people to get used to see women in leadership positions. This is not a symbolic position. Women participate in all processes that the male president and administrator participate in. Both men and women equally share power and responsibility. The co-chairship system, which is one of gender equality policies of the party, is often utilized by the party representatives and female activists in order to highlight that the pro-Kurdish party is the only political party that challenges the Turkish political system. Most of female activists have differentiated their party from others in terms of its practice of co-chairship. One of female mayors' statements addressed the importance of co-chairship system. She noted:

> Even though our party (DTP) is criticized to be ethnic based or to follow ethnic based policy, it has very influential works and policies, which serve as an example for other political parties. One of these model implementations is the co-chairship. There is no any other political party with such kind of practice. I believe none of mainstream political parties (ruling party AKP, main opposition party CHP and the second opposition party MHP) will ever practice any policies in favour of women because they are system parties, which never challenge existing rules. On the other hand, DTP challenges the existing system. It challenges all hierarchies and discriminative policies, which are maintained by mainstream parties. In this regard, co-chairship and its implementation throughout the party, which is co-coordinatorship, should be taken account as specificity of the party (Personal interview, Mardin, August 2009).

This quote clarifies that the co-chairship is not only a challenge to male domination in the party it also challenges the political system in Turkey. There is a significant point: while gender equality supportive policies contribute to feminizing pro-Kurdish party politics, they also contribute to differentiate the political party from the rest of political parties in Turkey. This is beneficial for the party to position itself as a significant actor for democratizing the country.

As the female mayor explained, the coordination is put into practice in the party administration, provincial organizations and central headquarters. In particular, all elected activists (14 in totals) involved in this research underlined that these kinds of practices have positive impact both on society and in the political arena because of their contribution in eradicating prejudices against women who are regarded as not qualified and capable enough to do politics in a male dominated society. These policies, while they reflect the ways a political party can act to incorporate women into every rank, provide them the opportunity to prove their ability and performance, giving them self-confidence. In addition, they make women visible in politics particularly in leadership positions and this transforms the gendered nature of politics and political institutions. Besides, women are encouraged to participate in politics and to take on more responsibilities when they see women in the higher positions. In this regard, a member of women assemblies expressed her opinions regarding the visibility of women in higher position in the party, which prove the positive impacts of women. They are considered as role models for many female activists. She said:

> To see a woman next to a man at the top of the party suggests many meanings. Firstly, it has symbolic meaning. Whenever people see this picture they internalize the presence of women in higher positions. For young activists they have the hope that they can be president, administrator, mayor and MP if they put their effort and they improve themselves in the political arena. As a woman activist, I believe that we have opportunity to take any position if we are qualified enough. These kinds of policies (co-chairship and co-coordinatorship) prevent discrimination against women (Personal interview, Diyarbakır, August 2010).

The interviews with the female activists pointed out that those female activists in the local governments play a significant role in putting these policies into practice at local level as well. The same system is also in place in the local administration. As one of female mayors underlined, although it is the party decision to implement co-coordinatorship in the local administration, it is the women who put effort to practice this policy every municipality running by the party's elected mayors.

The implementation of the co-chairship system demonstrates that political institutions, which are criticized as gendered institutions from a feminist perspective can be transformed if the required policies are carried out. The application of the co-chairship system by the pro-Kurdish party has played a major role in the elimination of the male domination within the party. As a result, co-chairship and its extension in other administration positions such as co-coordinatorship, is a policy that enables women to share with men the authority within party. They had the opportunity to be involved in the decision making processes which is a very important step towards the elimination of male authority in order to make feminization occurring within the pro-Kurdish party politics. At the same time that women strengthen their position with the applications of as co-chairship and quota in politics they become aware of the necessity of improving themselves and share their experiences in order to be qualified, capable and well-informed activists concerning various issues such as women rights, political agenda and struggle methods. This perspective, for sure, serves both the female activists objectives and the party's interests. As a consequence, the School of Politics for Women was established in order train them into their new roles. The next section will analyse its impact in the feminization process of pro-Kurdish party politics.

Training: the School of Politics for Women

The training as an insider strategy mentioned by Lovenduski (2005: 90) has been one of the significant strategies in feminizing pro-Kurdish politics. It was one of the most important processes that contributed to the construction of a political activist's identity. The type of training formations established by the political parties give an idea about their approaches toward their female members. In this sense, one of training formations founded by the pro-Kurdish party, the School of Politics for Women[122], which addressed the female political activists of the party, has played a major role in feminizing processes of pro-Kurdish party politics. It is a common practise among the political parties in Turkey to organize training programs for all its members, and when it was extended to women, it provided them the opportunity to become influential political actors.

An examination of the specific training school; the School of Politics for Women, provides to the members will clarify the significance of the training strategy of the pro-Kurdish party. This analysis shows to what extent the training policy of the

---

[122] It refers to "BDP Kadın Siyaset Okulu" in Turkish and "Dibistana Siyasetê ya Jinan a BDP' ê" in Kurdish.

party contributed to the development of women's political identity by raising their gender consciousness. In addition, a deep analysis of the school of politics for women, founded in 2008 in Diyarbakır, explains more about the reasons behind this new initiatives and its effect on the party members.

As it has pointed out the need to establish the School of Politics for Women emerged as result of various factors. One of these factors was the increasing number of women who joined the party lacked gender consciousness and were also not well informed politically in order to be influential actors. Secondly, female activists who have been involved in party politics for a long time and have become powerful within the party with the support of quota, co-chairship and assembly form of organization, pushed for such a formation. Thirdly, it is beneficial for the party to have politically conscious and well-informed political activists for reaching to the large masses. In this regard the below statements of the coordinator of the school, Mülkiye Birtane, clarified the idea and aims behind this formation and the pioneers who decided to establish it. According to her, women activists in powerful positions and the need of empowering women through a political education were determinant factors for the formation of the school. She said in the interview:

> Women played a big part in founding the school. Women who have experiences in politics for a long time; some of them elected representatives and some of them in administration positions in the party saw the need to raise consciousness among female activists; especially concerning gender consciousness, because most of female activists were not even aware of their rights as women. They needed to be informed in many areas; being aware inequality between genders, political rights, women rights, the party ideology and so on. As result of these concerns, women decided to found the School of Politics for Women (Personal interview Diyarbakır, August 2009).

Birtane stressed that the female activists in the party, DÖKH and women assemblies have played a role in establishing this school. In addition, she said that the necessities to extend the training programs that have been offered by the party until present and enhance the representation of women have pushed women to take action. Furthermore, the coordinator of the school, Birtane mentioned that the party also was supportive to open such a training centre for women. She stated that DTP (2005-2010), as a new party[123], considered fulfilling the society's expectations (that also refers to women's expectations from the party to take steps in favour of women). Thus it supported the establishment of the school. In addition, she underlined the influences of the Kurdish national movement in legal politics saying that the gender ideology of the national movement influenced the political party to be supportive in order to improve the status of women in pro-Kurdish politics. Besides, being the party with the highest percentage of female representatives in Turkey's politics it had to include more women through offering new applications in favour of women. She goes on:

> The party has implemented various works and training activities for its female members in different periods. But there was a need to have more organized and professional training. When all these (the reasons behind the party's support mentioned above) were incorporated there appeared a need to offer scientific training for which there was needed such schooling for women (Personal interview, Diyarbakır, August 2009).

There are also pragmatic reasons behind the party's support to open the school. As it will be mentioned below, among the courses of the school there is a focus on the party policy and ideology for instance. Well-trained women or party members will be able to transfer the party's ideologies and ideas to masses

---

[123] The DTP was considered to be the successor of the Democratic People's Party *(DEHAP)*. It was founded in 2005, as the merger of the DEHAP and the *Democratic Society Movement (DTH)*. DTH was founded by the veteran Kurdish politicians, former deputies Leyla Zana, Orhan Doğan, Hatip Dicle and Selim Sadak upon their release from prison in 2004. What made the party new was that it represented transformations in the tradition of pro-Kurdish party politics in many respects. For this research its gender policies are significant in creating differences in women's political representation. For a deep analysis of DTP see Şeref Kavak's published MA thesis. Şeref Kavak (2012) *Kurdish ethno-political transformation in Turkey: Democratic Society Party (DTP) experience (2005-2009): a pro-Kurdish party between ethnic & non-ethnic political agenda*. Saarbrücken: LAP: Lambert Academic Publishing.

effectively. The School of Politics for Women, which was founded to train female members of the party especially serves to convey messages to large masses and access to every segments of the society through well-informed women activists. As the research conducted during the election campaign of March 29, 2009 local elections indicated, this can be a very influential factor during the elections because a vast number of women are involved in the organisation of elections campaigns. They carry out elections campaigns of candidates, especially female candidates, in both national and local elections. In my observations during election campaigns of 2009 local elections, female activists take a significant role in access to female electors especially in rural areas of Kurdish region where male domination is highly visible and strict patriarchal norms are dominant. Both in rural and urban areas women activists who are well-informed, experienced and have effective communication abilities, are usually involved in mobilizing women electors through house visits and organizing meetings with them mostly at the party's local branches and encouraging them to participate in public meetings. In this regard, one of courses of the school which focuses on the effective communication trains to political activists how to be influential mobilizing actors which serves both women activists' gender identity based struggle and the party's aim of vote-maximization.

In addition, as it can be deduced from the name of the school, it only offers training for female activists and its training policy is not limited to political training such as the political ideology of the party. Birtane said that they have a training policy, which aims to enlighten women in every area. This approach certainly influences the political environment in the party in terms of creating gender consciousness among women activists, which is a determinant factor in questioning male domination in the political arena. This study will analyse who are the targets, who are the instructors, what kind of courses are offered and for how long and what are the teaching materials used in the school. Regarding the time period of training programs Birtane explained:

> We have short term, like 5 days, program. If there is a demand, we organize workshops. For instance, if a group of women want to train on a subject like philosophy we can organize a workshop about this subject. Moreover, there can be training programs for women who carry out organization works in neighbourhoods and those who take place in the party activities. These can be short one-day workshop, but if it is a comprehensive program, it is long term like 20-25 days (Personal interview, Diyarbakır, August 2009).

These courses are mainly for female activists involved in pro-Kurdish politics. Although they can join the training programs individually, however, training programs are mostly organized for group participation and they are tailored to their needs. This group-based organization is related to the women's organization form, which is based on assemblies. In this regard, Birtane noted:

> Our party's working style is based on assembly, which is an organization style within the structure of *Democratic Confederation*. For instance, the assembly organization on the base level starts from neighbourhood assembly, then namely district assembly and city assembly. Each has its members, representatives and spokespersons. There have to be training programs for female activists of these assemblies at all level. There is training for elected female activists. Then, there are training programs toward personnel of the party and individual female activists. Those who want to attend these programs have to make application (Personal interview, Diyarbakır, August 2009).

The coordinator of the school makes clear that the priority is given to the party personnel in the school's training programs. She continued:

> There are many women outside the party who have not taken place in the party activities but vote for the party want to join training programs. As I said at first we organize training programs to empower the female activists who take part in the party activities. However, in the future we intend to organize workshops for those who are not active in politics but have interest in our programs for personal development (Personal interview, Diyarbakır, August 2009).

As she noted, while there are training programs determined by the school, the school also arrange the programs in accordance with the female activists' demands. She said:

> Some of them especially group training programs are arranged on their request. We also have additional programs. We establish schools of politics in the places where our party has branches. We organize training programs in neighbourhoods. It would not be necessary to come the party building where the school is founded. I mean institutions can request for training programs for their members and our trainers will do training in their places (Personal interview, Diyarbakır, August 2009).

The subjects that are thought as part of training programs are significant in order to understand the role of the school in constructing the women's political identity. For instance, the approach towards ethnic identity and gender identity can be well figured through training subjects. At this respect, Birtane said:

> At first, it starts with an introduction about the importance of the training program, and then we want to know why they requested the training and we tell them why we prepared such a training program. There is a course related to Kurdish language. It aims to create language consciousness [this is one of main issues for the Kurdish national struggle]. It is one of a must courses in the training programs. On the other hand, we have lectures concerning method and style for effective communication for female activists who take part in political activities. Moreover, there is a course on the 'history of societies' focusing of women's history, which mainly emphasizes how women's position has changed historically. There are also for sure courses related to the party policy. But I can say that the courses, which specifically address women and women's issues such as gender inequality in the society and contribute to develop consciousness against gender inequality, take our priority (Personal interview, Diyarbakır, August 2009).

Basically, the training activities involve various courses covering discussion subjects such as history of societies, women's history, women and family issues, the party policy and ideology, Kurdish language, method and style for effective communication. There are many important points that can be raised regarding course subjects. Obviously these training courses address both national concerns and gender concerns. Women activists are trained in order to be strong political actors for their double struggle which meet objectives of both women's political movement and the Kurdish legal political struggle in general which has been primarily carried out by the pro-Kurdish political party since the 1990s. For instance, based on observations and statements of female activists involved in the training, it is evident that the language of instruction has been one of main concern of the director and the instructors. This reflects the national/ethnic concerns. In Birtane's words:

> Kurdish language has been banned in Turkey. The language of education is Turkish. Everything is in Turkish. Therefore many Kurds can't speak their language well. We carry out our lectures both in Kurdish and Turkish in order to make all participants to understand lectures because we do our lectures in an interactive manner, so that all participants can be involved in the discussions. In addition, we try to use both Kurdish dialects (Kurmanji and Zazaki). But we aim to teach only in Kurdish in the future. This can be possible if all our trainers and participants know their language well. For this, we will provide very intensive language course for all the party cadres and trainers (Personal interview, Diyarbakır, August 2009).

While the use of Kurdish language refers to national/ethnic concern, it also becomes a tool to communicate with women effectively. Since a considerable number of women still lack formal education, they cannot speak and understand Turkish well. Women can express themselves in their language easily especially they can explain their issues well and engage in debates during lectures as expressed by the instructors. Employing the Kurdish language as instruction language in training women shows that the language is considered as a tool to create both gender and ethnic identity consciousness among women activists.

As seen above, there is a wide range of subjects discussed in the training programs. Political, cultural matters and women issues are addressed during training but there is a point that the Kurdish national movement perspectives are quite dominant especially in the teaching material. This research revealed that most of this material comes from the ideological publications of the movement in particular from Öcalan's writings.

Another point is the profile of the trainers. The first distinctive point is about gender. While the background of trainers is varied, in terms of sex, they are predominantly female. On that matter Birtane confirmed:

> We give precedence to female trainers. We think if trainers are female participants feel more comfortable. In our observation during general works, we notice that female activists, especially in neighbourhoods and in districts can express themselves better in the presence of women. Those who have a long experience do not feel discomfort with male trainers but those who got involved in politics more recently, especially in the neighbourhoods, are the ones who participate more actively in lectures, join the discussions, ask questions and tell their opinions. Therefore, for now we prefer female activists in order to provide active involvements of participants during lectures and to have efficient training programs (Personal interview, Diyarbakır, August 2009).

Regarding the profile of trainers, she continued:

> They are chosen among those who have long-term experiences and are professional in their subjects. For example, if a female activist has been involved in politics for a long time she can be part of trainer groups and give lessons about politics in general as how to carry out political activities. In addition, if some has worked in women's units and dealt with gender issues and improved hers in the area of gender works this person can be capable to train in gender classes. In addition, we invite academics and experts in relevant subjects taught in school to participate in our training programs (Personal interview, Diyarbakır, August 2009).

During the fieldwork it was possible to attend a few classes and to observe the participants reactions and have an idea about courses, content and trainers. The participants were diverse in age, education and experiences. But the common point is the positive reaction of women to such service, which showed how women were ready to improve themselves. It also indicated their interest in politics, Kurdish struggle and gender issues. Birtane noted that such a school with the name 'for women' has generated excitement among them. They have received many applications both from inside and outside the party. There is a great interest during the lectures. She said:

> In respect to their education background female activists are differentiated from each other. The school has been founded recently so we have faced some problems in this sense. On one hand, there are uneducated participants on the other, there are university graduated. This creates difficulty during lectures because it affects the learning process of the participants (Personal interview, Diyarbakır, August 2009).

Offering training for women through the establishment of the BDP's School of politics for women primarily aims to construct and shape the political identity of female activists. Women activists who had already gained consciousness, whether this is about ethnic identity or gender identity, in a certain level however still need to enhance the level of consciousness and to expand their experiences in order to become influential political advocates of both their gender identity rights and national identity rights. Regarding its impact on feminization, training plays a crucial role in terms of creating female actors who question male domination and struggle for gender equality. Therefore these female activists who have already taken different roles in the party gain a consciousness to act for women's interests, which refer to substantive representation component of feminization.

While the school of politics can be regarded as a key institution for the feminisation of politics (through enhancing gender consciousness among female activists in particular, and encouraging them to act for women while fulfilling their political roles), it can also be regarded as an outcome of the feminization process of pro-Kurdish politics. Women who have already attained power at a certain level in the party, involved in decision making processes of the party, and have obtained positions in representation offices, want to be more professionalized through utilizing training facilities in order to reach their objectives at the desired level.

As seen above, these training programs also reflect an activity of sharing experiences and knowledge among female activities. The diverse profile of activists such as some of them work in women associations affiliated to the party, some work in pro-Kurdish media and some work in the women assemblies of the party and likewise the instructors who predominantly have been involved in pro-Kurdish politics for a long time are differentiated in personal and the areas of their political experiences their intellectual background. For instance, they share their experiences regarding men resistance they face and their strategies to deal with this. Another example: one of the instructors shared her experiences about her work during election campaigns and mobilization activities in the lecture about the effective communication. However, while internal training provides the opportunity for female activists to share their experiences and knowledge, female activists are also aware of the fact that, in order to enhance and share their experiences and deepen their knowledge, they need to be in contact and organize activities with different circles at both national and international level, which also bring forward the networking activities of female activists as one of substantial strategies to feminize the pro-Kurdish party politics.

Networking Activities

Kurds are spread over the world; not only Kurds from Turkey, Kurds from other parts of Kurdistan have left their homeland due to mainly political reasons. Fleeing abroad had massively occurred among politicized Kurds from Turkey in the 1980s and the

1990s. However, these Kurdish expatriates have continued their political activism in the countries such as Scandinavian and European countries[124]. They have established networks, organizations and institutions in these countries in order to mobilize Kurds, make the Kurdish cause known by the world's public opinion and provide support from the international organizations while keeping in constant contact with pro-Kurdish organisations in their home countries. Whether separately or within these organizations, many female activists act in the transnational Kurdish movement and carry out a struggle both for Kurdish rights and women issues. Today it is quite obvious that there is a transnational Kurdish women movement. In addition, the political activism of Kurdish women has been internationalising through the establishment of translational organizations and networks with international organizations. This international activism or internationalizing of Kurdish women's political activism has yielded significant results. However, the aim of this study is to analyse how network activities employed as an outsider strategy and international collaborations contribute to the political activism of women within the pro-Kurdish politics and thereby influencing the feminisation of pro-Kurdish party politics in Turkey. Networking activities of political movement of Kurdish women could be regarded as a strategy, which empowers women through presenting knowledge and experiences that they can use to develop their policies, projects and conduct activities for their benefit. More importantly, they can force the party to act in favour of women and they can implement policies and projects in the areas where they operate.

---

[124] For a detailed analysis of pro-Kurdish mobilization in Europe see Olivier Grojean (2011) "Bringing the Organization Back in: Pro-Kurdish Protest in Europe" in *Nationalisms and politics in Turkey: political Islam, Kemalism, and the Kurdish issue* (ed. by Marlies Casier and Joost Jongerden). Milton Park, Abingdon, Oxon, [England] ; New York : Routledge. P. 182-197

Obviously, female activists' network activities are not only on the international level. They have local and national collaborations as well. However, international based projects are more determining and influential. Primarily, they have contributed to the Kurdish women movement by integrating them with international women's movements and by enabling them to expand their experiences and knowledge. These contributions are very crucial because they enhance gender consciousness among female activists who become more concerned with substantive representation of women in the political area. National and international networking and collaborations are carried out with academics, politicians, political organizations and women's organizations in various countries such as Sweden, Germany, Belgium, Canada and Iraqi Kurdistan.

There have been a number of activities organized by female activists during the 2000s in particular, which illuminate how female activists are networking both at national and international levels and these networking activities have become a strategy to feminize politics. Some of these activities are examined in terms of their participants, discussion subjects and conclusions to find out what have been their impacts in the feminization process. In this regard, it is important to mention three conferences and their contributions to feminization of politics. The first one entitled "International Local Governments and Women Conference" was organized with the cooperation of Bağlar Municipality (Diyarbakır)[125], Rosa Luxemburg Foundation (Germany) and Centre for Social Research and Education [126] on the 3-4 May, 2008.

---

[125] An detailed analysis of the works of local governments running by female mayors will be made in the following chapter. The Bağlar municipality, which is governed by a female mayor will be included to the analysis as well.

[126] Toplumsal Araştırma ve Eğitim Merkezi (TAREM)

[127] The second one was the International Conference: "Towards Cities for Women" which was organized jointly by Diyarbakir Bağlar Municipality and Bağlar Women's Cooperative[128] on 5-6 February 2011, the third one entitled "women are creating a new life". These conferences which are organized with initiative of Bağlar municipality (Diyarbakır) to address local governments, local politics and women are good examples of these national and international co-operations to demonstrate women activists' connections with national and international associations, politicians, activists, academics and researchers. The profile of participants also shows the organisers' national and transnational networking efforts. Female MPs and mayors of pro-Kurdish political party, representatives of various women associations and non-profit organizations such as vice chairperson of Rosa Luxemburg Foundation, City Planning Expert (member of KA-DER)[129] Yıldız Tokman and the former mayor of Kreuzberg (Berlin/Germany) Cornelia Reinauer were some participants of the conference entitled the International "Local Governments and Women Conference". These activities contributed to enrich experiences and knowledge of women activists in political area and also provided Kurdish women movement to integrate with worldwide actors, organizations and institutions, which can be well understood when the discussion subjects and speeches of the participants are examined. All these

---

[127] "Yerel yönetimlerde kadın bakış açısı" 4 May 2008, http://www.emekdunyasi.net/ed/guncel/4700yerelyonetimlerde-kadin-bakis-acisi (Accessed 27 June 2011).

[128] Since 2004 the Bağlar municipality has been governed by a female mayor. From 2004 to 2009 Yurdusev Özsökmenler was mayor. After 2009 local elections Yüksel Baran was elected as mayor of Bağlar municipality.

[129] It stands for *Association for the Support and Training of Women Candidates* in English, *Kadın Adayları Destekleme ve Eğitme Derneği* in Turkish. It is founded in March 1997 with the aim of increasing the number of women in politics and in decision-making positions in order to achieve gender equality in politics. More information about the association can be obtained on http://www.kader.org.tr/en/index.php.

factors play a role in developing their movement, discourses and arguments to improve women's status.

Another activity, which is worth introducing is the First Kurdish Women Conference organized by DÖKH on the 24-25th of April 2010 in Diyarbakır.[130] The conference, which concentrated on "The Role of Woman in the Development of Democracy" aimed to bring together women from all part of Kurdistan (Turkey, Iran, Iraq and Syria) and other countries around the world. Although the majority of participants were Kurds, there was non-Kurd female participants as well. The participants consisted mainly of activists, academics, politicians and journalists. The significance of this conference is that it addressed the Kurdish women from four parts of Kurdistan in particular to create unity among women both their national rights and women rights. The focus of the conference were on social and political problems that Kurds have faced, the state policies that carry on the base of rejection and denial of national identity, the discriminations that Kurdish women have faced, their perspectives and struggle methods, the representation roles of women in the democratic struggle processes and the perspectives of overcoming sexism, and the women's methods to obtain democratic national solidarity.[131] This conference shows that female activists are aiming to strengthen their political struggle through cooperating with the Kurdish women in other parts of Kurdistan and the diaspora.

---

[130] Conference announcement text was with the name of Leyla Zana (The prize winner of Sakharov and the former MP of DEP and elected again in 2011 election as an independent candidate).
"Ulusal Kürt Kadın Konferansı 24-25 Nisan'da Diyarbakır'da", 23 April 2010,
http://bianet.org/kadin/bianet/121519-ulusal-kurt-kadin-konferansi-24-25-nisan-da-diyarbakir-da (Accessed on 01 July 2011).
"Diyarbakır'da Kürt Kadın Rönesansı!", 24 April 2010,
http://www.lekolin.org/news_detail.php?id=601 (Accessed on 12 June 2011)
[131] "Kürt Kadın Konferansından Barış İçin Dayanışma Çağrısı Çıktı"
http://www.bianet.org/bianet/siyaset/121585-kurt-kadin-konferansindan-baris-icin-dayanisma-cagrisi-cikti (Accessed on 22 June 2011).

The two above mentioned conferences organized with the initiative of Bağlar municipality are substantial in terms of their themes, discussion subjects and the speeches of the participants, which addressed to women's participation and representation in local politics and approached to local services from a women perspective. During the International Local Governments and Women Conference (3-4 May, 2008), whose slogan was "we are rewriting the future", the participants discussed the opportunities for women to participate in local governments. In the opening speech[132], the mayor of Bağlar municipality Yurdusev Özsökmenler emphasized that in the conference which brought together many women they share their experiences and they'll benefit from the conclusions that they will make end of the conference in order to be influential in the local elections[133]. She raised several issues concerning women and local politics. She underlined the low number of women in local governments, which influence the development of democracy at local level negatively. In this regard she stated:

> The rate of female mayor is 0.56 % and the rate of female assembly member is 2.37 %. The active participation of women in city governments is substantial due to the development of democracy from the local basis; in the sense of making the women's perspective dominant in local governments, which is democratic and rejects dominant hierarchical perspective.[134]

In addition, she notified that although many positive steps have been taken in Turkey and in the world to increase the number of women in politics, that it is not enough. She underlined:

> The equal number of women in politics is precisely an absolute must. However, it is not sufficient because, it is fundamental to come to power with

---
[132] "Uluslararası yerel yönetimler ve kadın konferansı yapıldı"
http://www.sendika.org/yazi.php?yazi_no=16888. (Accessed on 25 July 2011).
[133] She meant the next local elections, which was held on 29 March 2000.
[134] "Yerel yönetimlerde kadın bakış açısı", 4 May 2008,
http://www.emekdunyasi.net/ed/guncel/4700yerelyonetimlerde-kadin-bakis-acisi (Accessed on 27 June 2011).

> a woman perspective and with understanding of rejecting hierarchical and centrist view and governing the cities as such. When the budget is making how much men and women are going to benefit from it and for whom we are going to use it the question is if women do really have a plan. Thirdly, can we carry out horizontal organization both within the municipality and in the city, can we realize decentralization and can we achieve participation? These are important for us. [135]

As Özsökmenler recalled, other participants expressed the necessity of involvement of women in local politics, including woman perspective in the activities of local governments, enabling women to utilize local services and creating woman friendly cities in their speeches as well.

The significance of female perspective in local governments is underlined in the majority of speeches. In this regard, Stefanie Ehmsen[136] expressed: "Women in Diyarbakır have too many problems. But we have seen women here are very active and they have carried out substantial projects. This is a pleasing progression."[137] Furthermore, Kurdish MP Emine Ayna pointed to the importance of discussions in the conference in the sense of their contributions to achieve women's claim, 'we are rewriting the future' which is also the slogan of the conference. In addition, she highlighted:

> Creating woman perspective in the local governments is substantial for us. The most important feature of local government is to carry participatory democracy into effect. In other words, the basis, neighbourhood and village should participate in decisions and even they should have power to change them. We can develop women's perspective more according as this understanding is adopted. Women's participation will increase according as going down the local level. (...) We have carried out a struggle against gender inequality. Any party, any group has not discussed the subject of local governments and women as much as we have done."[138]

---

[135] "Yerel yönetimlerde kadın bakış açısı", 4 May 2008,
http://www.emekdunyasi.net/ed/guncel/4700yerelyonetimlerde-kadin-bakis-acisi
(Accessed on 27 June 2011).
[136] Vice chairperson of Rosa Luxemburg Foundation (Germany).
[137] "Yerel yönetimlerde kadın bakış açısı", 4 May 2008,
http://www.emekdunyasi.net/ed/guncel/4700yerelyonetimlerde-kadin-bakis-acisi
(Accessed on 27 June 2011).

[138] Ibid.

These quotes of Ayna reflect Kurdish female activists' approach towards local governments, which consider women's participation with their own perspective as crucial to create democratic local governments.

As previously stated, while the representation of women in the local politics in Turkey is generally low, Kurdish women representation is growing. The growing representation of Kurdish women in politics is also mentioned by some of the participants. Leyla Deniz who presented on the projects of Kurdish female activists and the formation and development processes of DÖKH stated that in the press organs the women in this region are brought to agenda mostly with backward values. However, this region with 8 MPs and 9 mayors is ahead of other regions. Additionally, concerning nomination of female candidates she noted that they regard the female candidates representing women from every section of the society when they nominate female candidates.[139] Similarly, in her speech Dr. Yıldız Tokman, member of KA-DER, presented the statistics regarding the numbers of women elected in the local governments. Tokman, who reported that there were 18 (9 of them elected from pro-Kurdish party) female mayors, stated this happened thanks to the female presence from the DTP.[140] Moreover, on account of solving the representation issue of women in local governments she suggested some actions. These are collecting statistical data based on sex difference, providing local services according to the needs of developing policies, solving the issues immigration and poverty, creating mentality change and awareness. Local women associations

---

[139] "Yerel yönetimlerde kadın bakış açısı", 4 May 2008, http://www.emekdunyasi.net/ed/guncel/4700yerelyonetimlerde-kadin-bakis-acisi (Accessed on 27 June 2011).

[140] Ibid.

should constantly monitor the activities of local governments and they should use all means for enforcing.[141] In addition, she suggested that the consideration of equal public service for everyone has not enabled women to benefit from local service equally. She added that a different local strategy is required in order for women benefit from urban services. Cities should be planned in the way being sensitive to gender. A woman friendly and egalitarian city is not imaginary; it is a synthesis of gender egalitarian local policies.[142]

As observed, the international participants make significant contributions in their discussions based on examples and experiences from their countries. They did not only make determinations regarding the situation of women in the local governments, they also produced ideas and shared their experiences in order to achieve the desired changes in the local politics. In this perspective, the former mayor of Kreuzberg Cornelia Reinauer who shared her experiences from Berlin - which is the only place where gender-based budget is implemented-, underlined that administrators should make their budget according to sex. She remarked that this is necessary in order to enable women to benefit from public services.[143]

Furthermore, Prof. Dr. Ramón Pérez, who is an academic at San Diego State University, made her speech in the context of 'women participation in the local governments and representation models' describing the women situation in Mexico.

---

[141] "Uluslararası yerel yönetimler ve kadın konferansı yapıldı", 7 May 2008,
http://www.sendika.org/yazi.php?yazi_no=16888 (Accessed on 25 July 2011).

"Yerel yönetimlerde kadın bakış açısı", 4 May 2008,
http://www.emekdunyasi.net/ed/guncel/4700-yerelyonetimlerde-kadin-bakis-acisi (Accessed on 27 June 2011).

[142] "Yerel yönetimlerde kadın bakış açısı", 4 May 2008,
http://www.emekdunyasi.net/ed/guncel/4700-yerelyonetimlerde-kadin-bakis-acisi (Accessed on 27 June 2011).

[143] "Uluslararası yerel yönetimler ve kadın konferansı yapıldı", 7 May 2008,
http://www.sendika.org/yazi.php?yazi_no=16888 (Accessed on 25 July 2011).

Peréz underlined that women in Mexico have faced various problems due to the decentralized regime, immigration, poverty and traditions. She noted that these issues share similarities with the situation of women in Turkey.[144]

In comparison to the above-mentioned example the second example of women's networking efforts has a specific concern. The aforesaid conference addressed women and local government in general however the conference which is entitled The International Conference "Towards Cities for Women (5-6 February 2011, Diyarbakir) focused on the theme "women are creating a new life". The call for papers stated that "this conference aims at providing an opportunity for various social groups including women's organizations, leaders, local, national and international administrations, academic and non-academic researchers to communicate, work together and mobilize along universal principles with the goal of creating free, democratic and gender emancipatory urban environments."[145] Basically, it addressed two main topics: how cities should be for women and in what kind of cities should women live in. In this sense, the wide range of participants made significant speeches, which reflect different ideas and suggestions regarding women, urban life and local governments.

As the participants' statements exposed, these events are not only considered by the Kurdish female activists as the opportunities for setting co-operations, sharing experiences, learning from experiences of participants and obtaining new ideas for creating democratic and liveable cities for women. The participants regard these

---

[144] "Uluslararası yerel yönetimler ve kadın konferansı yapıldı", 7 May 2008, http://www.sendika.org/yazi.php?yazi_no=16888 (Accessed on 25 July 2011).

[145] "International Conference: Towards Cities for Women", 5 February 2011, http://womenandhumansettlements.org/events/conference-towards-cities-women-diyarbakir-turkey-5-6-february-2011/ (Accessed on 19 March 2011).

"Conference 'Towards Cities for Women'"–Diyarbakir, Turkey 5-6 February 2011, http://womenandhumansettlements.org/events/conference-towards-cities-women-diyarbakir-turkey-5-6-february-2011/ (Accessed on 19 March 2011).

events from a similar perspective. For instance, one of participants Fatma Jaffer from British Columbia University stated there were two purposes for her to attend the conference. She said:

> The first reason is international solidarity. I will write about what I have experienced here. Secondly, it is actually main reason, we came here; we will organize a conference under the name of 'transformation in cities' in Vancouver. And we want to determine women from there that attend this conference. We invite women here to Vancouver. We do not want to stop here. We want to maintain dialogues through these kinds of conferences. We want to sustain our relations with women here. . We become stronger in our local areas according as we provide solidarity here because each of us carries on struggle in our locales areas. If we establish a wide network of solidarity here we would be more powerful in our struggle in our local.[146]

In addition, she expressed her observations concerning the Kurdish women movement in Turkey, which are significant to understand Kurdish female activists' efforts to feminize politics. Jaffer stated:

> Kurdish women movement has taken root within the Kurdish struggle for self-determination and it has expanded as part of this root. This is the source of its mobilization and dynamism. It does not only struggle on gender issues. It struggles for a total social change and transformation. That is why there is not fragmentation. It becomes integrative. Kurdish women movement does not proclaim that it just deals with gender side of problem. It approaches gender issue with other problems of the society. This is the origin of the movement's dynamism and power.[147]

Various issues were discussed by the participants in the context women and cities such as the exclusion of women from city life and local governments' services. Besides they share their ideas and experiences to overcome these issues and to create women friendly cities. From this standpoint, Prof. Dr Nermin Abadan Unat,

---

[146] "Conference 'Towards Cities for Women'–Diyarbakir," Turkey 5-6 February 2011, http://womenandhumansettlements.org/events/conference-towards-cities-women-diyarbakir-turkey-5-6-february-2011/ (Accessed on 19 March 2011).

"Kürt kadını toplumsal değişimi esas almalı", 5 February 2011, http://www.yuksekovahaber.com/yazdir/haber/haber/kurt-kadini-topglumsal-degisimi-esas-almali-45693.htm (Accessed on 16 February 2011).

[147] "Kürt kadın hareketi bütünleştirici". 7 February 2011, http://www.yeniozgurpolitika.org/?bolum=haber&hid=67650 (Accessed on 20 February 2011).

asserted that the discrimination starts in the cities and that "the urbanization is putting the women into prison". She went on saying, "in rural area, woman and man can work side by side but in the cities we see that the discrimination creates divisions. The discrimination starts in the cities." Then, she claimed that the change is possible with feminist philosophy: "Here, in Bağlar Municipality I saw two girls in the library. They were preparing for the university and they were determinate. I will sacrifice myself for a determinate person. Because she knows what to she will do. We will sacrifice ourselves for feminist politics."[148] Furthermore, some participants told about their experiences and implementations in their countries and about what improved the situation of women in politics as well as their life in the cities. Prabha Khosla, the city planner of the Canada Toronto City Woman Alliance, talked about her experiences and the politics applied in Philippines' Naga city. She informed that 'Enforcement Regulation' and 'The Development Code of the Women' are prepared in a way, which will be applied even though the governments will change. There is a mechanism, which is constantly supervising the application. In addition, she mentioned that 10% of the city budget is spent on projects determined by the Woman Council.[149] Another participant from Brazil, Emile Kosta, drew attention to the importance of quota. She informed that they work approximately with 200 municipalities and that they try to apply gender quota in the projects they support. She also stated that in 1999 in the constitution, against centralization, the

---

[148] İrfan Uçar "Unat: Kentleşme Kadını Hapse Sokmaktır", 7 February 2011, http://bianet.org/bianet/toplum/127710-unat-kentlesme-kadini-hapse-sokmaktir (Accessed on 10 February 2011).
"Urbanization is Putting the Women into Prison", 15 February 2011,
http://www.umut.org.tr/en/printpage.aspx?id=23578 (Accessed on 20 February 2011).

[149] İrfan Uçar "Unat: Kentleşme Kadını Hapse Sokmaktır" 7 February 2011, http://bianet.org/bianet/toplum/127710-unat-kentlesme-kadini-hapse-sokmaktir (Accessed on 10 February 2011).

responsibility for primary education was given to municipalities, thus participation was guaranteed as turned into a policy. In Brazil women participate in the budget meetings by 57% rate; women set the budget.[150] Regarding the implementation of quota, in her presentation on behalf of the BDP Local Governments Commission members and the Democratic Free Woman Movement, Gülay Calap said that they try to ensure the existence of women in the political life with a 40% quota. She added:

> We try to strengthen the representation of women. Our struggle is for reaching to a representation level, which serves to gender equality and freedom. We, women have made a significant headway in local governments for the third period. In 1999, out 37 mayors only 3, in 2004 out of 57 only 9 and in 2009 out 98 mayors only 14 of them are women.[151]

The profile of the participants and their speeches indicate that these above mentioned conferences which focused on women's participation and representation in local governments and women's exclusion from urban life and ways to struggle against issues women face in the local level best present the picture of sharing knowledge, experiences and suggestions between representatives from various national and international women associations and foundations. In addition, as participants' speeches prove, these types of conferences enable circulation of ideas regarding the role of women in improving and democratizing local governance by increasing their participation and representation.

In comparison to these two conferences the First International Kurdish Women Conference, which brought Kurdish women especially together from different countries regarding its concern on women's participation and representation

---

[150] Ibid.

[151] Ibid.

in politics remained weak. The conference, which drew great attention on Kurdish women from various countries (because it was the first international conference devoted to Kurdish women), addressed both Kurdish women's gender and national issues. Although the focus of discussions was on women issues and their struggle, debates regarding the unification of Kurds and Kurdish national rights also took place during the conference. During the conference the participants underlined their role in providing unity among Kurds and creating democratic national solidarity. While this indicates that they were not only concerned with women issues on the other hand, the mixture of gender and national concerns in the conference led to a less discussions about Kurdish women's situation and issues.

Alongside of those activities, mentioned above, organized by female activists in the country which are regarded as networking activities contributing to expand the experiences of elected female activists, the activities organized by female activists abroad are also considered as the transnational extension of the Kurdish women' political movement. In addition, the international activities that female activists are participated in are taken into account in this context. From this standpoint, some examples of these activities are examined in order to have an idea how these activities are contributing to the female activists' networking. Besides, this examination will reveal the aims behind organizing these activities and who organizes and who participates in. This analysis will expose the connections of women outside Turkey with the Kurdish women's movement in Turkey.

In order to show the level of internationalization of Kurdish women activism, this study presents the examples of activities organised in Europe. In this sense,

Zilan[152] *Festival* which has been organized every year since 2004 in Germany is a good example to show the links and parallelisms with the Kurdish women's struggle in particular and pro-Kurdish struggle in general in Turkey. The *Zilan Women Festival* was organized first in 2004 in Dortmund (Germany) by the Cenî-Kurdish Women Peace Office [Cenî-Kürt Kadın Barış Bürosu] and the Solidarity Initiative with Leyla Zana [Leyla Zana İle Dayanışma İnisiyatifi] as the first Kurdish women festival. The festival entitled 'women who cut across are coming together'[153] aimed to bring together women from various regions such as Africa, Latin America, Kurdistan, Turkey, Europe, Afghanistan and India. The organization committee underlined that it was not enough to meet only with Kurd, but it emphasized the need of meeting women from all over the world. In addition, they invited women from different professions such as writers, politicians, artists and sculptors; but regarding the connections between female activists in Turkey and outside Turkey two names that participated in the festival are worth to be mentioned due to their political role, the administrator of DEHAP Women Branch Gülbahar Gündüz and the mayor of Dersim (Tunceli) Municipality Songül Erol Abdil.[154]

The theme of the festival every year and the profile of participants correspond to the female activists' agenda and women reflect the relations with female women activists in the country. This festival organized by Kurdish women in European countries has a different agenda every year. Whereas the second one (June 2005) theme was 'Women want to justice and peace for a democratic and ecological

---

[152] She was a female guerrilla who committed a suicide bombing against soldiers who were performing flag raising ceremony in the centre of the city of Dersim (Tunceli) in June 30th, 1996. Her real name is Zeynep Kınacı.
[153] The festival theme in Turkish is "Sınırlarını Aşan Kadınlar Buluşuyor".
[154] "İlk Kürt kadın festivali 10 Temmuz'da Dortmund'da", http://www.rojaciwan.com/haber-755.html. (Accessed on 18 July 2011).

world'[155] the Third international Zilan woman festival was entitled 'Against war and against all forms of violence.'[156] In its fourth year in June 2007 the festival was organized under the slogan of 'woman is life; don't kill the life'.[157] The fifth year festival focused on the 'we are not honour of anyone; our honour is our freedom'.[158] On June 2010, the sixth of this festival took a stand against rape culture, which is considered as one of issues women face all over the world, and its slogan was 'promoting the struggle of freedom'.[159] As seen the struggle that women activists has carried for both national rights and women rights manifested in the slogan of the festival. For instance, women activists' campaigns against violence towards women under the name of honour and their slogans were used by the festival organizers as well.

In 2011 it was organized as the 7th International Zilan Woman Festival.[160] The slogan of the festival was announced as 'Overcome the Rape Culture Together/ No Woman Massacre.'[161] Considering the slogan and theme of the festival in each year pointed out the fact that they show parallelism with the activities and campaigns carried by female activists in Turkey. For instance, the campaign of "No Woman Massacre" was led by female activists of DÖKH on 8 March 2011.[162] The organization committee called women from every part of the world to come together to give a common woman perspective concerning 'peace, freedom and democracy',

---

[155] In Turkish it refers to "Demokratik ve Ekolojik Bir Dünya İçin Kadınlar Adalet ve Barış İstiyor".
[156] The slogan in Turkish is "Savaşa ve her türlü şiddete karşı".
[157] The slogan in Kurdish and Turkish refers to "Jin Jiyan e Jiyanê Nekuje- Kadın Yaşamdır Yaşamı Öldürme".
[158] "Kimsenin namusu değiliz, namusumuz özgürlüğümüzdür".
[159] İsmet Geleç "Kürt kadınları 7.Kez buluşuyor", 9 June 2011,
http://www.yeniozgurpolitika.org/arsiv/?bolum=haber&hid=71120 (Accessed on 15 June 2011).
[160] "Kürt kadınları Dortmund'da buluşuyor"
http://www.firatnews.tv/index.php?rupel=nuce&nuceID=44669
İsmet Geleç "Kürt kadınları 7.Kez buluşuyor", 9 June 2011,
http://www.yeniozgurpolitika.org/arsiv/?bolum=haber&hid=71120 (Accessed on 15 June 2011).

[161] In Turkish it refers to "Tecavüz Kültürünü Birlikte Aşalım/ Kadın Kırımına Hayır".
[162] "Kadın kırımına hayır' kampanyası yeniden canlanıyor"
http://www.durushaber.com/news_detail.php?news=5989 (Accessed on 5 July 2012).

specifying that the festival is a communion space for women. Moreover, the drafting committee of the festival expressed in its written statement that while Kurdish women have made a social revolution in Kurdistan they also pioneered the development of democracy culture against the dominant massacre mentality in Turkey. The committee who mentioned that, neither life nor politics would not be possible without women requested women's presence would be more stronger after June 12, 2011 national elections. It is underlined that because Kurdish women have achieved to be the driving force of freedom not only in Turkey, in the Middle East too conveying new democracy and work culture to society with co-presidency system which was developed under the leadership of them, their participation in political parties, becoming the voice of the peoples and their positive distinction in the area of social service in the municipalities. As it is understood, the drafting committee of the festival are very much involved in political issues of Kurdish women in Turkey. They demonstrated they have strong ideological connections with the female activists in Turkey in their messages. Their call for supporting the Labour, Peace and Democracy Block in which pro-Kurdish party took part in the June 12, 2011 national elections displayed their interest in pro-Kurdish politics in general and women's involvement in politics in particular. They call all women whether Kurdish or not to support the candidates of the block but female candidates first.[163]

The most important point about all these activities whether inside Turkey or outside is that Kurdish women have gained awareness of their condition as women and they managed, by networking with other women and confronting their experiences, to influence political institutions. Being in contact with other female

---

[163] "Kürt kadınları Dortmund'da buluşuyor",
http://www.firatnews.tv/index.php?rupel=nuce&nuceID=44669 (Accessed on 19 July 2011).
İsmet Geleç "Kürt kadınları 7.Kez buluşuyor" ,9 June 2011,
http://www.yeniozgurpolitika.org/arsiv/?bolum=haber&hid=71120 (Accessed on 15 June 2011).

activists, groups and associations they became aware of new developments and policies as two conferences organized with initiative Bağlar municipality. From this point of view, these activities have played a part in encouraging women to struggle for making changes in politics in favour of women.

Conclusion

This chapter revealed a number of strategies utilized by the pro-Kurdish political parties and female political activists that make possible the feminization of pro-Kurdish politics. The strategies examined were: the change of form of intra-party women's organizations (Commissions- Branches- Assemblies), the expansion of autonomous women's organization through the DÖKH, the implementation of the quotas, equal participation in leadership positions (co-chairship), training (the School of Politics for Women) and networking activities. This chapter demonstrated that all these strategies have contributed to feminization of pro-Kurdish politics in different ways. Among these, insider strategies have made very observable changes in favour of women. For instance, the quotas as equality guarantee strategies are found very influential in terms of changing gender composition in pro-Kurdish politics in a short time. Another strategy, which also differentiated pro-Kurdish party from other political parties in Turkey, is the co-presidency system. It has created a very significant change in the gender composition of administration positions, which are very difficult to access for women since politics and political institutions are male dominated.

As an outsider strategy, the role of the DÖKH, which is a feminist establishment founded in 2003 and concerned primarily with gender inequality issues of Kurdish women - is very significant in the feminization of pro-Kurdish politics. The DÖKH, which is an establishment outside the political party has direct influence in the party's processes because of the party's female members and women's assemblies being the main components of the DÖKH. As found out, since the establishment of the DÖKH in 2003 the activities of female political activists are organized under the name of the DÖKH. In this connection, the struggle of female political activists for achieving equal political representation corresponds to Lovenduski's finding: "[if it is assumed] sustained and substantial increases in the numbers of women representatives are necessary to the feminization of politics then insider strategies are essential. However, insider strategies work better when an autonomous women's movement is present in the system and active on the issue" (Lovenduski, 2005: 88). Thus, employing these insider strategies through autonomous organization of the DÖKH has been influential to increase women's descriptive and substantive representations in pro-Kurdish politics since the beginning of the 2000s. In this sense, the Kurdish case might be a good example for women's advocates who carry on a struggle for increasing women's political representation.

The following chapter concentrates on the implications and indications of feminization in Kurdish context through the analysis of political roles and acts of elected female representatives.

CHAPTER SIX

The Feminization of Politics in Practice

Introduction: Make a difference in (pro-Kurdish) Politics?

The arguments presented until now have focused almost entirely on how to equalize of women's political representation in pro-Kurdish politics, or on how the equal representation of women in pro-Kurdish politics has been promoted. As it has been pointed out earlier, the descriptive representation of women has significantly been increasing in pro-Kurdish politics. The question that remains to be answered is what difference women representatives have made in pro-Kurdish politics since then. In this regard, this chapter assesses whether descriptive representation links to women's substantive representation (attention to women's interests in debate, policy making, and in legislation). This chapter mainly aims to answer the question regarding results of the actors' efforts in pushing for feminization and can give new insights on what feminization actually is/does.

Although the research conducted with female political activists explored to what extent they consider themselves as representatives of women and asserting that they act to represent women's interests in representation bodies, the analysis in this chapter also focuses on the extent to which their descriptive representation affects their substantive representation. This analysis will present evidences that female officeholders are likely to act for women or women's interests throughout the policymaking process and beyond. This research will establish a clear, empirical link between women's descriptive and substantive representation by exploring what difference does the increasing numbers of women elected to public office make.

More clearly, to what it can be stated that the increasing numbers of women in public office mean that women's political interests, concerns, needs, preferences, and perspectives are better represented. In this analysis, substantive representation is conceptualized as truly giving voice to the experiences of women constituents in representative bodies by female representatives. This chapter examines the links between gender and representative roles relying on empirical data obtained from research conducted with female representatives. That is, the effect of gender on the expression of women's interests is scrutinized in the examination that follows.

As mentioned in the first chapter, the concept of *feminizing politics* was employed referring to Lovenduski's work (2005). Two dimensions of feminization which Lovenduski's definition put forward are descriptive representation, analysed in the previous chapters and substantive representation which is explored in this chapter. While descriptive representation referring to the numerical presence of women that has been remarkably increasing in pro-Kurdish politics, substantive representation refers to women's participation in decision-making with their ideas and perspectives in favour of women.

According to Lovenduski, feminizing politics is like many other political processes according to which *"if feminization is a cause of change, it is also a result of it"* (2005: 180). This statement indicates that while on one hand the roles and acts of elected women are regarded as the results of the feminization, on the other hand, they also contribute to the increasing presence of women in politics. In addition, practices and discourses of female political activists indicate that women's efforts in the political arena go beyond the achieving of equality of women's representation. It can be stated rather that they aim to transform gender relations in society at large. In other words, as this research indicates, in the Kurdish case the process of feminization has been multifaceted and comprehensive due to its specific conditions. As mentioned in Chapter 3, Kurdish women's political activism continued to emerge in the 1990s when they joined pro-Kurdish political party since the beginning of 1990s through mobilization under the influence of Kurdish national movement around national rights struggle. Their dual experience of oppression due to ethnic identity and gender identity determines their interests and understanding of feminization. Especially the experience of oppression due to belonging to a traditional patriarchal society has urged women representatives to make efforts to create a society that is egalitarian with respect to gender. In this respect, while the focus is on the transformations in politics in favour of women and on its effects, its reflections and intentions go beyond politics. The efforts of female activists such as their political acts, roles and works, their projects, campaigns, and policies addressed women's demands, needs, and interests, aiming to make structural changes in society through making changes in the existing political system. In fact, a new society, which is democratic and gender egalitarian, is aimed to be created by female political activists. In order to achieve this goal female activists employ their works to raise gender consciousness, improve women's lives and empower women in the society, eliminating gendered structures and male domination in every realm of life. These are focused in order to reveal what female representatives do on the ground to feminize politics for the purpose of creating a gender egalitarian society at large. Thus, the following sections will concentrate on substantive representation of women to demonstrate if feminization is happening. Since the following analyses focus on women representatives' works, activities and roles in the representation offices in the context of substantive representation in order to demonstrate if pro-

Kurdish politics has been feminizing, it is necessary to remember to which criteria substantive representation refers.

As explained in the first chapter, there are a number of definitions of substantive representation by different scholars. Among these the Pitkin's definition presents some aspects that are relevant to be mentioned for below analysis. Substantive representation, which is defined as "acting in the interest of the represented in a manner responsive to them" by Pitkin (1972: 209), introduces such elements concerning women's substantive representation. Firstly, this definition explains that substantive representation is about representative acts. Secondly, the outcomes of these representative acts should be in the interest of the represented; in this case, it is women. Lastly, the representatives should be responsive to those they represent. In short, Pitkin's definition presents that female citizens and their interests are central to representative process (Celis, 2009). In this respect, in Kurdish context, the following analysis explores that what 'substantive representation of women' actually is at first; what is it that is represented, 'women's interests', and what are they. These points are taken into account in order to determine to what extent substantive representation is achieved through women representatives' political acts and roles. Therefore, the analysis of behaviour, acts, experiences, roles and accomplishments of women in pro-Kurdish politics demonstrate that to what extent feminization is occurring and what feminization actually means on the ground.

Substantive representation in this study is regarded as the representation of women's interests and inclusion with their own ideas and perspectives into political decision-making. Thus, the concept of women's interests, which was elucidated in the first chapter, is also worth to be mentioned in this chapter briefly. Although there are several debates concerning what women's interests are, one classification, which can contribute importantly to this analysis of the Kurdish case, belongs to Maxine Molyneux (1985) who coined the concepts of practical and strategic gender interests. Practical gender interests are those needs which are formulated from the concrete conditions women experience in their engendered position within the sexual division of labour which derives from their practical gender interests for human survival (Moser 1989:1803). According to Molyneux, the 'practical gender interests are given inductively and arise from the concrete conditions of women's positioning by virtue of the gender division of labour and are usually a response to an immediate perceived need' (Molyneux (1985: 233). They do not generally involve a strategic goal such as 'women's emancipation' or 'gender equality'. She also added that they cannot themselves challenge the prevailing forms of gender subordination, even though they arise directly out of them. On the contrary, according to Molyneux, the 'strategic gender interests' derive from 'an analysis of women's subordination and from the formulation of an alternative, more satisfactory set of arrangements' (1985: 232). They are formulated from the analysis of women's subordination to men. They focus on the fundamental issues related to women's/men's subordination and gender inequities. 'The demands that are formulated on this basis are usually termed 'feminist' as is the level of consciousness required to struggle effectively for them' (1985: 233). In addition, Moser (1989: 1803) added that women's subordination varies depending on the cultural and socio-political context within which they are formulated. Therefore, gender strategic interests are contextual. These theoretical approaches regarding women's interests enable us to contextualize the interests of female political activists in pro-Kurdish politics in order to analyse what feminization refers to in the Kurdish context.

Substantive representation is mostly examined within parliamentary representation. Regarding parliamentary representation, many scholars have analysed, legislation that meets women's needs, interests and demands as the key element of substantive representation. It is legislation more than any other parliamentary activity that affects the lives of female citizens both directly and indirectly. In addition, legislation is also considered a more intensive form of substantive representation (Kathlene, 2001; Swers, 2002; Tamerius, 1995). However, this research does not only regard women's substantive representation in the parliament. It also addresses women's substantive representation in local governments and the party as well but in the sense of the influence of women's increasing representation of women's interests in the party on women representatives to improve women's substantive representation in the parliament and local governments. Since women representatives are members of the same party, their roles and acts in all of these areas (the parliament, local governments and the party) are interconnected and influence each other as show in the following analyses.

In order to explore the extent to which that female political activists act to represent the interests of the represented (women) through analysing political roles, actions, perspectives, attitude and discourses of female representatives, the following section focuses on political arenas where substantive representation takes place and women representatives in these arenas.

Practice of Politics: Women Activists in Offices

This section focuses on significant characteristics of women representatives, which contribute to the enhancing representation of women's interests in representative institutions. It is pointed out that descriptive representation (the women's presence) has been increased in both parliament and local governments since the end of 1990s in parallel with the growth participation and political power of women in the party.

After Leyla Zana, the first female Kurdish representative elected to parliament in 1991, Kurdish women elected to representative institutions in 1999 local elections. That is, Kurdish women's presence and visibility both in national politics and in the local governments have become notable since the end of 1990s. Kurdish women's representation in national politics significantly changed in the 2007 national elections, when 8 female MPs were elected out of 21 from the pro-Kurdish party (DTP). In addition, in the most recent elections on June 12, 2011, the numbers rose to 12, bringing a total number to 35. Women were elected to local governments in 1999 for the first time as well. There were four female mayors elected from pro-Kurdish party (HADEP). While there were only nine female mayors elected from the pro-Kurdish party (HADEP) in 2004, their numbers increased to 14 in 2009. A total of 18 women were in charge of the mayorships in Turkey at that time. As many female political activists and the party administrators mentioned, the number of women activists in the administration of the party has considerably increased as well. This indicates that Kurdish women have started to have positions in representation offices for more than a decade.

The significant point about women's representation is that in contrast to the general tendency in Turkey where women participate more in national politics rather than in local politics, as the numbers of elected representatives indicates, in pro-Kurdish politics women's participation in local politics is considerably higher. Regarding the poor representation of women in local governments, İlknur Üstün, chairperson of the Ankara branch of KA-DER[164] stated that, *"Usually in the world, it is just the opposite. Women are represented more in local politics compared to national. But in Turkey the situation is different. Local administrations, due to regulations of the Constitution, were turned into a sort of rant arena and a place where economic power comes from. Men usually do not want to share this arena with women."* [165] In the Kurdish case, women's representation in local politics is connected to the Kurdish political struggle, which focuses on obtaining Kurdish national rights through self-governance in Kurdish region from the beginning of 2000s, formulated under the political project of *Democratic Autonomy*. The political struggle for achieving self-governance has urged women's participation in local governments. The growth of participation in local governments has processed to development of a gender-egalitarian approach by women activists, which prioritizes representation of women's interests in local governments.

As the research points out there have been significant numbers of women in pro-Kurdish politics elected to representation bodies and also, as will be seen below, these female representatives have been acting for representing women's interests in political arena. These female representatives who have contributed to improve substantive representation have close ties with the women's movement and some female political activists during interviews mentioned about their relations with

---

[164] It stands for *Kadın Adayları Destekleme Derneği* in Turkish and *Association for the Support of Women Candidates* in English. KA.DER, which is founded in March 1997 aims to increase the number of women in politics and in decision-making positions so as to achieve equal representation of women and men. More information can be obtained on http://www.ka-der.org.tr/en/index.php.

[165] Ayşe Karabat, "Women face more difficulties in local polls than general elections", *Zaman*, 5 April 2009, http://www.todayszaman.com/tz-web/detaylar.do?load=detay&link=171521 (Accessed on 16 December 2012).

Turkish feminist groups in 1980s and 1990s. The profile of female representatives indicates that, although they are involved in all the party's activities, they had mainly gained political experiences through women's organizations and by being involved in women's works. Their political engagement through the party's women's organizations have made them to become aware of and to be more experienced about women's interests, demands and concerns in order to represent them substantially. As chapter 5 explained the party's women's organizations, which contribute to mobilize women in political arena and provide space for women to gain political experiences regarding both national identity rights and women's rights, are employed by female political activists to negotiate for improving women's status in the party. Besides, female representatives are still members of the Kurdish women's movement organized under the umbrella of DÖKH (Democratic Free Women Movement- *Demokratik Özgür Kadın Hareketi*). In this sense, women representatives can be identified with what Suzanne Dovi (2002) would label 'preferable descriptive representatives'. According to Dovi (2002), not every woman can represent women's interests in representative offices. Regarding the link between women's descriptive and substantive representation, Suzanne Dovi (2002) asks the question that will 'any woman' representative do. Her answer is no. Instead, it is important to specify criteria for selecting 'preferable group representatives', who she defines as those who experience a "reciprocated sense of having [their]... fate linked" with other women. They should also have "strong mutual relationships with dispossessed subgroups". Through these connections, preferable female representatives should reach out to, and participate in social networks with, dispossessed subgroups of women (Dovi, 2002: 729, 736). The point here is that whom the representatives know and interact with is an important dimension of 'good' 'acting for' representation (Dovi, 2002: 736). Similarly, Young (2002: 128) describes the representative connected to the represented in determinate ways. Women representatives in pro-Kurdish politics are supported by the women's movement on the purpose of encouraging them to act for the interests of women in representative institutions. Therefore, women representatives who have mostly experienced within the women's movement are bounded to cooperate with the movement that supported them.

Furthermore, there is a significant body of research that shows that female politicians are more likely than their male colleagues to be supportive of women's interests and concerns (Carrol, 1985; Duerst-Lahti and Kelly, 1995; Haavio-Mannila et al., 1985; Vallance and Davies, 1986). This suggests that men and women have different values and priorities, which reflect their political acts. In this research, it is pointed out that female representatives regard women's interests and issues as their primary tasks, which can be observed at their works in representation offices. Although they expressed their commitment to represent women's interests, depending on the representation bodies they are elected for and their positions in these representation bodies their political acts and roles concerning women's interests are differentiated. In this regard, the following section concentrates on finding out what change women representatives have made in pro-Kurdish parliamentary representation in favour of women.

Feminizing the Parliamentary Politics

This section attempts to find answer to the question as to what difference Kurdish female parliamentarians have made in pro-Kurdish parliamentary politics in terms of representing women's interests. It primarily addresses what those women do in office to act for women. In this respect, this section asserts parliamentary politics of pro-Kurdish party is feminizing on the basis of the impacts that women parliamentarians have made in the parliamentary politics of pro-Kurdish party. Examining to what extent women's interests are represented, their influences on representative process, organizational culture, the difference they have made in women's roles and tasks in the parliamentary representation illuminate their contribution in feminizing politics both in the context of parliamentary politics of the pro-Kurdish party in particular and of Turkey in general. The research demonstrates that Kurdish female representatives have had significant impacts through their parliamentary roles and acts in the sense of raising women's issues and introducing women's perspectives in the legislation process and creating a new female political image in Turkey. It is not realistic to expect pro-Kurdish women representatives as a small group to have a major impact on the policy making process in the parliament, but they have been influential to raise attention and to bring women's issues into the political agenda and challenging male domination in parliamentary representation. Two female MPs (Istanbul Deputy Sebahat Tuncel and Diyarbakır Deputy Gültan Kışanak) interviewed during the fieldwork mentioned that, because of their small number and of the lack of cooperation with female MPs from other political parties in the parliament, their impact is limited in the legislative process. However, female deputy Sebahat Tuncel, regarding importance and the contributions of being in the parliament in terms of making changes in women's lives in Turkey stated: "The Parliament has the following significance: Laws are passed there, and this is affecting our life. Therefore it is important to enter there (the Parliament) as women."

166 These statements of Tuncel demonstrate that female representatives are aware of importance of being there as women to influence legislative processes and to introduce women's perspectives through parliamentary actions.

Through an examination of the parliamentary records it is clear that female representative regulate legislative processes and influence parliamentary agenda by carrying a number of representation actions such as offering law proposal, giving parliamentary questions and research proposal, and making parliamentary speeches regarding women's issues. These parliamentary works contribute to raising awareness of women issues and bring women's issues into the political agenda. Besides, they sometimes become successful in shaping laws for the benefit of women. The same parliamentary records show that they have been effectively raising women's issues whether individual cases or common issues women face in different areas. The analysis of female deputies' parliamentary works since 2007 when the pro-Kurdish party (DTP) managed to enter the parliament with 21 MPs and 8 of them were women, confirms the argument that they act for women's interests. In addition, the parliamentary records of MP's parliamentary works demonstrated that the numbers of parliamentary actions that female MPs have taken concerning women's issues is more than male MPs.

From 2007 to 2011 (23rd legislative term) there were about 250 parliamentary research proposals[167] presented by pro-Kurdish party lawmakers and at least 15 of them concerning women's issues. Out of 15 parliamentary research proposals three

---

[166] Esra Aşan and Seda Saluk, "Kadınlar, Siyaset ve Genel Seçimler Üzerine Sebahat Tuncel ile Söyleşi", *Feminisite.net,* June 2011,
http://www.feminisite.net/news.php?act=details&nid=878 (Accessed on 25 September 2012).

[167] It is one of parliamentary acts aims to get information on specific subject through making a parliamentary inquiry to be launched in the Parliament. Detailed information about parliamentary inquiry and parliamentary research proposal is available at Turkish Grand National Assembly (Türkiye Büyük Millet Meclisi/ TBMM)'s website, visit
http://www.tbmm.gov.tr/yayinlar/Yasama_El%20Kitabi.pdf. (Accessed on 20 March 2013).

of them were given by male lawmakers.[168] These research proposals addressed issues such as violence against women, gender-based discrimination, sexual abuse, child marriages, discriminatory and sexist approaches against women in the media, discriminatory practices faced by women in working life, gender sensitivity in education, female employment issues, women suicides in the Eastern and South-Eastern Anatolia region of Turkey (predominantly Kurdish populated region) and specific cases of sexual abuse, sexual harassment and rape in different part of Turkey. Through these research proposals relevant governmental bodies were asked to investigate these problems in order to determine measures to be taken.

Since 2011 until present[169] the pro-Kurdish party has given 300 parliamentary research proposals and 27 of them are related to women. Out of 27, 7 research proposals were given by male MPs. In comparison to the previous term there is an increase in number of parliamentary research proposals presented by pro-Kurdish parliamentarians and the number of research proposals concerning women's issues is higher. Besides, in comparison to previous term (23rd legislative term) there is an increase in the number of parliamentary research proposals given by male MPs concerning women's issues. The increasing interest towards women's issues among pro-Kurdish parliamentarians demonstrates that there is a progress in feminization of parliamentary politics. Besides, this can be explained with the impacts of women in political arena to encourage male politicians to represent women's interests.

Among female MPs, during the 23rd term (2007-2011), Fatma Kurtulan,[170] who had primarily worked in the parties' women's organizations, had the highest

---

[168] For more information regarding parliamentary works of 23rd term MPs visit http://www.tbmm.gov.tr/develop/owa/milletvekillerimiz_sd.sorgu_donem?p_donem_kodu=23.
[169] This is current legislative term (24th term) started after on June 28, 2011 after 2011 elections.
[170] MP Fatma Kurtulan's parliamentary works during 23rd term can be accessed on http://www.tbmm.gov.tr/develop/owa/td_v2_istatistik.tutanak_hazirla?v_meclis=&v_donem=&v_yasam

number of written questions. She had 204 written questions and 25 of them were with regards to women's problems. Another female MP Ayla Akat Ata.[171] Ata had 140, and 19 of them regarding women. Whereas female deputies raised women's common issues such as domestic violence, gender discrimination in work place, sexist approaches in the media and female unemployment, they also brought specific cases to the Parliament's agenda in order to enforce the relevant governmental bodies to take actions. For instance, Fatma Kurtulan who was elected from the province of Van gave written questions concerning women in Van such as education issues, female employment, and women suicides in Van.

The most important of parliamentary actions is legislative proposals which usually recommend making a new law or to suggest changes to the existing law. If a parliamentary proposal, which meets women's interests is approved in the parliament; it would improve legal rights of women. In this sense, legislative proposals offered by female lawmakers during 23rd term (2007-2011) indicate that female lawmakers attempt to make changes in laws in order to enhance equality between men and women and provide protection for women against any acts of violence. Three significant legislative proposals were offered in that term and all of them were proposed by female MP Sebahat Tuncel with the support of the party's MPs. For instance, the first law proposal offered arrangements in the Turkish Civil Code to ensure equality for men and women regarding the use of surname in marriage and, in the context, the freedom of choice to children in terms of the use of

---

a_yili=&v_cilt=&v_birlesim=&v_sayfa=&v_anabaslik=&v_altbaslik=&v_mv=FATMA%20KURTULAN&v_sb=&v_ozet=&v_kelime=&v_bastarih=&v_bittarih= (Accessed on 20 March 2013).

[171] See MP Ayla Akat Ata's parliamentary works during 23rd term at
http://www.tbmm.gov.tr/develop/owa/milletvekillerimiz_sd.sonuc_donem?p_donem=23&adi=ayla&soyadi=&il=&parti=&kelime= (Accessed on 20 March 2013).

surname.[172] The two other law proposals, which offered amendments to the Turkish Penal Code and the Law on Protection of the Family regarded rearrangements of penalties for people who use both sexual and non-sexual violence against women and children.[173] Furthermore, the legislative proposal offered by Tuncel to amend the law on political parties proves that female representatives concern to improve status in political arena through legislative regulations. The legislative proposal on the amendment of the law on political parties envisages women's participation and representation in the organisations of political parties at the rate of at least fifty percent in order to ensure equal participation of women in politics[174]. It offers women's representation and participation at all levels party leadership, Parliament, municipal councils and provincial councils at least fifty percent. In this regard, female representatives emphasized that women's equal representation in politics and their presence in decision making mechanism is significant for the elimination discriminatory and unequal policies against policies. However, none of these legislative proposals have been approved by the Parliament yet.

The report regarding parliamentary works of MPs during the 23rd legislation term (2007-2007) points out that Kurdish female MP Ayla Akat Ata was the most hardworking parliamentarian in terms of her parliamentary activities during the 23rd period which include parliamentary speeches, research proposals, parliamentary

---

[172] Information about this legislative proposal which was proposed on October 6, 2010 can be found on http://www.tbmm.gov.tr/develop/owa/tasari_teklif_sd.onerge_bilgileri?kanunlar_sira_no=86628 (Accessed on 15 March 2013).
[173] The second law proposal was offered on October 6, 2010 to make amendments to the provisions of Turkish Penal Code. More information on the law proposal can be obtained on http://www.tbmm.gov.tr/develop/owa/tasari_teklif_sd.onerge_bilgileri?kanunlar_sira_no=86998 (Accessed on 15 March 2013).
The third law proposal, which was offered on March 2, 2011 proposed amendments to the Turkish Penal Code and the Law on Protection of the Family. The detailed information about the law proposal can be found on
http://www.tbmm.gov.tr/develop/owa/tasari_teklif_sd.onerge_bilgileri?kanunlar_sira_no=8938 (Accessed on 15 March 2013).
[174] Detailed information about this legistaive proposal can be acessed from http://www.tbmm.gov.tr/develop/owa/tasari_teklif_sd.onerge_bilgileri?kanunlar_sira_no=83595

questions and law proposals. According to the report, she had 140 parliamentary questions, 26 research proposals and 7 law proposals. Her parliamentary activities address a wide range of issues: Kurdish problem, poverty and inequality, discriminatory practices against women, violence against women, human rights violations, unemployment and environmental problems.[175] The success of Ayla Akat Ata is significant to show the active role female deputies have played in politics and their roles in representing women's issues.

During the 24th legislation term (June 2011-) there have been 4 legislative proposals[176] concerning women's issues that have been presented so far by female deputies, addressing various issues similar to the previous legislative proposals made by female MPs during the 23rd legislation term. They aimed to prevent issues such as sexual assault, women killings and lack of social support, and to provide assistance to women. Only one of these law proposals was passed by the parliament so far, on March 8, 2012 (it had been presented on October 24, 2011); it included changes to the Turkish Penal Code and the Family Protection Law in order

---

[175] "En çalışkan vekil: BDP'li Ayla Akat Ata",
http://yeniozgurpolitika.org/arsiv/?bolum=haber&hid=70436, (Accessed on 14 March 2013).
"BDP'li Ayla Akat en çalışkan vekil", http://www.yuksekovaguncel.com/politika/bdpli-ayla-akat-ata-en-caliskan-vekil-h21048.html, (Accessed on Accessed on 14 March 2013).
[176] The first law proposal was proposed on October 24, 2011 to make changes to the Turkish Penal Code and the Family Protection Law. Information about the proposal is available at
http://www.tbmm.gov.tr/develop/owa/tasari_teklif_sd.onerge_bilgileri?kanunlar_sira_no=97204
(Accessed on 15 March 2013).
The second law proposal was offered on November 18, 2011 to make amendments to the Turkish Penal Code, was passed by the parliament on March 8th, 2012. Information about the proposal can be accessed on
http://www.tbmm.gov.tr/develop/owa/tasari_teklif_sd.onerge_bilgileri?kanunlar_sira_no=98443
(Accessed on 15 March 2013).
The third legislation proposal was offered on December 19, 2012 to make changes to the Social Assistance and Solidarity Law. Information about the proposal is available at
http://www.tbmm.gov.tr/develop/owa/tasari_teklif_sd.onerge_bilgileri?kanunlar_sira_no=117182
(Accessed on 15 March 2013).
The fourth law proposal was offered on January 24th, 2013 to make amendments to the Law of Municipalities. Information about the proposal can be found at
http://www.tbmm.gov.tr/develop/owa/tasari_teklif_sd.onerge_bilgileri?kanunlar_sira_no=1273
(Accessed on 15 March 2013).

to re-arrange penalties for those who commit crime and violence against women.[177] Since March 20th, 2012 when the law enters into force, 20,000 people's registered gun that perpetrates violence against their partner were confiscated.[178] Furthermore, another law proposal presented on January 24th, 2013 offered the establishment of gender equality commissions in all municipalities and imposed the municipalities with a population over 10,000 to open shelters for women and children.[179] Female deputy Sebahat Tuncel who presented this law proposal indicated that women are not represented in local governments and that local governments do not respond to women's needs.[180] So, by this law proposal, she aims to ensure women's interests are represented in local governments. These parliamentary actions of female MPs prove that they have intensively raised women's issues and put efforts to make changes in the interests of women. Furthermore, these parliamentary works prove that female activists have tackled issues that meet both women's practical and strategic interests of women.

Women parliamentarians can represent different interests because of the experiences they gained in wide range areas of socio-economic and political life. For instance, in terms of political experiences the majority of them have participated in

---

[177] Information about the proposal is available at
http://www.tbmm.gov.tr/develop/owa/tasari_teklif_sd.onerge_bilgileri?kanunlar_sira_no=97204 (Accessed on 15 March 2013).
This law proposal was discussed in the parliament along with other proposals concerning to same subject offered by mainstream political parties. The parliament discussion concerning to these proposals can be accessed on http://www.tbmm.gov.tr/tutanak/donem24/yil2/bas/b076m.htm (Accessed on 15 March 2013).
[178] Rifat Başaran, "5 bin polis ve askerin silahına el konuldu", 20 April 2013,
http://www.feminkurd.net/content.php?newsid=13768 (Accessed on 22 April 2013).
[179] Information about the proposal is available on
http://www.tbmm.gov.tr/develop/owa/tasari_teklif_sd.onerge_bilgileri?kanunlar_sira_no=120173 (Accessed on 15 March 2013).
[180] "Yerel yönetimlerde kadınlar yok, sığınma evleri yetersiz"
http://www.ka-der.org.tr/tr/container5.php?act=sayfa&id00=113&id01=-198 (Accessed on 17 February 2013).
"BDP Milletvekili Sebahat Tuncel: 'Yerel yönetimlerde kadınlar yok, sığınma evleri yetersiz'"
http://haber.sol.org.tr/devlet-ve-siyaset/bdp-milletvekili-sebahat-tuncel-yerel-yonetimlerde-kadinlar-yok-siginma-evleri (Accessed on 17 February 2013).

the Kurdish political movement since the 1990s. Besides, many of them were active in the women's organizations of the party and were elected with the support of the Kurdish women's movement and are still members of the women's movement. This encourages them to raise gender inequality issues and to get involved in representative process as to make legislative changes to promote gender equality.

Pro-Kurdish female representatives have also attempted to collaborate with female representatives from major political parties in the parliament in order to be influential on the legislation process, to make legal changes and to create pressure in the parliament in their favour. As result of these efforts, all female parliamentarians released a joint statement on 25 November 2010 (the Day to Combat Violence against Women) and made a joint press release about *Violence against Women,* which was a first in the parliament that brought together female members of parliament regardless of political party.[181] However, regarding this cooperation among female parliamentarians, pro-Kurdish female MP Sebahat Tuncel underlined that there is an issue of a lack of cooperation among female parliamentarians, which creates difficulty in making legal changes for the interests of women.

Apart from their parliamentary works, the roles and tasks that female parliamentarians undertake show the impact of their presence in the party's parliamentary politics. There is a great deal of evidence that female representatives have undertaken equal roles and responsibilities in the Parliament. The attendance of female representatives in any meeting regardless of its significance has become a common practice in pro-Kurdish party politics; female MPs indicate that this is an established practice. They are actively involved in public statements, speeches and political debates. They have taken part in different parliamentary working groups and

---

[181] "Milletvekilleri kadına şiddeti "tartıştı", *Hürriyet,* 25 November 2010,
http://hurarsiv.hurriyet.com.tr/goster/printnews.aspx?DocID=16378319 (Accessed on 15 October 2012).

commissions although some of these have been dominated by male lawmakers such as the planning and budget commission and national defence commission. For example, the planning and budget commission had 40 members to refer but there was no female member from any political parties except female MPs Gültan Kışanak. Furthermore, female representatives began to have equal roles and to take equal responsibility especially since the co-chairship system has been implemented in pro-Kurdish politics. Since co-chairship has been implemented in all administrator levels in the party from 2005 and on its effects on the party's parliamentary politics regarding women can be observed in roles that women parliamentarians undertake in the parliament. For instance, co-chairs participate in most significant meetings together and the party's weekly group speeches are carrying out by both co-chairs. In addition, Diyarbakır deputy Gültan Kışanak stated[182], for the first time a political party in the Parliament nominated a woman for the group deputy chairman. Regarding the implementation of co-chairship system, the pro-Kurdish party has two group deputy chairs (one female MP and one male MP) which previously has been perceived as male duty in Turkey as female deputies expressed. In this respect, Kışanak expressed:

> The group deputy chairman has been defined as male job up to this time. This duty has not been assigned to women because the group deputy chairman is expected to be able to control everything in the parliament and the deputy chairman should be able to shout around, walk all over the platform and should be able to silence other MPs and dominate the party group. These attributes are commonly accepted as male attributes. That is why women have not been charged with this duty until now (Personal interview, Diyarbakır, August 2009)

Obviously, women parliamentarians undertaking duties, which have traditionally been attributed to men contribute to changes in perception concerning women's roles, which have been identified with women's traditional gender roles. Furthermore,

---

[182] Personal interview conducted with MP Gültan Kışanak in August 2009 in Diyarbakır.

in the parliament, female deputies represent their party not merely as individual party members, but also as group speakers. They delivered speeches on a broad range of issues from foreign policy to economic and education policies, from Turkey's relations with U.S., European countries and neighbourhood countries to budget talks.[183]

Taking critical positions in the parliament, positions, which used to be fulfilled by male deputies, enable them to challenge the gendered structure of the parliament and gender based distribution of tasks and to change the perception that politics is a man's activity. Female parliamentarians who undertake different roles and tasks in the parliament, especially those regarded as men's, have contributed to change perceptions about women representatives. Their visibility in political arena has an impact in Kurdish society. As the research conducted with female political activists underlined that is due to growing number of female MPs and MPs' active roles in the parliamentary representation that they have become role models for many young female political activists who believe that, one day, they might be the deputies as those female MPs. In this regard, one of members of women assemblies stated:

> Whenever I saw our women deputies speaking in the parliament I want to work harder to become such a strong woman. Kurdish women are very strong. Leyla Zana, Gültan Kışanak, all of women politicians have gone through a very difficult struggle. They fight for our rights. We, women, follow in these women's footsteps (Personal interview, Diyarbakır, April 2010).

---

[183] The parliamentary records are available at
http://www.tbmm.gov.tr/develop/owa/tutanak_dergisi_pdfler.meclis_donemleri?v_meclisdonem=0 (Accessed on March 2013).
Pro-Kurdish party MPs' parliamentaryy works can be accessed; for the 23rd legislation term on http://www.tbmm.gov.tr/develop/owa/milletvekillerimiz_sd.sonuc_donem?p_donem=23&adi=&soya=&arti=BDP&kelime= (Accessed on March 2013) and for the 24th legislation term on http://www.tbmm.gov.tr/develop/owa/milletvekillerimiz_sd.sonuc?p_donem=24&adi=&soyadi=&il=&paBP&kelime= (Accessed on March 2013).

Similarly, these statements of one of female activists, who have two young daughters, demonstrate that parents hold up female politicians as role models for their daughters. She expressed:

> I want my daughters to fight for their rights. I want my daughters to be free. I do not want my daughters to be oppressed by men like us. There are many examples of strong Kurdish women. They came from women's movement. We can see Kurdish women in the parliament, in municipalities and they are everywhere. They are right next to men. They do not stand behind them. This is very important for us, for Kurdish women. We see these women and young women see these women. Of course they impress us. I am telling this to my daughters (Personal interview, Diyarbakır, September 2010).

These expressions explain that female representatives become influential not only through their works but also influential by their positions in representation bodies.

Kurdish women representatives who have displayed a role of strong advocacy of women rights and presented a feminist stand in discussions regarding women have displayed a different political image for women in Turkey's politics. Although it is assumed that women bring supposedly feminine qualities of consensus building to politics, female Kurdish politicians have challenged this assumption. Female Kurdish deputies mostly appear to outsiders as hard-liners or assertive deputies. They have presented this picture by representing both their gender and ethnic identity rights. It is important to observe their commitment and determination for their causes: national rights and women's rights struggle, and their political mobilization processes which include various forms of oppression such as arrest, detention and torture have influenced female political activists to be assertive, active and conspicuous in their work. Regarding the political image of Kurdish women politicians, the statements of Deputy Prime Minister Bülent Arınç are interesting as they show a male politician's perceptions against Kurdish female representatives. In a meeting with journalists a question about a 'women quota' with reference to the implementation of gender quotas in pro-Kurdish politics was asked by a well-known journalist Meral Tamer,

Arınç stated, implying Kurdish MP Sebahat Tuncel's slapping in the face of a police in the argument with the polices because of their attack on people during Newroz celebration in Şırnak in 2011[184], *"There is no need for BDP's to increase woman quota. How you view those [Kurdish female politicians] as women?" "Each of them boosting the police, slapping..."*[185], was the answer. While these statements apparently expose a racist, nationalist and sexist approach towards Kurdish female politicians, this reaction proves that Kurdish female politicians have made changes to break male domination through their active role in politics and this makes men uneasy. Besides, this reaction against Kurdish female politicians is mainly related to women who act in opposition to the traditional roles assigned to them by patriarchal society. Bülent Arınç who is the deputy prime minister in the AKP government which is an Islamist-leaning and conservative political party, reflects the general attitudes of its party and a great number of male deputies in the parliament. The AKP government's policies and discourses concerning women such as abortion law[186] and Prime Minister Recep Tayyip Erdoğan's call for women to have 3 children[187] which are regarded as sexist and authoritarian and have received reactions from feminists, activists, and women rights advocates.[188]

---

[184] "Sebahat Tuncel'e, Polise Tokat Atmaktan Para Cezası", 28 March 2013, http://www.bianet.org/bianet/siyaset/145430-sebahat-tuncel-e-polise-tokat-atmaktan-para cezasi (Accessed on 5 April 2013).
[185] Aslı Aydıntaşbaş, "Ah Sayın Arınç orada duracaktınız!", *Milliyet*, 18 September 2012, http://siyaset.milliyet.com.tr/ah-sayin-arinc-orada-duracaktiniz-/siyaset/siyasetyazardetay/18.09.2012/1597872/default.htm (Accessed on 10 March 2013).
Murat Sabuncu, "Bülent Arınç, Leyla Zana ile Merve Kavakçı'yı bir hatırlasa...", 18 September 2012, http://t24.com.tr/yazi/bulent-arinc-leyla-zana-ile-merve-kavakciyi-bir-hatirlasa/5633 (Accessed on 10 March 2013).
[186] "Kürtaj Yasası geliyor", *Sabah*, 29 May 2012, http://www.sabah.com.tr/Gundem/2012/05/29/kurtas-yasasi-geliyor (Accessed on 13 June 2012).
[187] "En az 3 çocuk yapın", *Hürriyet*, 8 March 2008, http://www.hurriyet.com.tr/gundem/8405007.asp (Accessed on 21 February 2012).
"Erdoğan neden 3 çocuk istediğini açıkladı?" *Milliyet*, 2January 2013, http://siyaset.milliyet.com.tr/erdogan-neden-3-cocuk-istedigini-acikladi-/siyaset/siyasetdetay/02.01.2013/1650260/default.htm (Accessed on 23 March 2013)
[188] "BDP'li vekilden Başbakan'a '3 çocuk' tepkisi!." 8 March 2013,

Consequently, the parliamentary works of female politicians and their political image demonstrate that they are not passive actors. They represent the transformations in pro-Kurdish party politics through their political roles and works in the parliament. Although Kurdish female parliamentarians have not been able to make deep and large scale legal changes to weaken male domination in the parliament to a considerable extent in order to improve women's substantive representation, they have been remarkably successful in raising women's issues and creating a new female political image that represents a strong advocacy for women's rights and challenge existing gendered political culture. They have attached attention the role of women in politics to make difference for women. From this standpoint, since feminization is regarded as a process, developments in pro-Kurdish parliamentary politics in favour of women through inclusion of women in decision-making and female deputies' works demonstrate that there is a process of feminization happening in pro-Kurdish politics.

In comparison to female representatives in the Parliament who are active and very visible and challenge the existing perceptions and beliefs regarding women's roles and tasks in political arena but could not make a very direct impact in improving women's lives, female mayors have been able to do concrete works and policy changes which have contributed to make changes in women's lives as analysed below.

---

http://www.habervitrini.com/haber/bdpli-vekilden-basbakana-3-cocuk-tepkisi-673273/ (Accessed on 26 March 2013).
"Kadinlardan başbakana protesto", 27 May 2012,
http://www.sendika.org/2012/05/kadinlardan-basbakana-protesto/ (Accessed on 26 March 2013).

Feminizing Local Governments

The section examines the roles and activities of female mayors are in order to find out what differences they have made in local governments regarding the representation of women's interests since their descriptive representation has increased in two recent elections. It examines the relationship between women's descriptive representation and substantive representation in local governments running by pro-Kurdish female public officials. This analysis reveals the actual impact of women on policy outcomes and political processes, which proves elected female officials in local public offices act for women. In this section, it is aimed to find out to what extend the process of feminization is happening in pro-Kurdish local politics since women have increasingly been elected to local governmental offices.

The local governments model developed by pro-Kurdish political party to be implemented in the municipalities run by pro-Kurdish elected public officials has contributed to enhance women's representation in local governments. The research conducted with female political activists and elected representatives pointed out that a model known as the Democratic Ecologic and Gender-Egalitarian Local Governments Model[189] is adopted by the municipalities governed by pro-Kurdish party elected representatives in running local affairs. In particular, female political activists from local governments and mayors mentioned that their works within the local governments refer to this model. Explaining this model will help to understand to what extent women enable to act in favour of women by undertaking their activities and tasks in local governments and to what extent women's participation in local governments is encouraged in order to be gender-egalitarian political arena.

---

[189] It refers to *'Demokratik, Ekolojik ve Cinsiyet Özgürlükçü Yerel Yönetimler Modeli'* in Turkish.

This local government model which has been promoted and adopted by pro-Kurdish party since mid-2000s is related to the political projects of *Democratic Confederalism, Democratic Republic and Democratic Autonomy* explained in Chapter 2, developed by the leader of PKK, Abdullah Öcalan after his arrest on February 15, 1999, in order to offer a democratic solution for the Kurdish question in the Middle East in general, and in Turkey in particular. Since these political projects, especially the one of *Democratic Autonomy,* have been adopted by the pro-Kurdish political party DTP (2005-2009), then BDP (2008-), which replaced DTP in 2009 as a democratic self-government model since the mid-2000s, political objectives, policies, and organization style of the party have changed accordingly. In fact, the DTP (2005-2009) was founded in accordance to these political projects. The DTP started to voice overtly its political project, the *'Project for Democratic Autonomy',* very much in line with Öcalan's concept of *Democratic Confederalism.* Since *Democratic Autonomy* has been adopted as self-government project by pro-Kurdish political party (DTP) important changes have been made in the party's structure, objectives and policies as mentioned in the Chapter 3. In the line of these changes the *Democratic Ecologic Gender Egalitarian Local Governments Model* has been developed and explicitly implemented by the pro-Kurdish political party.

The Democratic Ecologic and Gender Egalitarian Local Governments Model was developed at the DTP's 3rd Ecologic Local Governments Conference [1-3 February 2008][190]. As a member of DTP's ecology and local governments commission and the conference's preparation committee Alican Önlü stated, *"this*

---

[190] "DTP'nin Yerel Yönetimler Modeli Netleşiyor", *ekolojistler.org,* 3 February 2008, http://www.ekolojistler.org/dtpnin-yerel-yonetimler-modeli-netlesiyor.html (Accessed on 4 February 2013).
"3. Ekoloji ve Yerel Yönetimler Konferansı", *haberdiyarbakir.com,* 1 February 2008, http://www.haberdiyarbakir.com/3-ekoloji-ve-yerel-yonetimler-konferansi-7648h/ (Accessed on 4 February 2013).

local governments model has been developed through utilizing experiences of running municipalities in Kurdish region since 1999, when pro-Kurdish political party [HADEP] first time won some [38] municipalities in Kurdish region, and the results of conferences addressed local governments and local governments models in Europe and worldwide."[191] The reason for adopting a new local government model was, as he specified, *"the party believed that the local governments cannot be carried out with the current policy and understanding and thus it became a need to develop a unique local government model."*[192]

Although it is emphasized that a pro-Kurdish party developed this local government model due to the existing local government model being inefficient, antidemocratic and centralized however, this research determined that the political project of *Democratic Autonomy* has basically influenced pro-Kurdish party and party activists to seek for a model of decentralized local government. This model, as a member of DTP ecology and local government commissions and the *DTP's 3rd Ecologic Local Governments Conference's [1-3 February 2008]* preparation committee Alican Önlü stated, is a system located within the *Democratic Autonomy*. This serves as a model within the administrative structure of the state. This model once is applied to local governments running by the pro-Kurdish party it will contribute to the *Democratic Autonomy* project. This model is not just for the local governments run by pro-Kurdish political party; it will contribute to the democratization of Turkey and the formation of a democratic system based on the people's participation. This model raises debates regarding local governments in the

---

[191] Hikmet Erden, "DTP'nin Yerel Yönetimler Modeli Netleşiyor," *Haftaya Bakış*, 2-9 February 2008, www.ekolojistler.org/dtpnin-yerel-yonetimler-modeli-netlesiyor.html. (Accessed on 3 February 2013).
[192] Ibid.

current system and addresses that centralization in Turkey does not propose solution for any social, political and cultural issues.[193]

While the *Democratic Ecological and Gender-Libertarian Local Governments Model* has been promoted by pro-Kurdish party and political activists for creating a democratic society it refers to changing the existing governance system in Turkey to a new system which will meet the demands of Kurds and open space for Kurdish cultural and political rights within the legal political structure. However, for this research, this new local government model is taken into account to show what opportunities it offers for women and how it affects the representation of women in local governments and what roles do women play in its implementation. As women politicians' statements in the *1st Ecology and Local Governments Women Conference* (20-21 February 2010)[194] and *2nd Ecology and Local Governments Women Conference* (26-27 May 2012)[195] demonstrated that this model is connected to the *Democratic Autonomy* project and they emphasize they have significant roles in building this project. This approach influences their works in local governments.

The main distinctive characteristic of this model emphasized by female mayors is that it promotes gender equality. The model proposes the ways in which women's participation and representation is increased in the local governments and women's interests are represented and the role of women was specified as

---

[193] Hikmet Erden, "DTP'nin Yerel Yönetimler Modeli Netleşiyor," *Haftaya Bakış*, 2-9 February 2008, www.ekolojistler.org/dtpnin-yerel-yonetimler-modeli-netlesiyor.html (Accessed on 3 February 2013).
[194] "BDP'de Kadın Odaklı Yerel Yönetimlere Doğru" bianet.org, 23 February 2010, *http://www.bianet.org/kadin/toplumsal%20cinsiyet/120236-bdp-de-kadin odakli%20yerelyonetimleredogru* (Accessed on 24 April 2012).
"BDP '1. Ekoloji ve Yerel Yönetimler Kadın Konferansı' sonuç bildirgesi açıklandı", 23 February 2010, *http://www.emekdunyasi.net/ed/guncel/6970-bdp-39-1 ekolojive-yerel-yonetimler-kadinkonferansi 39-sonuc-bildirgesi-aciklandi* (Accessed on 14 October 2012).
[195] "2. Ekoloji ve Yerel Yönetimler Kadın Konferansı", 26 May 2012, http://www.diyarbakirhaber.gen.tr/haber-5745-2-Ekoloji-ve-Yerel-Yonetimler-Kadin-Konferansi.html (Accessed on 14 October 2012).

fundamental for the success of the project. It advocates and institutionalizes the formation of an autonomous organization of women and mechanisms to make their own decisions in local governments such as a municipality and provincial councils in order to incorporate their distinctive features (ideas and perspectives) into the local political processes. It insists on coordination and cooperation between women's assemblies, associations, and local governments. The model suggests a policy to be established in local governments, which ensures gender equality; for instance, it ensures local services to be provided from a gender egalitarian perspective and that women benefit from local services equally. In this regard, it entails the implementation of a 40% gender quota, forming women and men equality commissions in local government bodies, and introducing a separate budget for women in the local governmental bodies. In this connection, female mayors situate their works, policies and applications in the municipalities within the scope of this model, which they believe allow women to create gender egalitarian local governments. During the fieldwork, almost all female mayors interviewed referred to this model in order to express that they act for women and represent women's interests. One of the district mayors of Diyarbakır province stated that:

> We have a democratic, ecologic, gender egalitarian local government perspective, which has determined our works. Our local administrative mentality is based on this democratic gender egalitarian model. We work to establish this model (Personal interview, Diyarbakır, March 2010).

Similarly, Edibe Şahin, the mayor the city of Dersim/Tunceli, stated:

> We form and develop our local service planning based on democratic, ecological, gender egalitarian, anti-sexist and participatory economics strategies. The local governance model, which is implemented by our municipalities, offers the ways to overcome gender inequalities (Personal interview, Dersim/Tunceli, August 2009).

In addition, another female mayor Ayşe Gökkan said:

> We want to build local governments as political areas where women have to be there with both their presence and opinions equally with men (Personal interview, Mardin/Nusaybin, July 2009).

All female mayors underlined that the local government model, which they have implemented promotes more democracy and gender equality in the society. In addition, they aimed to develop this model through their works that contribute to advance gender equality in the society.

While this model of local governance encouraged female mayors to carry works to improve substantive representation of women in local governments a gender egalitarian approach is not the only aspect that women mayors mentioned. In addition, for instance, exercising multilingual municipality conception[196] is explained within the scope of the party's local government model. In this regard, one of women mayors expressed:

> We want to provide service in people's mother language, which is more democratic and make people to get benefit from municipality services. As we know the vast number of people especially women cannot speak Turkish which is official language (Personal interview, Diyarbakır, July 2009)

Thus, it is clear that this model has provided significant contributions especially in terms of its gender egalitarian perspective. It requires women's needs and demands to be taken into account and women to be included in local decision-making.

Advocating Kurdish women's involvement in local governments which have been male-dominated areas requires overcoming women's under-representation in local-decision making and the exclusion of women from local governments' services. In this regard, women's efforts are essential in advancing more women-friendly policies and applications, which contribute to women's inclusion in local

---

[196] In Turkish it refers to 'çokdilli belediyecilik anlayışı'.

governments. It is worthwhile to explore to what extent the increase in descriptive representation of Kurdish women in local governments has generated to substantive representation, what Kurdish women in these municipalities practically do for the improving the lives of women, and what difference they have made in the interest of women.

This research regarding the feminisation of local politics reveals that female mayors and female political activists are making changes through their works in local governments. Both with their presence they represent women's interests in the decision-making process or *"inter-esse"* (literally to "be amongst"), which shows control over the conditions of choice rather than over their consequences (Jónasdóttir, 1988) and with employing women's perspective or their specific social perspectives in Iris Marion Young's (1997; 2000) terms, they represent women's interests while carrying their duties and activities. The observations during field research and the statements of female mayors indicate that in municipalities run by female mayors woman perspective and women's interests are central in decision-making processes, which is reflected in their works. In this regard, the works carried by the Bağlar municipality (Diyarbakır) explains the influences of women's perspectives in decision-making clearly. For instance, the municipality which has initiated a number policies and activities supporting women has established an equality commission and woman unit to develop projects for women and dealing with the problems of female personnel of the municipality in order to ensure women to be more active in local governments and in every spheres of life.

In addition, the works of female mayors in local governments addressed both women's strategic interests and practical interests by eliminating male domination and achieving gender equality both in society and local governments and opening space for women and organizing vocational courses for women in order to improve their life conditions. In the long term these activities contribute to advance women's status in society. For example, women who become economically independent from men gain self-confidence and are able to resist male oppression, controlling and violence, as many female mayors emphasized during interviews. Implementing women friendly policies, mobilizing and organizing women around gender identity concerns, establishing women consultancy centres, and developing projects that contribute to improve women's lives socially and economically lead to eliminate the patriarchal structures in order to achieve a gender egalitarian society.

Female mayors' works concerning women include policy changes, awareness-raising activities, organizing social and cultural activities which encourage women's participation in public life, and life improving works which include various training courses that enable women to become employed. One of the influential works of municipalities that make change in women's life is to establish women's cooperatives. For instance, the Bağlar Woman Cooperative (Diyarbakır), which was established in 2005, provides employment-oriented activities such as computer courses and textile workshops, organizing seminars concerning women's health, family planning, human rights, gender and women's legal rights. It has provided employment for 760 women. Regarding the role of women's cooperatives in creating change in women's lives the president Bağlar Woman Cooperative stated:

> In order to eliminate all forms of violence that women are exposed in private and public sphere we make awareness-raising activities, which create awareness to all segments of society and we are working towards strengthening of positive discrimination towards women. We see it as our responsibility to increase awareness through starting economy under the leadership of women and to meet the economic needs of society.[197]

---

[197] "Kadın kooperatifleri çocuk ve kadınların alternatif eğitimi" http://www.diyarbakirhaber.gen.tr/haber-9501-Kadin-kooperatifleri-cocuk-ve-kadinlarinalternatifegitimalanlari.html. (Accessed on 19 March 2013). More information can be obtained on http://www.baglar.bel.tr/BaglarBelediyesi.

Moreover, the Bağlar municipality has initiated another project to ensure the participation of women in economic life. In this regard, the municipality opened *Jiyan Semt Pazarı* (Life Neighbourhood Market) in August 2013 to create job opportunities for women. The importance of this market is, only women are allowed to work. Regarding the opening of the neighbourhood market for women, Yüksel Baran stated, the municipality intends to ensure greater participation of women into economic life of the city through implementing these sorts of projects.[198]

The research conducted with female mayors points out that having a woman's perspective is regarded as their distinctive characteristic which they argue influencing their political roles and works for the benefits of women. Their shared gender identity brought similar experiences among women that make female mayors able to understand women's needs and interests better. There are also two other factors that make women to act in favour of women in local governments as this research revealed. First, they are mainly nominated by the female activists of the women's movement with implementation of gender quotas. Secondly, the party's local government model and gender ideology and policies allow female mayors to make policies and to develop projects which contribute to eliminate gender inequality and improve women's lives. Based on these findings it can be stated that Kurdish women who are elected to representative bodies have already had woman's perspective and objective of representing women and giving priority to women's

---

[198] "Bağlar'da Jiyan Semt Pazarı Açıldı", http://www.anfnuce.com/news/kadin/baglar-da-jiyan-semt pazari acildi.htm, (Acessed on 25 November 2013).
"Bağlar'da Jiyan Semt Pazarı törenle açıldı", http://www.baglar.bel.tr/bilgi1259-Baglarda-Jiyan-Semt Pazaritorenle-acildi.baglarbelediyesi, (Acessed on 25 November 2013).
"Jiyan Semp Pazarı, kadın istihdamı için yola çıktı", http://www.ka-der.org.tr/tr-TR/Page/News/2424/jiyan-semp-pazari-kadin-istihdami-icin-yola-cikti.html?bid=515, (Acessed on 25 November 2013).

interests and issues. Attitude change in the way of recognizing and supporting women's interests among female representatives does not happen after they have been elected. Women mayors' gender consciousness and the party's women-friendly policies such quotas and co-chairship facilitate to carry out works in local governments to promote gender equality both in political areas and society.

Furthermore, there is an elector's pressure on female mayors pushing them to carry out works and make decision that respond to women's demands. Based on the observations during field research conducted with female candidates in Diyarbakır and Mardin provinces in the period of election campaigns for 29 March 2009 local elections it can be stated that women were main supporters of female candidates both as electors and activists working in election campaigns. That is to say, female candidates are elected, mostly thanks to women's effort. Besides, there is a two-way effect here. On one side, female candidates encourage women to make their voice through voting for them. On the other side female candidates oblige to carry works in order to respond the needs of women when they get elected. In this respect, one of female mayors underlined:

> We have a responsibility towards female electors. We, female candidates put so much effort to access to female voters and get support from them because our gender identity is important and it affects our works. We want to women voters to be aware of this. Since we are elected as female mayors we have to act in the way to respond the demands of women (Personal interview, Diyarbakır, August 2009).

In addition, when the research conducted after 29 March 2009 local elections it was observed the close relations that were established between female voters and female candidates during election campaigns continued after female mayors started to run municipalities. In the course of my field research in different periods between 2009 and 2011, I had the opportunity of observing interactions between female mayors and their constituents. Especially, during my visit to female mayors' offices I encountered a number of cases that female residents sharing their issues, asking for help and suggesting projects and activities for the interests of women. Women were expressing openly that they were going to the municipality because the mayor was a female. For example, two young women were visiting female mayors in Diyarbakir province to thank them for their help; one for getting job in one of women organizations and other one for attending vocational courses. Another young women in Mardin province was asking help to get rid of family pressure and allow her to continue her education. As expressed by many of female mayors, another reason why women request for help because they believe female mayors put all their efforts to respond their demands.

The research explored that the concrete developments in favour of women have happened when women began to be elected to local offices. Female mayors have changed and implemented a number of policies in favour of women since 2004 in particular when a significant number of women (9 Kurdish female mayors out of 14 totals) were elected to local governments. Although there are legal obstacles due to the centralized government system, which does not give opportunity to local administrators implementing policies complying with central rules, to carry out some of these policies, however women still push to make policy change in order to ensure that women's interests are equally represented in local governments. Many of these new policies initiated by women mayors that challenge the state authority and male domination in politics and in society are also implemented in all municipalities governed by the mayors elected from pro-Kurdish party. In this regard, some of the first significant policy changes which have been made by one of female mayors, Leyla Güven was first elected in the 2004 local elections as mayor for one of Adana's town, Küçükdikili, and re-elected in 2009 local elections, as the mayor for

Şanlıurfa's district Viranşehir, have led to consequential transformations in favour of women. Regarding her works concerning women especially during her first mayoral period between 2004 and 2009 this female mayor stated:

> When we formed the collective labour agreement [Toplu İş Sözleşmesi] I wanted to add some articles for the benefit of women. Then 4 articles were included to the agreement. These were: 1) Those who do not allow their daughters to go to school, monetary assistance for their sons will be cut too; 2) Those municipality staffs who commit violence against their wives their half of the salary will be paid to their wives; 3) Those that get second wife will be fired without compensation; 4) Municipality staffs have holidays with pay in March 8 International Women's Day, March 21 Newroz day [Kurdish new year] and May 1 Labour Day (Personal interview, Dersim/Tunceli, August 2009).[199]

Güven's previously mentioned policies were included in the Collective Labour Agreement signed with the General-Work Union on 09 February 2006. This was the first time a mayor initiated such actions for improving status of women and protecting rights of women despite the legal restrictions.[200] These policies were implemented in order to prevent common law marriage and domestic violence, and to provide education for girls, which are some of women's common issues as the female mayor emphasized. For the application of the "domestic violence" article the worker's spouse, child, or a relative reference to the municipality is enough to begin an investigation by the municipality staff. According to the article of "common law marriage", the employee of municipality lived with his wife making this wedding without official marriage contract; his employment contract shall be terminated without the payment of compensation. The aim behind these applications is to prevent polygamy and violence against women. In this regard, Güven stated:

---

[199] Leyla Güven was interviewed after she was elected as mayor for Şanlıurfa's Viranşehir district, which is her second mayoralty. She was interviewed when she was in Dersim/Tunceli for participating Munzur Festival (30 July- 2 August 2009).

[200] According to lawyers collective labour agreements regulate working life whereas these new articles are concerned private life therefore the applicability of these articles are disputed they argued.
Yüksel Eker, "İş sözleşmesinde nikahsız evlilik ve aile içi şiddet", *Hurriyet*, 10 February 2006, http://arama.hurriyet.com.tr/arsivnews.aspx?id=3914041 (Accessed on13 December 2012).

> Our goal is to protect legally the wives of 32 employees and to prevent domestic violence as much we could do. In addition, we want to prevent common-law marriages what we call co-wife [kuma in Turkish], protecting the rights of women and to raise the status of women. Second marriages are pleasure marriages. We do not allow a second marriage. We will end his job when we found out the employee [married worker] is having a common-law relationship[201] (Personal interview, Dersim/Tunceli, August 2009).

These policies in favour of women received great attention especially from female representatives because the rules for the first time in local governments were made uniquely for women and concerning women's issues. Regarding reactions toward her new applications in the municipality Güven stated:

> Female MPs called me and they congratulated me. On the other hand, some lawyers called me and stated that there is no legal status of these articles. But I said the important point from my perspective is to make people think about women's situation. They should think about why we included these clauses to the contract and why there is a need for these clauses. That indicates there is a problem. Consequentially they have had positive impacts. After that, nobody has attempted to have a second wife for instance; not only among personnel also among the community of Küçükdikili- a town of Adana province (Personal interview, Dersim /Tunceli, August 2009).

As Güven, other female mayors mentioned that they, too, struggle to solve these problems. They underlined the importance of these policies initiated by Leyla Güven and encouraged them to make further works in favour of women. In this regard, another female mayor explained that her municipality rejects traditional gender roles and implements strategies and policies that have an impact throughout society. She expressed:

> What we do is that in all our contracts, we clearly state that if violence against women is committed, this contract is invalidated. For instance, if a place is rented out, one of the provisions of the contract is that if violence is committed against a woman, it is immediately cancelled" (Personal interview, Mardin, August 2009).

---

[201] Yüksel Eker, "İş sözleşmesinde nikahsız evlilik ve aile içi şiddet", *Hurriyet*, 10 February 2006, http://arama.hurriyet.com.tr/arsivnews.aspx?id=3914041 (Accessed on 13 December 2012).

As it is pointed out not only female mayors adopt new rules and policies and applications protecting women and eliminating male domination, male mayors have implemented these policies as well. The pro-Kurdish party controlled municipalities in an attempt to promote women's rights have implemented similar rules and policies. For instance, the municipality of Viranşehir district [Şanlıurfa] that was run by a male mayor [2004-2009] also added these articles in the collective labour agreement, which was signed with General-Work Union [Genel-İş Sendikası] on 28 February 2009.[202] This stresses both the influence of female mayors' works and the party's local governments' policies and in particular its local governance model- *Democratic Ecologic Gender-Egalitarian Local Governments Model,* which promotes gender-egalitarian policies to be implemented by the local administrators. The female mayors' statements indicate the party's role and approach in feminizing local governments. One of the female mayors regarding the party's approach toward female mayors' works on women stated:

> Our party has a wide perspective on women's municipality [Kadın belediyeciliği]. It [the political party] has constantly been in solidarity with us [women political activists] in the matters of democratization of society, emancipation of women and reconsidering politics from a woman's perspective within the context of women's liberation ideology[203] (Personal interview, Diyarbakır, July 2009).

There are some critical points that these statements address. Firstly, it points to the overlapping of the party's local governments' model and the women's liberation ideology. The works and efforts of female mayors to promote gender equality in local governments and in society are supported by the party and this is expressed with the concept of women's municipality. The concept of women's municipality is very

---

[202] "Viranşehir Belediyesi'nde Toplu İş Sözleşmesi İmzalandı", 28 February 2009, http://www.genel-is.org.tr/diger_incele.php?id=MjEy (Accessed on 14 December 2012).
[203] "Leyla Güven (Adana Küçükdikili Belediye Başkanı)", 5 July 2012, http://sosya.wordpress.com/2012/07/05/leyla-guven-adana-kucukdikili-belediye-baskani/ (Accessed on 4 Mach 2013).

significant in the sense of promoting the feminization of local governments in Kurdish context. The concept gives the meaning of feminization of local governments when it is pointed out that what it refers to. It refers to women's participation and representation in local governments and representation of women's interests in local governments particularly. It signifies the running of local governments from a woman's perspective, which concerns for women's needs and interests. According to female mayors' statements women's municipality which promotes representation of women's interests and participation of women in local governments is achieving a considerable extent with the efforts of not only female mayors, all the female political activists organized under the umbrella organization of the Democratic Free Women's Movement [DÖKH].

Female mayors have carried out works, which have contributed to make a change in women's lives. Regarding her works during her first experience of mayoralty [2004-2009] in Küçükdikili [a town of Adana province], Güven said:

> I set relations with young women to encourage them to be involved in the municipality activities. We opened vocational courses for women. We met women in different platforms. We founded Kırçiçeği Women's Association [Kırçiçeği Kadın Derneği] in Küçükdikili. We celebrated March 8 International Women's Day. All of these were the first there (Personal interview, Dersim/Tunceli, August 2009)

These statements address very significant points regarding the works of female mayors and explaining what roles they play to generate changes on the ground. Female mayors, as Güven did, have opened women associations to raise consciousness among women regarding gender inequality, to provide guidance and counselling services to women victims of violence and to offer skill courses in order to create employment opportunities for women. In this respect, the Bağlar municipality [district of Diyarbakır province], which has been run by a female mayor since 2004 has become a model for other municipalities for its activities concerning women as many female mayors mentioned.

Based on a survey conducted in March 2012, the mayor of Bağlar, Yüksel Baran, took place in the seventh successful mayors among 75 central district mayors and she was the only female mayor among them.[204] The municipality has provided a number of services through Kardelen Kadın Evi [Snowdrop Women Home]; the first woman home was opened in 2005 and the second one in 2009. The main aims of Kardelen Kadın Evi are presented to ensure the woman's effective participation in economic, social, and cultural life; to conduct research for the problems women face, to improve ways and methods of solution, to offer support; to encourage solidarity, to raise the status of women through empowering them, and to contribute to the struggle for gender equality. In order to achieve these goals, it carries out works such as skills-building courses (such as computer class, handicrafts course and reading-writing course)[205], guidance and counselling services, cultural activities and awareness-raising trainings. For instance, within the context of awareness-raising training seminars on topics such as gender, gender awareness, women's rights, maternal and child health, family planning, and hygiene are offered.[206]

Another municipality, Bismil municipality (Diyarbakır), which is governed by a female mayor, Cemile Eminoğlu opened a women centre to provide similar services to its female constituents. In the opening of Nujin Kadın Evi [New Life Women Home] Eminoğlu stated, it is established to provide health, counselling and education services, vocational courses and training to create employment opportunities for

---

[204] "Kürdistan'da örnek belediye başkanı" http://www.feminkurd.net/content.php?newsid=13583. (Accessed on 5 April 2013).
[205] "Kursiyer Kadinlar Sertifikalarini aldi" 26 February 2013, http://ozdiyarbakirgazetesi.com/index.php/home/news/1594 (Accessed on 6 March 2013).
[206] Detailed information regarding the works of Kardelen Woman House and statistics concerning number of applications for consulting can be found on http://kardelen.baglar.bel.tr/hakkimizda.htm.

women and to gain economic independence of women.[207] The centre offers computer, cooking, hairdressing, handicrafts, sewing and language courses (English and Kurdish). In addition, it provides awareness raising training as well as family counselling and psychological support for women. The statements of one of participants prove that the services offered by the centre have created a change in the lives of women. The participant stated that she has learned a lot in a short period of time. She added there is a very limited area of social life for women in the county. Through this centre, women in the county have gained a wider area of social life.[208] From this standpoint, the female mayors interviewed during the research emphasized that these works of their municipality for women aim to empower women in the society by building self-confidence among women and providing economic independence for women.

During research it has been observed, the female mayors make efforts to provide the same services to women in their constituencies and they cooperate with each other in order to share experiences. In this connection, one of female mayors expressed:

> We, female mayors have close relations with each other. We come together from time to time. We discuss issues in local governments especially our works concerning women. We share our experiences in order to provide better services to our people. Bağlar municipality has long experiences to work for women since 2004. Female mayors have established a system in the municipality. We ask them to help us to implement projects in our municipalities such as opening women houses, consultancy centres and proving training courses (Personal interview, Diyarbakır, July 2009).

---

[207] "Bismil Kadın Kültür Evi Törenle Açıldı", http://www.bismilhaber.com/bismil-kadin-kultur-evi-torenle-acildi-5082h.htm (Accessed on 14 April 2013).
[208] "Nujin'de yaşam yeniden inşa ediliyor",
http://ozgurgundem.com/?haberID=89546&haberBaslik=Nujin'de%20yaşam%20yeniden%20inşa%20ediliyor&action=haber_detay&module=nuce (Accessed on 25 November 2013).

While this cooperation between female mayors enable them to share experiences and develop their works concerning women also it enables them to influence male mayors to implement some of the same projects because some expressed the aim is to eliminate gender inequality in society therefore male mayors have to carry works to improve women's status in their places in order make change in the society.

The presence of women in local governments, their works, attitudes and behaviours in the municipalities which have been identified as male domains refer to significant connotations and have created major impacts on the local community. In this regard, Leyla Güven who was elected a second time as mayor in 2009 and therefore had significant experiences in local governments, having worked in Küçükdikilli (Adana) for 5 years, highlighted some significant points regarding how a female mayor could contribute to changing gender relations in the society through her works, perspectives and attitudes in the support of women. She said:

> Besides the municipality's basis services such as road and water and sewerage which have to be done as determined by law, I have also concerned what I can do for women. During my 5 years mayoralty I think I have contributed to create a (gender equality) culture at least among local community. For instance, whether in public area or at home women were sitting on one side, men on the other side; women and men were separated but this has changed among families which I visited. In places I visited women had to attend to the meeting too otherwise I was not doing the meeting only with men. Also, I encouraged women to participate in the municipality activities. Thus, women began to participate in political discussions and to express their demands and problems during my period. Men have gotten used to see women in public sphere (Personal interview, Dersim/Tunceli, August 2009).

The gender identity of female mayors has influenced women's participation in municipality activities. Almost all female mayors emphasized that after they were elected, they made efforts to put municipalities into women's services and to make municipality buildings open for women's use. They were concerned that, since municipalities have predominantly been governed by men, they have become gendered spaces and excluded women in terms of both their presence and their interests. One of female mayors stated:

> Since I began I don't remember any day without a female visitor. Women in every age come to municipality. I meet all of them. They share their problems and demands such as employment, men oppression and training courses. Women contact me without any hesitation and they feel confortable to speak about anything because I am a woman. Many of them stated that they hadn't been in the municipality before at all (Personal interview, Diyarbakır, August 2011).

During my field research I came across a number of examples that a group of women from different ages were visiting municipalities. They were not only going to the municipality for a special request. Women as a group were visiting female mayor to share their opinions and to establish a social relationship with the mayor.

Furthermore, recruiting female staff is also regarded as a mean for opening municipality spaces for women's usage. For instance, as female mayors informed, more women personnel started working in municipalities while previously there had been a limited numbers of women in municipalities. One of them stated that,

> Before me, the municipality was run by a male mayor. There was only one woman working here and she was a secretary. Now, we are six women in the municipality. We want to include more women in local governments. We need women's perspectives in the management of local governments (Personal interview, Diyarbakır, August 2011).

In addition, female mayors attempt to implement a 50% quota in recruiting staff. Thus, women mayors' efforts contribute to a change in the gender composition of municipalities' workers. They have been transformed into a place where men are no longer dominant. While there are outcomes for advancing women's position on the other hand, increasing women's power in the local politics may provide the party a chance to mobilize women to join the political movement.

All these efforts of female representatives have contributed to raise awareness of the challenges women face, in the Kurdish region. Most of female activists interviewed during research underlined that society has changed a lot since women have taken active roles in local governments. Member of women associations such as Selis Women Association and Gökkuşağı Women Association informed that although they never knew exactly how many were taking place, they believe honor killings have considerably declined. Early marriages, *kuma* (second wives) are also decreasing. This is due to women activists, who have succeeded in changing societal perceptions.

The statements of female activists who participated in this research indicate that significant progress has been achieved in recent years and awareness of the issues such as honor killing, violence against women and early marriage has increased in the region, largely thanks to the work of women activists who take roles in local governments and women's associations.

Conclusion

This chapter primarily aimed to determine what differences women representatives both in national representation bodies and local representative offices have made in terms of women's participation and representation in pro-Kurdish politics through analysing their political roles and acts in these institutions. It focused on effects of elected Kurdish female representatives in the Parliament and local governments. The analysis revealed a wide set of indicators on the importance of gender in the parliamentary process and local governments decision-making process.

The picture that emerges shows that female politicians contribute to strengthening the position of women's interests.

The research shows that there is a link between women's descriptive and substantive representation. Since women's numbers have increased in representative bodies, they are able to voice women's issues and to influence the decision-making processes as the analysis of women's representation roles and works in the parliament and local governments have demonstrated. The increasing proportion of female in representative bodies has provided the inclusion and integration of their perspectives and ideas in political arenas and to better political representation of their interests, concerns and needs.

This research demonstrates that although at both national and local representation levels, women representatives have made a number of significant contributions; it is in local governments that women representatives could make the difference through their works, policies, and projects. Local governments allow women to do more concrete and wider range of works, which create differences in women's lives. Female have initiated a numbers of policies, activities and projects which meet women's both practical and strategic interests.

Furthermore, this research points out that the roles of women in local governments have increased especially with the changes in pro-Kurdish parties' political projects since the mid-2000s. The adoption of *Democratic Ecologic Gender Egalitarian Local Government Model* since the mid-2000s has contributed to changes in favour of women. It is clear that female mayors have created a new concept of a "women's municipality" to describe their works and to explain their perspectives and approaches in governing local governments. This is actually within the context of this research refers to feminization of local governments.

The increasing visibility of Kurdish women's representatives in national politics and the roles and tasks they undertake in the parliament indicate that women representatives play a substantive role in parliamentary politics. They are influential in the legislative process through introducing women's perspectives, raising women's issues through parliamentary debates, and acts. On the local level where women have been excluded, female mayors have challenged the opinion that local governments are male arenas. They have changed the perception that only men can be mayor. Through employing a gender egalitarian approach and encouraging women to participate in local governments, local governments run by female mayors have become women-friendly places and provide services that contribute to women to gain gender awareness, participate in public life, and improve their status in society. The changes women representatives have made in representation bodies in the context of pro-Kurdish politics, in line with women's growth-role in the party's decision-making demonstrate that pro-Kurdish politics in these political arenas is feminizing. Women are participating in the political arenas in a growing number representing their ideas and perspectives. That is to say, the process of feminization is happening since women have increasingly included and integrated in decision-making and made visible and concrete changes both in national and local level.

CHAPTER SEVEN

Conclusion

Findings and Theoretical Implications

The thesis is based on the argument that pro-Kurdish party politics in Turkey have been feminizing since the 1990s. On the basis of this argument, I aimed to explore how the pro-Kurdish party politics have been feminized by looking at the evidence of feminization within the Kurdish context. It was in this respect that the thesis analysed the changing dynamics in Kurdish women's political participation and representation since the 1990s on the basis of the experiences of female political activists.

The process of changes in pro-Kurdish party politics in both the sense of increase in women's descriptive representation and substantive representation is termed as the feminization of pro-Kurdish party politics based on Lovenduski's work (2005). In this regard, this research focused on the actors, strategies, and outcomes of changes in women's increasing numbers and roles in pro-Kurdish politics. I aimed at showing that female political activists who have struggled to make changes in pro-Kurdish party politics through pursuing a number of gender equality strategies are determinative actors in the process of the feminization of pro-Kurdish party politics.

The concept of feminization which encapsulates the two main components- descriptive and substantive representation were found useful in examining the changes in the Kurdish women's political participation and representation since 1990s.

Findings

Since women's political representation in Turkey is quite low, as the statistics, which were mentioned in Chapter 1, proves any change in the political gender gap particularly at political party level is worthy of examination. On that account, it is important to find out how women can be empowered to carry on struggling for gender equality in politics and to pressure political parties to make changes in favour of women while also finding ways in which the party can play a constructive role in narrowing this gap. In this respect, examining the Kurdish women's gender-based political activism aimed at increasing women's representation in pro-Kurdish politics and political party's role in the inclusion of women in decision-making presented a number of substantial findings.

The research findings identify factors behind women's political activism, obstacles to women's political participation and women's taking part in decision-making, strategies for *feminizing politics* and evidences of feminization in pro-Kurdish party politics. The Kurdish case's findings contribute to scholarship concerning party politics and women's political representation while expanding the concept of *feminizing politics*.

The research demonstrates that the political activism of Kurdish women originated at the intersection of their ethnic and gender identities. The experiences of Kurdish women as members of subordinated categories (due to their gender and ethnic identities) influence their political activism. The intersection of identities influences state policies towards Kurdish women as well as their political demands and actions. They have experienced oppression, discrimination, and disadvantage in their society and politics. However, the multiplicity of their subordinated positions provided them organizational resources for mobilization and more ideological motivation for collective action, thereby encouraging them to get involved in non-governmental organizations and political parties during 1990s. These mobilizations resulted in an intersection of ethnic and gender identities, which drove women's activism for gender equality in politics in the end of 1990s and began positively effecting changes in their representation at the beginning of 2000s. Thus mobilization, via intersecting identities, was an influential factor in improving the representation of Kurdish women in politics.

Furthermore, this study revealed that the transformations in women's political participation and representation over the last two decades, informed by the feminizing pro-Kurdish party politics, are the result of the influence of several actors and the interplay of various factors. The Kurdish national movement, the party and female political activists are three critical actors that have contributed to the feminization process of pro-Kurdish party politics differently.

First of all, this study revealed that the PKK, which has been leading the national movement since end of 1970s has become a major actor in mobilizing Kurdish women for the Kurdish national cause since the beginning of 1990s when the first pro-Kurdish political party was established. Their influence was especially felt in influencing them to join the political party. The ideological discourses of the movement and its mobilization strategies have played a role in shaping gender discourses, the organizational structure of the pro-Kurdish political party and constructing the political identity of activists.

Secondly, pro-Kurdish political parties are identified as actors that have played a decisive role contributing to the feminization of politics. The role they have played in the feminization process proves that political parties matter in terms of making changes in women's political representation. Political parties are the real gatekeepers to elected offices. Their attitudes and approach toward gender equality in political decision-making can be drivers of positive change in terms of women's representation thereby influencing society as a whole. This research proved the significance of the political parties' gate-keeping role for women's participation in politics, women's access to powerful positions and women's inclusion in political decision-making through their policies. As I noted the pro-Kurdish party has always encouraged women's participation without broader concern for gender equality in politics. By the 2000's, however, the party observably began to be supportive of gender equality and responsive to female political activists' demands for equal political representation. The change in the party's approach to gender equality, which could be determined by looking at its program and statutes, has been affected from the Kurdish national movement's gender ideology, which addresses women's emancipation. This research found that the party has been influenced ideologically by the Kurdish national movement both in terms of its political objectives and projects. The findings showed that the party has been responsive to female political activists' demands for equal political representation in accordance with its approach to gender equality and political objectives, which have been shaped by the national movement.

The analysis of the pro-Kurdish parties' ideology in the broader context of in relation to the Kurdish national movement suggested that the party's ideology has been a substantially open space for women in the political domain. However, female political activists remain critical actors to improve women's representation through employing this as tool for their gender equality claims.

Based on the case of pro-Kurdish political party it can be stated that political parties are dynamic organisms. Their ideological standing can change because of external and internal factors such as outside pressure and a country's changing domestic political environment. While at one point in time a party may have been less likely to support women's equal representation and may have created obstacles against it, at another, the same party might change its stance and support higher women's representation. Therefore, those aiming to increase women's representation should seek to develop strategies to push for change without solely examining the parties' ideological standing. From this standpoint, the Kurdish case reflects a good example in terms of strategies female political activists pursued and policies implemented by the party with efforts of the female activists in order to promote gender equality in politics. The changing political objectives and projects of the Kurdish national movement, which were formulated under the name *Democratic Cofederalism* from the beginning of 2000s, together with the adjustment of the pro-Kurdish party according to new political objectives, encouraged the party to be responsive to female political activists' demands. The party's focus on a political solution for the Kurdish question in Turkey through political projects- *Democratic Confederalism* and *Democratic Autonomy*- has influenced its discourses and policies towards women's political representation. As found out in Chapter 3 during the analysis of the party's program and statutes, pro-Kurdish party has stressed the significance of gender equality in the context of democratization. Because of its gender ideology and egalitarian policies, the party seems to have been promoting transformations in favour of women in politics. However, the main driving force behind these transformations is the female political activists who were identified as the most influential actors in the feminization of pro-Kurdish politics, and their gender-based rights struggle, which forced the party to take further steps.

The party's decision to carry on Kurdish national rights struggle through electoral politics has created opportunities for women to join political parties since the first pro-Kurdish party established in 1990. The findings regarding Kurdish women's experiences specifically the party's women's organizations have ensured space for women to both become active in politics as well as to claim more representation by making clear their demands to the party leadership. Female activists have utilized the party's gender approach, which has nevertheless improved in time thanks largely to the efforts of women's activism for gender equality, ideological shifts in the Kurdish national movement and the parties' efforts to adopt international standards, to make their claims for equal representation. The research pointed out female political activists who made their arguments for equal political representation based on three arguments; *justice, pragmatic* and *difference* arguments which have contributed to facilitate the process of feminization by urging the party to be responsive to women's demands. Besides, it is pointed that the party's support for gender equality is primarily in the context of *justice* argument as mentioned in Chapter 3.

In the analysis it became evident that numbers do matter which have encouraged female political activists to argue for equal political representation. The growth of statistical representation of women in the party's decision-making, local governments and in the Parliament makes a difference. When there are few women in political institutions women's ability to manoeuvre is limited in having less influence in making changes within a gendered structure of political institutions, less ability to transform masculine political culture, decreased lobbying strength in areas of concern, and marginalization from committee collaboration in decision-making. A number of female activists expressed in my interviews, involvement in politics increased especially since the end of 1990s when they joined the party's women's organizations. These organisations have enhanced the strength of women by demanding for a more equal participation in decision-making. Women felt strong and confident about making claims for equal participation and representation in decision-making and representative bodies; the party was forced to respond to the female activists' demands. An increase in the number of women within the party elected to local government and the Parliament brought out the female women's perspectives and experiences into politics in the interests of women.

This study demonstrated that feminization is a process that includes various factors promoting gender equality, strong commitments of actors', especially female political activists' struggle against gender inequalities not only in politics but also in society at large and a numbers of strategies employed by female political actors. On the other hand, the process of feminization includes a number of obstacles for female political activists who seek a change in politics. To achieve and exercise real power, women must overcome a multiple of obstacles.

The study's findings brought out significant points regarding obstacles to women's entering in politics and their gaining access to powerful positions. While some obstacles encountered by the Kurdish women I have researched overlap with the obstacles facing women in Turkey and other parts of the world, some are specific to Kurdish women. Political, socio-economic and cultural factors became apparent in distinguishing Kurdish women's challenges. The role of state politics is of particular salience since it frequently designates pro-Kurdish politics as a "high risk area" thereby adding specificity to the Kurdish set of obstacles that distinguish it from the rest.

The analysis of political factors, which included the political and electoral systems, the party system and the political culture, demonstrated that these institutions have been heavily shaped by men due to men's historical domination of the political domain. This reality poses a major obstacle to increasing women's political representation. This opened up an exploration in the way socio-economic development can regulate social roles in a society, especially when relating to financial resources and education. However, as this study revealed, while economic resources and education levels are two interrelated factors that generally determine women's political participation and representation in Turkey, in the Kurdish case, they have not been primary determinant factors. Female political activists, despite poor economic conditions and low levels of education, have been able to become political actors. When women do attempt to become political actors, the social norms circumscribing women's expected roles and duties come into play. Men will often resist movements that modify and expand women's roles, duties, and capabilities. Traditional gender roles attributed to women create obstacles for women's entry into politics as well as for those who are already active in political arenas. Finally, my research figured out state politics involving the pro-Kurdish political "high risk area" is unique to the Kurdish case. The state targeted women's political activism using measures that included a number of violent and non-violent acts aimed at female activists' sexual identity in order to impede women from joining pro-Kurdish politics to create obstacles for everyone associated with women in pro-Kurdish politics. Overall, the research found the main reason behind all these obstacles is the patriarchal ideology that dominates society and is promoted and reproduced by the state institutions based on the respondents' testimonies.

Since the findings of my research have shown that the pro-Kurdish party politics has been experiencing a feminization process, then an explanation is needed to show what the contributing factors are to this process of feminization is occurring. This indicates the success of strategies that were employed by female political activists in order to achieve gender equality in pro-Kurdish politics. In addition, the discussion regarding the roles of these strategies in the feminization of pro-Kurdish politics holds pertinence to aims of increasing descriptive representation and improving substantive representation of women.

The Role of Gender Equality Strategies in *Feminizing* pro-Kurdish Politics

As the findings of this thesis illustrated, female political activists play a key role in changes for better representation. A number of strategies are employed by female political activists to strengthen women's claims to better representation; these provide answers to the question of how pro-Kurdish party politics has been feminizing. This includes enabling women's involvement in decision-making mechanisms and changing the gender representational balance in pro-Kurdish party politics. Women have engaged in various strategies aimed at enhancing the descriptive and substantive representation of women in politics. These strategies can be discerned in the change of form of intra-party women's organizations (Commissions- Branches- Assemblies); the expansion of autonomous women's organization, DÖKH[209]; the implementation of the quotas; equal participation in

---
[209] It stands for *Demokratik Özgür Kadın Hareketi* in Turkish and *Democratic Free Women Movement* in English.

leadership positions (co-chairship); training (the School of Politics for Women) and networking activities. Each of these strategies has played an integral role in the feminization of pro-Kurdish politics.

The research revealed that *the change of form of intra-party women's organizations* which first established at mid-1990 has contributed to the strengthening women's position within the parties. Despite a variety of views concerning the role of women's organizations, for enhancing women's representation in political parties, this study firmly establishes that women's organizations within parties play a transformative role if women use the power of these organisations to negotiate better self-representation. In the Kurdish case the changes in the composition of the women's organizations within the parties; first took the form of commissions and then turned into branches, and finally, running in the form of assemblies due to the growth of the number of women joining the parties. Women's efforts at becoming independent of the centralised party power showed that female political activists used these intra-party organizations as a strategy to feminize pro-Kurdish politics.

Women's organizations justified expanding female participation by arguing that women contribute to parties by offering access to wide segments of society, vote-canvassing and mobilization during electoral campaigns. These contributions reinforce the recognition of women as actors in party politics, especially by male elites of a party. At the same time, these organizations empower women through creating a consciousness and developing a sense of women's collective interests. Such empowerment and awareness allows women to not only maintain their rights in the political arena, but also raise an agenda concerning women's interests and issues which are accompanied by women's demands for taking up positions in decision making bodies of the party.

Women's organizations in political parties can also contribute toward better representation, especially if their demands are asserted firmly. If women's organizations established coalitions across parties to work on representation and collaborated with non-party women's networks, they would be more influential in voicing their demands and putting pressure within the political parties and on legislative bodies. The experience of Kurdish women's activism demonstrates that collaboration with unaffiliated women's networks which has been observed since the beginning of the 2000's empowers women within the party to voice their demands. Female activists in pro-Kurdish party acted with women organized outside the political party in improving women's status in general. This was especially the case since Kurdish women activists began to organize under the name of DÖKH in 2003. That organisation has allowed them to become more able to influence and monitor the political activities the party to make them more sensitive to women's interests and issues and to make policies in favour of women. These mechanisms have been effective in the process of increasing women's representation.

My research points out that female political activists employed the DÖKH as an autonomous women's organization as a strategy to influence political arena through expanding women's movement. The DÖKH as an umbrella organisation for the all Kurdish women' activism that was created in 2003 by Kurdish women activists to link together Kurdish women in different areas such as the political party's women's organizations, Kurdish women's associations and women who hold positions in public offices has taken the representative role for the Kurdish women's rights struggle. As an autonomous organization it has become influential in enhancing women's activism, mobilizing women and raising women's issues through the organization of various activities such as campaigns, conferences, demonstrations and public statements. The unification of socially and politically active Kurdish women from various organizations under the banner of the DÖKH enabled women to create pressure and negotiate for women's taking part in decision-making and elected to representative institutions in different organizations whose female cadres joined DÖKH. My research points out that a number of changes have occurred in political party since the formation of DÖKH in 2003. This includes the changing organizational style of intra-party women's organizations from commissions to assemblies, the implementation of a co-chairship system and a 40% gender quota. As the research revealed, DÖKH's role in the feminization of pro-Kurdish politics became apparent since it has gained power to regulate the processes of accessing representational bodies and to observe the works of representatives in the representative bodies. This means the DÖKH, as an embodiment of Kurdish women's unified power, is able to penetrate political areas with the aim of advancing gender equality through determining female candidates of gender quotas and monitoring the works of elected female politicians. These active roles of the DÖKH have ensured both increase of descriptive and substantive representation of women in politics.

This research shows that the claims and arguments of the party's female activists for equal representation made possible the implementation of affirmative action policies such as gender quotas as an insider strategy. The evidence of the study suggests that the implementation of gender quotas is one of the most effective strategies enabling women's access to political decision-making. Since women are disadvantaged in many respects, including financial and educational factors, politics is internally perceived as a masculine vocation. Political institutions are indeed male dominated. When in use, gender quotas are considered as the only means to achieve an increase in women's descriptive representation in politics over short period of time. This research brought out some distinctive aspects regarding the implementation of quotas in pro-Kurdish politics, which could allay their critics' fears. First of all, the gender quotas which are currently at 40% and implemented in various areas such as the deputy candidate list in national elections, the candidate list of mayors and the party's organs, has contributed to the institutionalization of women's roles in all these areas. Secondly, the determination of women nominated by the quotas by female political activists themselves ensures that the elected women are qualified to represent women's interests. In order to ascertain which female candidates are to be elected, female political activists put pressure on the party's male elites to nominate female candidates in their constituencies. Thirdly, by monitoring the works of female representatives elected through gender quotas by the DÖKH, and collaborating between those elected women and female activists, obliges elected representatives to act for women in representative bodies. The female activists who have organized under the DÖKH umbrella since 2003 have gained authority in the implementation of gender quotas. They have made the use of quotas an effective strategy for enhancing both the descriptive and substantive representation of women in pro-Kurdish politics.

As findings on *the implementation of gender quotas* in the case of pro-Kurdish parties demonstrated, the descriptive representation of Kurdish women has dramatically increased in decision-making bodies by virtue of gender quotas; these support the argument that quotas can make important improvements in women's representations as recent experiences worldwide have shown. It is with this in mind that, based on the experiences of Kurdish women regarding the implementation of gender quotas, this thesis suggests that an active role of women in the implementation of gender quotas is required in order to ensure that quotas are applied properly and to prevent the women included in quotas from being treated as merely symbolic in their political roles.

Furthermore, the case of Kurdish women demonstrated that women's efforts are critical for both the introduction and proper usage of quotas. Without the efforts made by women activists within the party for its introduction, male leaders would not have made it. The presence of quotas in pro-Kurdish party provides a positive look for the continuity of women's achievements in the political arena even after the Kurdish political movement accomplishes its goals and no longer needs women's political mobilization. The quotas guarantee that women will be represented in the pro-Kurdish party and in the representative offices. The pro-Kurdish party would not be able to withdraw the decision to increase women's representation by means of gender quotas, because women's organizational power, the rising egalitarian political culture in pro-Kurdish party and changing gender roles within Kurdish society will grow stronger as time passes and women consolidate their gains.

Another strategy, the system of co-chairship which literally refers to the fact that the party is headed by one male and one female and has provided women equal participation in leadership positions ensures the institutionalization of women's equal participation in the party's administration. From this standpoint, this system of sharing equal political power in the party, despite not being legitimated according to the law on political parties in Turkey, has contributed to the feminization of pro-Kurdish politics. To begin with, this research revealed that the implementation of power-sharing has contributed to the decline in male domination of the party's administration; secondly, women have been enabled to exercise power in leadership positions; and thirdly, the application of this policy throughout the party has been felt from the local governments, to the Parliament, and all the way to the executive level. Based on the findings of this study it can be stated that exercising political power in leadership positions throughout the party structure by virtue of *the co-chairship system* has enabled women to claim more equality, by raising women issues, eliminating male dominated culture and attitudes, and encouraging female activists to become active in the party politics.

This study found that offering *training* to female activists in the party was regarded as a strategy for empowering women politically by the female political activists, especially by those had been involved in politics for a long time. Based on their experiences and observations in pro-Kurdish politics, these female political activists considered *training* as a necessity for the female activists of the party who have a lack of political experiences and gender identity consciousness. In this regard, *the School of Politics for Women* which was established to train female activists on various subjects such as the history of societies, women's history, women rights, women and family issues, and the party policy and ideology to female activists within the party, has played a role in the feminization of pro-Kurdish politics. The research revealed that *training* is a conscious strategy pursued by female activist to create political actors who are advocates of both their gender identity and national rights. These conscious actors have made changes on the ground through the mobilization of women around their gender identity rights, taking up active roles in elections campaigns in order to get female candidates elected and standing up against gender inequality, all of which have contributed to feminize pro-Kurdish politics.

This study focused on *networking activities* as a strategy that included conferences, meetings, and collaborations with academics, politicians, political and women's organizations at both the national and international levels. These have played a role in the feminization process of pro-Kurdish politics in terms of their contributions to the strengthening of the Kurdish women's struggle in general and political identity of individual activists in particular. These activities provided opportunities for the Kurdish women's movement to integrate and form relationships with worldwide actors, organizations and institutions. While they consolidated gender awareness among female activists, they also provided women activists the chance to enrich experiences and knowledge regarding women's rights struggles and the ways to achieve gender equality, especially in the political arena. For example, female political activists elected to local governments have drawn from these networks to develop policies and projects for better representation. The research pointed out that, *networking activities* which link women in setting both national and international cooperation's and expand their experiences; these in turn, are utilized by female political activists as a strategy to maintain changes for women in the political arena and to improve women's substantive representation.

The strategies that are produced in the Kurdish case as effective means to feminize politics also correspond to experiences across the world in areas such as quotas. The Kurdish case can also contribute to scholarship by bringing new understandings how feminization takes place. The study indicated that achieving full equality in politics requires a multi-faceted struggle incorporating multiple strategies by women themselves.

These strategies mainly explained how women got into the party's decision-making and representative bodies at a growth number and penetrate the party's politics to weaken male domination in pro-Kurdish politics by furthering women's interests. But this study also concentrated on the political roles and works of female political activists who have accessed powerful positions and elected representative bodies. These are important in understanding to what extent substantive representation is occurring within pro-Kurdish representation politics. Additionally, this analysis provided evidences of feminization in pro-Kurdish representation politics, which expand on how *feminizing politics* has been redefined by the Kurdish case.

The developments in women's political participation and representation, especially since the beginning of 2000s, were interpreted as the feminization of pro-Kurdish party politics. The evidences of feminization in the Kurdish context was primarily identified through examining the roles and actions of female political activists and elected politicians and tasks that they undertook in the party, in the local governments and in the Parliament in the context of substantive representation. This research found that the increasing numbers of women in representation bodies have leaded to substantive representation of women in those areas. That is to say, women's interests are represented by female representatives in representative bodies.

The research revealed that at the parliamentary level female representatives have been active in bringing women's issues into the political agenda through such efforts like offering law proposals, raising parliamentary questions, tabling parliamentary research proposals, preparing reports and addressing speeches and involving projects. I have pointed out how female MPs' concern to raise women issues and to represent women interests more than male MPs. Through their parliamentary actions which address such issues as; violence against women, gender-based discrimination, sexual abuse, child marriages, discriminatory and sexist approaches facing women in the media, discriminatory practices faced by women in working life, gender sensitivity in education and female employment issues that attempt to meet both women's practical and strategic interests. Moreover, the parliamentary works of female politicians and their political image prove that they are not passive actors. They undertake roles equal to male MPs. Their projects strengthen their presence in the parliament to be the voice of women and change the perception that politics is a man's job. They have created a new female political image that is equal to their male colleagues in terms of sharing power and undertaking roles, but different due to their gender identity, which encourages them to act for representing women's interests. They have been successful to a considerable extent in raising women's issues and constructing a new female political identity that represents a strong advocacy for women's rights.

Concerning the female mayors' work in the local governments the research revealed that female mayors have initiated policy changes and carried out a large number of works such as applying quotas in recruiting personnel for local governments, conscious-raising activities, mobilizing and organizing women around gender identity concerns, establishing women's consultancy centres, opening training courses, forming women and men's equality commissions, introducing a separate budget for women within the municipality and developing projects that contribute to improving women's lives socially and economically that enable them to stand against men's domination. Therefore, they respond to both practical and strategic interests of women. The research demonstrated that local governments are becoming political areas in which women's representation is increasing both in numbers, and ideas, and interests. Furthermore, this study brought out the process of feminization in local governments that has been escalating since the *Democratic, Ecologic and Gender Libertarian Local Governments Model* which was promoted by the pro-Kurdish political party from the beginning of 2000's. This model, which presents gender equality as one of its central elements, has encouraged female mayors to carry on their works in the local governments in favour of women. The research showed that female mayors have developed the concept of *women's municipalism* to define their governance approach in local governments, which can be interpreted as feminization of local governments in the context of pro-Kurdish politics.

This study also introduced theoretical implications in the light of empirical findings, which contribute to expand scholarship on political representation and women.

Theoretical Implications: Re-Defining *Feminizing Politics* in Kurdish Context

The analysis of the Kurdish women case presented several insights about the women's political representation, and how political party and political actors strategically interact in changing women's representation in representative institutions. Theoretically, this research offered an opportunity to widen the scope of descriptive representation, and substantive representation by analysing party related factors and especially the role of female political activists. Empirically, it provided data collection at the sub-national and party level. Some of the approaches employed in this study might be useful in studying gender and gender representations in general. First, the present literature at the global level (Lovenduski, 2005; Norris – Inglehart, 2001; Matland – Studlar, 1996; Matland, 1998;

Norris 1985, 1997, 2006; Paxton, 1997) and in national level (Arat, 1989 & 2005; Talaslı, 1996; Güneş-Ayata, 2001; Saktanber, 2002; Tekeli, 1981; White, 2002; Turam, 2008) is mostly to evaluate women's representation by the number of women in parliamentary office. The prominent literature focuses less on women's representation in local office and does not take into account their representation in party organs. This study, by contrast, considered all three areas as indicators of women's representation. Secondly, this thesis attempted to explain the Kurdish case with regard to an actor-based approach by considering the agency of women. It demonstrated the presence of a dynamic relationship between institutions and [women's] agency, indicating that this relationship continues even during the process of institutional change as observed in the party's organizational structure and in the party's policies toward women. Thirdly, this study intended to analyse women's representation based on the experiences of one group - Kurdish women in pro-Kurdish party politics by employing an in-depth analysis and chronological analysis perspective instead of group comparisons [women in mainstream political parties]. It contributes to existing studies, which have focused on political parties' relationship with women and questioned conditions under which political parties are more likely to include women in their ranks. Most studies (Caul, 1999; Leyenaar, 2004; Paxton et al., 2007) have pointed out that party ideology, especially from further left political leanings, is the major factor determining the party's policies regarding women's representation. However, this research found out it is the women activists who form part of the party who are the most influential factor in enforcing for change in favour of women in political areas. They can push the party to act in accordance with its ideology if it encourages gender equality as some studies of political parties with left wing political leanings demonstrate. The party's political ideology by itself is not a determinative factor. In addition, examining the Kurdish case specifically for exploring experiences and developments in women's representation, offers other groups the chance to benefit from experiences of Kurdish cases as a role model.

The examination of Kurdish women's representation based on the *feminizing politics* approach theoretically contributes to broaden the scope of *feminizing politics* but also broadens the scope of the concepts of descriptive and substantive representation included in this approach. The categories of descriptive and substantive representations are broadly utilized by feminist scholars analysing women's political representation (Pitkin, 1969& 1972; Goetz and Hassim, 2003; Mansbridge 1999; Lovenduski, 2005; Wängnerud, 2000; Celis 2008a, b). Each of these categories defines the different strands of discussion within women's representation literature. The findings of this study contribute to expand this discussion in many respects. This exposes the link existing between substantive and descriptive representation. That means according to the numbers of women in representative bodies increased the representation of women's interests increases as this study demonstrates. Similar to a number of studies which focuses on the relationships between substantive and descriptive representation (Lovenduski et.al. 2005; Bratton and Ray, 2007; Celis & Childs, 2008; Mackay, 2004; Reingold, 2008) this study introduces that women's presence will improve their substantive representation depending upon some factors. That means, descriptive representation is a necessary, yet not a sufficient, condition for substantive representation of women interests. Analysing the relationship between them on the basis of the Kurdish case suggests that descriptive representation does not automatically lead to substantive representation, there have been different relationship patterns that are influenced by various factors including the political context, party control, women's institutional power, the presence of strong women's movements and the profile of women.

Employing the concept of *feminizing politics* based on the Lowenduski's work- Feminizing Politics (2005) but applying it as both a concept and approach to the Kurdish case contributes to broaden the definition of this concept.

In the case of pro-Kurdish party politics the changes and developments in terms of women's representation are framed as a process of feminization. It can be defined as a process for women to be included in political decision-making numbers and ideas for representing women's interests and concerns (Lovenduski, 2005: 12-13). However, this study, which also addressed the feminization in sense of women's political representation, found out that its impacts and intentions are beyond the politics. It is approached as a process of transforming existing political system that leads to advancing gender equality not only in politics but it also has influences to change society more broadly. Based on testimonies of the interviewees, this study produced that *feminizing politics* in the Kurdish case is perceived as a project started in the political area to include women into decision-making in equal numbers and ideas but which can expand to the whole of society with the aim of changing gender relations in the society. In other words, feminization in politics is considered as an initial step to create a gender egalitarian society. The efforts of female political activists in the political area and their works, projects and campaigns in either the party or representational bodies, address women's interests and issues and aim to empower women in the society in order to improve their status. That is to say, in this research, *feminizing politics* refers to penetration of women into political institutions in equal numbers where they can contribute their perspectives to transform the existing political system. Feminization, then, helps bring about a new democratic and gender egalitarian system, which consequently ensures gender equality both in politics and in society at large. It can be stated that the broader aims behind the efforts to feminize politics is to make structural changes in society in terms of improving women's status and ensuring gender equity. These findings for the Kurdish case regarding feminization suggest that *feminizing politics* should be considered in a broader sense for further studies.

www.ingramcontent.com/pod-product-compliance
Lightning Source LLC
LaVergne TN
LVHW021234080526
838199LV00088B/4340